tear here

Geologic Time Table

Millions of Years Ago	Era	Period	Evolutionary Event
		Quaternary	First humans
65	Cenozoic	Tertiary	Mammals dominate
		Cretaceous	Last non-bird dinosaurs
			First flowers
		Jurassic	First birds
			Dinosaurs dominate
			Pangaea breaks up
250	Mesozoic	Triassic	First dinos and mammals
		Permian	Great extinctions
		Carboniferous	First amniotes
		Devonian	First amphibians
		Silurian	First jawed fish
		Ordovician	Jawless fish only
544	Paleozoic	Cambrian	Sea creatures with shells
4500	Cryptozoic	Pre-Cambrian	Bacteria and algae

alpha
books

Dino Lifestyles

Dinosaurs had similar lifestyles to those of modern mammals:

Dinosaurs	Mammals
Sauropodomorphs (such as "brontos")	Elephants and giraffes
Heterodontosaurs and Hypsilophodonts	Gazelles and antelopes
Iguanodonts and Hadrosaurs (iggies and duckbills)	Horses and buffalo
Pachycephalosaurs (dome heads)	Goats
Ceratopsians (frill heads and beaked dinos)	Rhinoceroses
Dromaeosaurs and Troodonts (raptors)	Lions and wolves
Carnosaurs and Tyrannosaurs (big killers)	Tigers
Ankylosaurs and Nodosaurs (armored dinos)	Extinct mammals known as glyptodonts, which resembled giant armadillos with tail clubs

T-Rex Classification

Full classification of T-rex, according to the Linnaean Classification System:

Kingdom Animalia (animals)

Phylum Chordata (animals with spinal cords)

Subphylum Vertebrata (chordates with backbones)

Class Dinosauria (terrible lizard vertebrates)

Order Saurischia (lizard butt dinosaurs)

Suborder Theropoda (meat-eating Saurischians)

Family Tyrannosauridae (tyrant lizard theropods)

Genus Tyrannosaurus

Species Rex

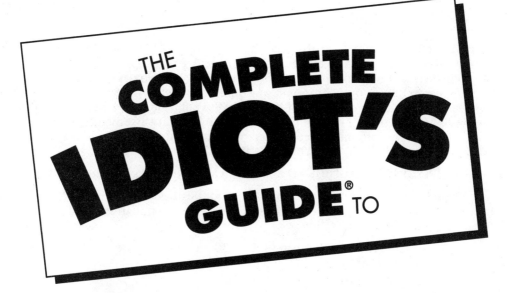

Dinosaurs

by Jay Stevenson, Ph.D,
and George McGhee, Ph.D.

A Division of Macmillan General Reference
A Simon & Schuster Macmillan Company
1633 Broadway, New York, NY 10019-6785

Macmillan Publishing books may be purchased for business or sales promotional use. For information please write: Special Markets Department, Macmillan Publishing USA, 1633 Broadway, New York, NY 10019.

International Standard Book Number: 0-02862390-8
Library of Congress Catalog Card Number: 98-89574

00 99 98   8 7 6 5 4 3 2 1

Interpretation of the printing code: The rightmost number of the first series of numbers is the year of the book's printing; the rightmost number of the second series of numbers is the number of the book's printing. For example, a printing code of 98-1 shows that the first printing occurred in 1998.

Printed in the United States of America

Alpha Development Team

Publisher
Kathy Nebenhaus

Editorial Director
Gary M. Krebs

Managing Editor
Bob Shuman

Marketing Brand Manager
Felice Primeau

Senior Editor
Nancy Mikhail

Development Editors
Phil Kitchel
Jennifer Perillo
Amy Zavatto

Editorial Assistant
Maureen Horn

Production Team

Production Editor
Stephanie Mohler

Copy Editors
Geneil Breeze
Krista Hansing

Cover Designer
Mike Freeland

Photo Editor
Richard Fox

Color Illustrator
Michael W. Skrepnick

Cartoonist
Jody P. Schaeffer

Designer
Glenn Larsen

Indexer
Sandra Henselmeier
Nadia Ibrahim

Layout/Proofreading
Angela Calvert
Kim Cofer

Contents at a Glance

Contents

Foreword

One of the best things about talking to kids about dinosaurs is their excitement. They *love* dinosaurs. They know *everything* about dinosaurs. They can't get *enough* about dinosaurs. If you have a child, then you know what I mean.

Even though I'm a paleontologist with decades of experience, I'm still awed by what kids know about dinosaurs. When I lecture, they correct me. They've memorized all the books their parents read to them. They even correct my pronunciation. ("No, no, it's Dine-oh-NIKE-us!", I have been informed on more than one occasion.) And why not? Dinos are big, they're fun, they're dead, they can't hurt you, and you can fantasize about them eating your sister. (Or your lawyer, if you've seen *Jurassic Park*.)

Some kids grow up and continue their fascination with dinosaurs as adults. Others lose that joy as they get older, but then find themselves parents of dinosaur-crazed kids and realize they need to brush up on some quick facts to answer those difficult scientific questions. And that leads to the point of this book.

If you're feeling inferior because your kids are geniuses about dinosaurs, then this book is for you. It tells you all you need to know about dinosaurs to hold up your end of an intelligent conversation with your kids. This is no mean feat.

And it's written by one paleontologist and one dino-freak. This is good. Too often, the stuff purveyed to kids is produced by people who don't really know the subject. You can see this when you watch documentaries on TV. You know how the crew goes out to the dig site, finds the skeleton, painstakingly uncovers it, gets excited, wraps it up in plaster jackets, drinks a bunch of beer, and goes back to the museum until next year? End of story. Dude, that's when the work *begins*!

All the fun stuff we know comes from the lab work, the comparisons with other skeletons, integrating the field data with the bones, and using new technologies from different fields to ask newer and neater questions. You'll learn about all that cool stuff here. (Though we all will admit that the field work is the *huge* fun!)

Another thing. Some of what you'll read in this book may turn out to be wrong. *"Whoa,"* you're thinking, "why don't I just put this back on the shelf and buy *The Complete Idiot's Guide to Elvis* instead?" Because this is science, that's why. It's *meant* to change, to evolve with new knowledge and new ways of looking at things.

Scientists disagree on a lot of things about dinosaurs. Most arguments are based on the interpretation of evidence, and the methods we use to study it. Very few paleontologists who actually work on dinosaurs think that an asteroid knocked them all off at the end of the Cretaceous Period. We've got a bunch of possible explanations of what the heck those duckbills were doing with those crests on their heads. Did pachycephalosaurs head-butt or only flank-butt? We don't always have enough evidence to satisfy everyone on these questions. Heck, a few scientists still don't accept the evidence that birds evolved from dinosaurs. So if this book gives you a better idea of how we know what we know about dinosaurs—and where the limits of our knowledge are—then it's done its work.

And when you're on *Jeopardy* competing against two 5-year-olds and the category is "Dinosaurs," you'll be ready to play!

—Kevin Padian, Ph.D., professor and curator, University of California, Berkeley

Kevin Padian, Ph.D., is Professor of Integrative Biology and a Curator of the Museum of Paleontology at the University of California, Berkeley. His research specialties include early dinosaur evolution, carnivorous dinosaurs, the origin of birds and their flight, the flying reptiles called Pterosaurs, dinosaur footprints, and the history of evolutionary thought. His books include *The Beginning of the Age of Dinosaurs* (1986), *The Encyclopedia of Dinosaurs* (with P.J. Currie, 1997), and the translation of *Dinosaur Impressions* by Philippe Taquet (1998).

Introduction

Dinosaurs were amazing creatures. They disappeared from the planet some 65 million years ago, and there hasn't been anything like them since. Lots of different kinds existed, and each kind had its particular traits that make it appealing—and dinosaur appeal is spreading like crazy. Growing numbers of scientists, 7-year-olds, and all kinds of people in between are catching on to dinosaurs.

Magnificent as they were in their own right, a lot of what makes dinosaurs really special is the fact that human beings have discovered and, in effect, re-created them. This re-creation is a careful scientific process, involving a patient, ongoing search for data and meticulous analysis of evidence. At the same time, it is an imaginative enterprise, the fleshing out of a world no one has ever seen.

Science and imagination work together in bringing dinosaurs back to life, and we've all seen the results of this collaboration in movies, on TV, in books, and in museums. The great thing is, anyone who wants to can be part of this group effort. In fact, lots of us begin to participate as kids when we first realize the earth was once inhabited by strange, terrifying, and fascinating creatures no longer alive today.

We need to use our imaginations to understand dinosaurs because we're a long way from being able to clone new, living dinos from fossilized DNA, despite what we see in the movie *Jurassic Park*.

A scene from Jurassic Park, *1993.*
(Universal Studios/ Photofest)

This film was a big hit, largely because the terrific special effects—with recently developed computer technology—filled the screen with moving, breathing dinosaurs. This movie was perhaps the most realistic dinosaur film ever because it drew on recent scientific ideas about dinosaurs. It shows the more you know about dinosaurs, the more your imagination starts working and the more fascinating they become.

Looking Back

As you probably already know, dinosaurs dominated the planet long before the first people came along. In fact, compared to dinosaurs—who evolved about 200 million years ago and hung around for about 140 million years—people only just arrived on the scene. Although the two million or three million years we've lived on earth may seem like a long time to us, human beings are really just evolutionary upstarts. We have a long way to go before we even begin to rival the dynasty of the dinosaurs.

The view of dinosaurs as big losers in the game of evolution couldn't be more wrong—the dinos developed a whole arsenal of effective survival strategies. While our distant ancestors, the early mammals, were little pip-squeaks whose best defense was running and hiding, the saurians found all sorts of ways to fit in and take over.

Many had sharp teeth and claws; some had horns, tusks, and skin like armor; many had great speed and agility; many had highly developed social skills—the ability to signal one another, hunt in packs or forage in herds, and perform mating rituals and displays—and some could even fly. And some, as everyone knows, had tremendous size.

Thanks in part to a newfound respect with which scientists have come to look at these weird, various, and complicated creatures, dinosaurs are as big as ever, attracting at least as much public attention as any other scientific topic.

In fact, dinoscience has recently made gigantosaurus-size steps backward to bring the past to life. Within the past 20 years, some major missing pieces of the dinosaur puzzle have been found and put together, giving us a paleo-picture that non-scientists as well as scientists find meaningful and exciting.

The story of dinosaurs is fascinating not only because of what we know about them but also because of how we know it—and because figuring out what they were like involves figuring out the unwritten history of our planet and our place in it. Dinosaurs have found new life in our time and have taken a lasting place in our thoughts about existence on earth. All these aspects of the dinosaur story are the subject of this book.

Part 1, "Boning Up on the Big Lizards," describes the science behind the dinosaur scene of today, including how the dinoscientists do their jobs and flesh out the bare bones of the fossil record. Included in this section are accounts of how fossils are formed and what they tell us, how we know how old the dinosaurs are, how the various kinds evolved, how they are related, and how they are classified.

Part 2, "The Lizard Butts," talks about the first of the two main group of dinosaurs, the saurischians or "lizard butts." This section explains what the saurischians were like, how they lived, what they could do, and how they evolved. This group includes the meat-eating theropods (those who survived by preying off others) and the lumbering sauropods (who survived by being just too darn big to be killed easily).

Part 3, "The Bird Butts," talks about the second group of dinosaurs, the ornithischians or "bird butts." These are the leaf-eaters who adapted a whole range of unusual survival traits, including thick, scaly armor, specialized teeth, and complex social behaviors that let them stay a half-step ahead of their meat-eating cousins.

Part 4, "They Also Ran, Crawled, Flew, and Swam," explains the lifestyles of the beasts who shared the planet with the dinosaurs: the pteranodons and other flying things, the lizards left out of the dinosaur clans, and the early mammals and fishy critters of long ago.

Part 5, "Famous Finds," is an account of the important fossil finds and the people who made them; it relates a history of the ongoing discovery of the dinosaurs.

Part 6, "Earthshaking Theories," heats up with the controversies, oddball ideas, and brilliant insights that have colored dinoscience since the earliest discoveries through the present day.

Part 7, "Paleo Fever," wraps things up with an account of the phenomenon of dinomania—their place in the books, movies, lives, and hearts of dinophiles everywhere.

Finally, at the back of the book are appendices for helping you dig still deeper into dinosaurs: a list of museums with large dinosaur fossil displays, a list of dinosaur names with a pronunciation key and an explanation of what they were, a set of outlines that show how the dinosaurs were related to one another, a glossary of technical terms, and a list of books on dinosaurs for further reading.

Extras

This book takes you through the nitty gritty of dinoscience, dinoscoveries, dinostories, and dinodiversions, and it includes some features to aid your reflection along the way. These include encapsulated facts, definitions, misconceptions, and suggestions falling under these headings:

Fossil Fallacy

Here you'll find some interesting bones of contention that got thrown out of—or never made it into—the respectable theories file. These fallacies illustrate how perilous dinoscience can be, relating some of the more notable mistakes along the way.

Boning Up

This feature is intended to help put the big, the old, the difficult, and the bizarre into perspective by supplying tips on how to wrap your brain around a prickly issue without unnecessary neural hemorrhaging.

Definosaurus

This feature takes the binomial nomenclature, paleojargon, technoterminology, and geekspeak, and puts it in plain language—because it's no fun reading something if you don't know what it means.

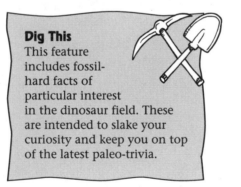

Dig This

This feature includes fossil-hard facts of particular interest in the dinosaur field. These are intended to slake your curiosity and keep you on top of the latest paleo-trivia.

Acknowledgments

Thanks to Vic Tulli and Jenn Dussling for consultation and bibliographic assistance.

Part 1
Boning Up on the Big Lizards

Scientists haven't had an easy time coming to terms with our older saurian siblings. Their task has been to make sense of a world no one has ever seen—literally from a couple of truckloads of ancient bones and teeth, a few thousand funny-looking footprints, and the rock and sediment that has built up over the planet's shifting, crumbling crust over the past quarter billion years. This section describes how they do it.

Chapter 1

The Dinosaur Underground

In This Chapter

➤ What fossils tell us

➤ How fossils are formed

➤ What kinds of fossils there are

➤ How fossil evidence gets interpreted

Dinosaurs have come to life all over again in the past 20 years, thanks to the dinoscientists who study their ancient, fossilized remains. From a growing number of fossils and some inspired ideas about them, we're getting a new, more vivid sense of just what the dinos were like.

Unfortunately, getting from a petrified bone to a good understanding of a living, breathing, well-adapted saurian romping through its environment involves painstaking, sometimes tedious work. The inspired flashes of theoretical insight come only after much digging, picking, and peering at bones.

Paleontologists, the scientists who study ancient life, spend their days poking around in search of bonebeds, digging out fossils—oh so carefully—with little shovels, brushes, and dental equipment, figuring out how all these scattered, broken, fossilized, incomplete bits of lizard once fit together. Finally—perhaps the most difficult job of all—they read about, examine, and compare all the various finds to try to make sense of them, to see what these bones were once part of, how these beasts once lived, how they evolved, and why they died off.

Much of their work may be tedious, but how they do it is rather fascinating, involving the ability to see a dynamic, unknown, by-gone planet in some broken, dead remains.

A Saury Lot

Definosaurus

The **fossil record** is the total amount of evidence of the existence of creatures no longer living. The word *fossil* comes from a Latin term meaning "dug up." **Taphonomy** is the study of what happens to remains from the time of death to the time of discovery, including how bones turn into fossils. The word comes from the Greek words *taphos*, for burial, and *nomos*, for law.

Our knowledge of dinosaurs is far from complete. After all, it depends entirely on the 250-million-year-old fossils we've been able to find. We rely on fossils to help us understand what the dinosaurs were like and what a variety of dinosaurs existed. Fossils help us see how evolution works, and how all the different kinds of dinosaur are related to one another and to the creatures who came before and after them.

As long ago as dinosaurs lived, we're pretty lucky to have as much evidence of their existence as we do. Fossilized dinosaur bones have been discovered on every continent, including Antarctica. About 300 distinct kinds of dinosaurs have been discovered and identified, and this may be as much as a quarter or a third of the number of different dinos thought to have existed.

The available evidence for dinosaurs is the *fossil record*, the buried and preserved remains and other traces of the dearly departed dinos. How to interpret this evidence is an important branch of dinoscience known as *taphonomy*—the rules governing how stuff gets buried.

Interpreting the fossil record is serious work!

(Special Collections and Archives, Rutgers University Library)

Turned to Stone

Most dinosaur fossils consist of bones and teeth that have turned to stone. This happens through *petrification*, or mineralization. Bones and teeth are made up partly of living tissue that decays fairly quickly, and elements like calcium and phosphorus that are slow to break down. After the soft part wears away, the hard part sometimes holds its structure long enough to soak up moisture with minerals dissolved in it. When the moisture dries, the minerals remain in tiny hollow spaces of bones, preserving their original shape.

Sometimes minerals completely replace the original tissue that formed the bone. In many dinosaur fossils, though, much of the hardest bone material remains intact. This is especially true of certain dino bones found in Alaska, where frigid conditions have kept the bones much as they were back in the big-lizard times. Thanks to finds like this, scientists are just starting to study some of the organic material that once belonged to dinosaurs, including dino DNA!

Sedimental Journey

For a skeleton to become fossilized, it usually has to be buried fairly quickly in sand, mud, or some other dusty, oozy stuff, so that the bones don't just crumble away. Eventually, this sand or mud has to dry out and get compressed into sedimentary rock—sandstone, clay, shale, chalk, or limestone—any kind of rock that forms from the build-up of layers of sediment. Non-sedimentary rock, namely igneous and metamorphic rock, doesn't ordinarily contain dinosaur fossils because these rocks are formed under such tremendous heat and pressure that any remains they contained have been destroyed.

Because only certain kinds of rock can contain dino-saur fossils, we can't be sure that a fossil record exists for all dinosaurs. For example, there may have been dinosaurs specially adapted for life in mountainous areas. Because sedimentary rock is unlikely to form on mountaintops, dinosaurs living on mountains would not likely become fossilized. This is one reason that most scientists think there were more dinosaurs than we will ever know about.

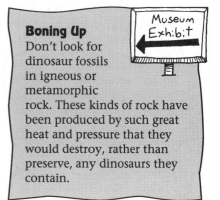

Boning Up
Don't look for dinosaur fossils in igneous or metamorphic rock. These kinds of rock have been produced by such great heat and pressure that they would destroy, rather than preserve, any dinosaurs they contain.

Older and Wiser

Because the fossil record is incomplete, it's important to learn all we can from the fossils we have. This means not only studying the bones of a particular dino, but also trying to figure out how the bones got where they were found and what the environment was like when the dinosaur died.

5

The study of prehistoric life, including the world of the dinosaurs, is known as *paleontology*. Paleontologists attempt to reconstruct the past to provide the fullest possible understanding of prehistory.

Paleontologists who study dinosaurs look at dino fossils in relation to all the other ideas scientists have formed about prehistory. As a result, a theory about a particular dinosaur may stand or fall based on knowledge of the plants or animals it may have eaten, the climate in which it might have lived, or the rock in which it lies buried.

Scattered bones of a single dino may mean it was killed by predators. The same can be said of a complete skeleton found together with the tooth of a meat-eater. A big jumble of bones belonging to different types of dinos may mean that they were deposited that way by a river or an avalanche. These scenarios provide clues about whether certain kinds of dinos lived in the water or on land, lived alone or in herds or packs, migrated or stayed in one place. The most direct clues about dinosaurs, though, are found in the fossils themselves.

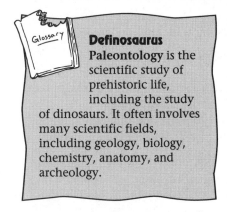

Definosaurus
Paleontology is the scientific study of prehistoric life, including the study of dinosaurs. It often involves many scientific fields, including geology, biology, chemistry, anatomy, and archeology.

Remains to Be Seen

There are two main kinds of fossils. The first kind, known as *body fossils*, are the preserved remains of the actual living dinosaur. The most common body fossils are the *hard parts*—mineralized bones and teeth. Occasionally, softer skin tissue remains after it has been dried and mummified. *Mummy fossils*, though rare, are also considered body fossils. Eggs and eggshells are also important.

The other sort of fossil are *trace fossils*, or *ichnofossils*. These fossils consist of pieces of evidence a dinosaur has left behind other than parts of its own body. The most significant trace fossils are *footprints and tailprints*.

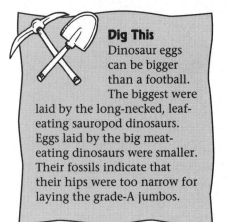

Dig This
Dinosaur eggs can be bigger than a football. The biggest were laid by the long-necked, leaf-eating sauropod dinosaurs. Eggs laid by the big meat-eating dinosaurs were smaller. Their fossils indicate that their hips were too narrow for laying the grade-A jumbos.

Other trace fossils are *natural casts* formed when sedimentary rock holds the shape of the inside of a skull or other hollow place. In addition, polished rocks called *gastroliths* have been left by dinosaurs who swallowed them to help them grind their food. Finally—you guessed it—there's petrified dino doo! These stools of stone are called *coprolites*.

Here's the whole list of dinosaur fossil varieties for easier perusing:

➤ **body fossils** Parts of the body that have been preserved, usually through mineralization but also through mummification.

➤ **hard parts** Teeth, bones, and bony structures that become mineralized.

➤ **mummy fossils**   Soft tissue that becomes dried and resistant to decay.

➤ **ichnofossils**   Traces left by a creature that are not actually part of its body.

➤ **footprints and tailprints**   Ancient trails that lead us back to the past.

➤ **skin impressions**   Scaly skinprints that have been preserved in sedimentary rock.

➤ **gastroliths**   The equivalent of modern-day gizzard stones, these polished rocks have been swallowed by paleo-plant-eaters to help them digest their dinner.

➤ **natural casts**   Lumps of hardened mud or clay formed inside a skull or footprint.

➤ **coprolites**   Mineralized monuments of some of the major movements of prehistory, including one fecal find that logs in at close to a foot long!

> **Boning Up**
> Coprolites, or petrified lumps of dino dung, have their tale to tell. Dinoscientists have discovered tiny tunnels preserved in certain samples. These may have been left by Mesozoic dung beetles. If so, it means dung beetles have been around many millenia longer than was previously thought.

Body Language

Dinoscientists turn to all the fossils they can find for clues that will tell them more about dinosaurs. By far the most valuable fossils are the body fossils, the petrified skeletons that provide the hardest evidence that dinos once walked the earth.

Shaping Up

Among the most important things body fossils tell us is the shape, or *morphology*, of the dinosaurs. If we can find most of a skeleton and figure out how the bones fit together, we can get a basic idea of the dinosaur's size and shape.

We get an even clearer idea of the physical shape of a dinosaur from marks in fossilized bones left from the muscles that were attached to them. By studying these marks, paleontologists can estimate the size and shape of the dinosaur meat that once covered the bones.

Reconstructing dinosaur morphologies, though, isn't as easy as it sounds. As we'll see in Chapter 21, a number of dinosaurs have been mistakenly put back together! This has happened when dinoscientists, often working with incomplete skeletons, made false assumptions about what the dinosaurs looked like.

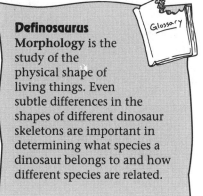

> **Definosaurus**
> **Morphology** is the study of the physical shape of living things. Even subtle differences in the shapes of different dinosaur skeletons are important in determining what species a dinosaur belongs to and how different species are related.

Fossil Fallacy

One of the first dinosaur skeletons ever discovered belonged to a beast called iguanodon because it had teeth that looked like dino-sized versions of a modern-day iguana's. Richard Owen, the famous Victorian scientist who first reconstructed iguanodon, assumed that his big lizard was shaped like the little iggies we all know and love—slow, squat, and four-footed. Only years later, after more iguanodon bones were found, did people realize Owen's mistake: Iguanodons trot around on two feet, more like kangaroos than today's lizards.

Lifestyles of the Extinct

In revealing clues about the physical characteristics of living dinosaurs, body fossils give us clues as to how they lived. Teeth and claws indicate what they ate and how they got their food: whether they hunted and killed their prey, scavenged for meat already dead, or ate plants. Skeletal structure suggests how they moved: whether they walked upright, on all fours, or crawled; whether they climbed trees, swam, or flew; whether they were fast or slow, agile or plodding; and whether they had hands capable of grasping things or forepaws with claws.

Bony structures such as horns, tusks, crests, frills, and armor provide clues about how dinosaurs may have interacted, whether they were capable of attacking or defending themselves, and whether they could get themselves noticed when a good-looking dinosaur of the opposite sex was around.

Boning Up

Some scientists believe that, just as love makes people do crazy things, love made many dinosaurs evolve some wacky physical characteristics that don't seem to be of much use outside of flirting. Triceratop frills, stegosaur plates, and duckbill honkers may have evolved as attention-getters for dinos who were hot to trot!

Time to Make a Change

Finally, body fossils provide important clues about evolution. By carefully examining similarities and differences among skeletons, paleontologists try to figure out how dinosaurs evolved and how they are related to one another. As we'll see in Chapter 4, this is especially challenging and controversial because structural similarities between two kinds of dinosaur do not necessarily mean the two are closely related. Instead, similarities may develop as a result of adaptations to similar environments.

A porpoise, for example, is not closely related to a fish, even though the two look fairly similar. The similarity stems from the fact that the porpoise, a mammal, developed fish-like characteristics while adapting to life in the water. Similarly, two dinosaur skeletons that resemble each other may have adapted in similar ways without being closely related. It's hard to tell because all we have to go by are fossils.

The Name Game

To make matters even more difficult, fossils are sometimes in short supply, undiscovered, or perhaps even nonexistent for some kinds of dinosaurs. Where fossils are scarce, it's especially hard to draw sound conclusions. It can be difficult to see not only how two species of dinosaur are related but even whether different bones belong to dinosaurs of the same or different species.

Fossil Fallacy

Technically speaking, there's no such dinosaur as a *Brontosaurus*. The name was given to a set of fossils that turned out to belong to a species that already had a different name: *Apatosaurus*. Dinoscientists go by the rule that says the first person to discover a species gets to name it. Of course, this rule sometimes causes problems because the first person to name a species of dinosaur may base that name on mistaken information. Also, as in the case of the *Brontosaurus*, a name may catch on before people realize the species already had a name.

Skeletons that are shaped differently may belong to the same species if they were left by dinosaurs that reached different ages when they died, or if they belonged to a male and female of a species in which males and females had different shapes. What's more, different-shaped skeletons may result from pressure exerted on one set of bones by the rocks in which they were fossilized.

If You've Seen One, You've Seen Them All

To keep the fossil record organized, paleontologists designate the best set of fossils they can find for each species as the measuring stick for that species. This is the most complete and most representative skeleton, called the *holotype*. New finds are compared to holotypes to see whether they belong to a species that has already been discovered, or whether they belong to a kind of dinosaur that no one has known about for two million years.

Definosaurus

A **holotype** is a fossil skeleton that best represents the species it belongs to. Other skeletons can be compared to the holotype to determine what kind of dinosaur they are.

Lasting Impressions

Because body fossils don't always tell us everything we want to know about dinosaurs, it's nice to have the trace fossils, or ichnofossils, to fall back on. By studying trace fossils, paleontologists can supplement what they learn from petrified body parts.

Organ Grinders

Some of the most ordinary-looking fossils are actually among the most peculiar. For example, gastroliths, or gizzard stones, look like—in fact, are—ordinary polished rocks, smaller than your fist. As ordinary as they appear, they hold a special place in the history of food as the first eating utensils.

A number of plant-eating sauropod dinosaurs have surprisingly small teeth and weak jaws that seem poorly designed for eating the tough stems, leaves, grass, and pine needles that formed their diet. For years, dinoscientists have taken this as evidence that the sauropods had a low metabolism—a low rate of burning food energy. This low metabolism would make them so sluggish that they wouldn't need to eat much. (We'll say more about high versus low metabolism in Chapter 23.)

Dig This

Some creatures today use gizzard stones just as the dinosaurs did. These include certain birds, as well as the crocodile, which uses them not only for digestion, but for ballast for staying underwater more easily.

This view downplays the significance of gizzard stones. In fact, many today accept the opposing view: That the big browsers swallowed enough rocks to line the walls of their gizzards and used them to grind down all the leafy greens they could swallow. The stones did the chewing, keeping the strain off the dinosaurs' delicate dental work.

Walk This Way

Like other kinds of fossils, preserved dinosaur footprints can be difficult to interpret. Different kinds of tracks have special names given to them by dinoscientists, who acknowledge that they are often unable to tell what kind of dinosaur made what kind of track. In fact, funny things can happen to prints in the millions of years since dinosaur feet made them. For example, only part of a set of prints may harden and be preserved, making it seem like they were made by smaller feet.

Dino footprints have been at the center of a number of kooky controversies. A famous fallout over footprints took place in Texas in the 1930s, when fossilized human tracks were identified side by side with tracks made by dinosaurs. The claim was startling because the dinos died out more than 60 million years before human beings emerged. The discovery fueled the belief held by many creationists that evolution is a myth and attracted much attention from the public. Locals even began carving new human footprints in the old rock and selling them to tourists!

Dinoscientists came to realize that people had been fooled by the many forms dinosaur footprints can take. Agile theropods, in particular, can leave tracks of several different shapes, depending on whether they walk on their toes, their toes together with their heels, or, in some cases, back on their heels with their toes up in the air. This last kind of print resembles human footprints and accounts for the appearance of 65-million-year-old people prints.

Fossil Fallacy

A set of sauropod tracks has been found that retained the impression only of the tips of the toes. Were these traces left by a 2-ton dinosaur tiptoeing through Triassic tulips? One explanation, widely accepted until only recently, held that the dainty dino was walking underwater, where, partially buoyed, its feet barely reached the bottom. Lately, dinoscientists believe that the original footprints were made in soil that has since partially eroded, leaving the shallow prints.

Geologic Time Trials

In spite of the uncertainty, footprints can say a lot about the dinosaurs that left them. For example, they can confirm whether a dinosaur walked with its legs splayed or together, and whether it walked upright or on four feet. Dinoscientists can also figure out how fast a dinosaur was moving based on its footprints.

This involves some complicated mathematical maneuvering, but the idea is that if you measure how far apart the prints are and you have a good idea of the length of the dino's legs, you can come up with a formula relating pace length to leg length and compare that to modern walkers whose speeds can be measured.

In fact, many dinosaur tracks suggest a vogue for Jurassic jogging and paleo-powerwalking. Five miles per hour is a typical pace—this would get most people's blood pumping. Many other dino tracks indicate a more leisurely strolling pace.

One set of theropod tracks sets a fossil record Olympic sprinters would be proud of: 100 meters in under 10 seconds. Of course, the dinosaur has a height advantage. The footprints in this trackway were planted 5.3 meters apart. That's about 14 feet, or about the length of a stretch limo! And for all we know, it may not even have been going full speed.

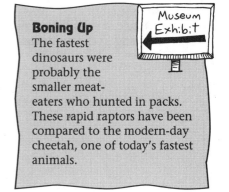

Boning Up
The fastest dinosaurs were probably the smaller meat-eaters who hunted in packs. These rapid raptors have been compared to the modern-day cheetah, one of today's fastest animals.

The Mommy Track

One of the most exciting bits of information revealed by paleo-footprints has to do not with how fast the dinos moved but how long they hung around. Footprints left by a certain kind of hadrosaur have been found together with nests, eggs, and baby skeletons of the same species. This means that not all the big lizards were deadbeat dinos! Some evidently took care of the kids, perhaps keeping the eggs warm, feeding the hatchlings, protecting them, and maybe even showing the little ones the reptilian ropes.

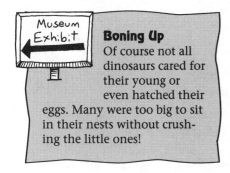

Boning Up
Of course not all dinosaurs cared for their young or even hatched their eggs. Many were too big to sit in their nests without crushing the little ones!

The idea that dinos provided kiddy care contrasts drastically with the traditional view of dinosaurs as being, in essence, overgrown lizards. As a rule, lizards of today lay their eggs and don't look back, leaving the hatchlings to fend for themselves. If young dinos had even a little parental upbringing, the result would be a more social sort of saurian who may have relied on the company of its kind in various ways throughout life. In honor of this model of paleo-parenthood, the species is named *Maiasaurus*, after Maia, the Roman goddess of nature. The discovery has led to speculation that other dinosaurs may have cared for their young as well.

Happy Trails

Footprints suggest a good deal about social behavior—as well as antisocial behavior!—among dinosaurs. Group tracks provide indications of herding together among plant-eating dinosaurs, and of hunting in packs among some meat-eaters. There are also a number of tracks that may show meat-eating dinosaurs stalking their prey. These tracks provide evidence against the view that many meat-eaters were scavengers who simply waited for their food to die rather than killing it themselves. They also depict dramatic, if speculative, scenarios.

Some trackways, because of their direction, location, and the large number of footprints they contain, have suggested to paleontologists that certain dinosaurs migrated. For example, a number of trackways consist of prints made by 30 or more different dinosaurs all going in the same direction. They must all be going off somewhere!

Excavating a dinosaur footprint in Woodbridge, New Jersey.

(Special Collections and Archives, Rutgers University Library)

The Least You Need to Know

➤ We learn virtually everything we know about dinosaurs from fossils.

➤ Fossils provide clues about dinosaur physical characteristics, way of life, and evolution.

➤ Dinosaur skeletons are generally preserved only in sedimentary rock.

➤ Dinosaur body fossils are preserved parts of once-living dinosaurs.

➤ Trace fossils are marks and remains that are not actual body parts.

Chapter 2

Using Rocks as Clocks

In addition to the fossils that tell us about dinosaurs, there's rock. You may be surprised to find out how much rock can say, not only about the creatures preserved in it but also about the long-ago world those creatures lived in. Rock readers have learned to retrace the sedimentary steps that lead from outcroppings of sandstone, shale, and limestone back to a lush, green, dino-inhabited planet.

The papers may say that more fossilized bones were found at a construction site in China or a desert in South America. The rocks, though, have the real scoop: the late-breaking story of a pack of velociraptors hunting on the mild plains of Laurasia; or an *Apatosaurus* that died during a Gondwana monsoon; and perhaps Pangaea was unusually cool that millennium.

Paleo-geologists want to know how the world of the dinos came about and what happened that made it change. To do this, they figure out what happened when the rocks and fossils they study were formed. In doing this, they reconstruct an entire chain of events that unfolded throughout the dinosaur era. This involves placing each rock and fossil as accurately as possible in time.

Two Kinds of Time

As we saw in Chapter 1, fossils are the basis of our understanding of dinosaurs, but they need to be interpreted in light of the environment in which they were found. Paleontology's task is to put these environments together into an understanding of the ancient world as an ongoing, evolving whole. This means, for the most part, using the layers of rock and soil that have been built up through the ages as a measure of passing time and evolutionary change.

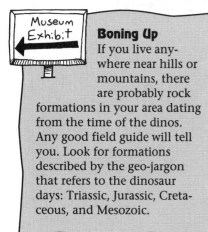

Boning Up

If you live anywhere near hills or mountains, there are probably rock formations in your area dating from the time of the dinos. Any good field guide will tell you. Look for formations described by the geo-jargon that refers to the dinosaur days: Triassic, Jurassic, Cretaceous, and Mesozoic.

There are actually two different ways of measuring the huge expanses of time that have passed since the earth was formed four and a half billion years ago. The first involves looking at the planet as a whole and noticing how it is made of layers of rock that were formed during different periods of time. Each layer tells part of the story of what happened long before human beings came on the scene.

The second approach to prehistoric time-telling involves looking at tiny, isolated atoms and calculating the incredibly slow and steady rate at which they give off minute amounts of energy. Both measuring methods are used together to put dinosaurs into better focus, letting us see just how old they are, what their lives were like, how long they were around, and how suddenly they disappeared.

Going Down in Time

A couple of hundred years ago, geologists began noticing rock's tendency to form in layers. Outcroppings of sedimentary rock take the shape of big stone sheets spread out one on top of the other. They figured out that the upmost layers, those closest to the surface of the earth, had formed most recently, and the farther down you go, the older the layers of stone. What's more, each layer has its own particular characteristics, setting it apart from the surrounding layers.

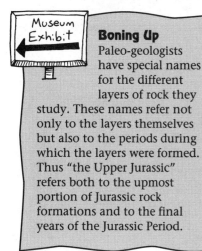

Boning Up

Paleo-geologists have special names for the different layers of rock they study. These names refer not only to the layers themselves but also to the periods during which the layers were formed. Thus "the Upper Jurassic" refers both to the upmost portion of Jurassic rock formations and to the final years of the Jurassic Period.

The layers are different for two main reasons. For one, they were formed at different times under different climates and geological conditions. The formation of layers of sediment isn't always a steady process. Long periods during which rocks form may be interrupted by equally long periods in which they don't.

It takes the right circumstances for a layer of sedimentary rock to form. Wind, gravity, the flow of water, and volcanic activity may combine in different ways to pile up sediment in any particular place. Because these circumstances are always changing, old layers may be interrupted, and new layers may be laid down for a whole new set of reasons. As a result, each new layer is noticeably different from previous layers.

What's more, layers of rock are different because each one contains the residue of different life-forms, reflecting evolutionary changes as new species developed and old ones died off. As a result, the earth's crust is like a big pan of lasagna in which each layer consists of different ingredients.

Blankets of Time

The layers have all been given different names and put into groups that have names too. As we said, the names refer to layers as well as to periods of time. Here's how geologists divide up pre-history.

➤ **eon**   The biggest segments of geologic time. In fact, there have only been two since the earth was formed: the Cryptozoic, which lasted about 4 billion years, and the Phanerozoic, which has only been going on for about 540 million years.

➤ **era**   The present eon is divided into three eras. These are, from oldest to most recent, the Paleozoic, the Mesozoic, and the Cenozoic. The Mesozoic Era included the days of the dinos.

➤ **period**   Eras are divided into periods. The Mesozoic Era includes, from oldest to most recent, the Triassic, the Jurassic, and the Cretaceous.

➤ **epoch**   Each period is divided into two to four epochs. The Cretaceous Period, for example, is divided into the Early Cretaceous and Late Cretaceous.

➤ **stage**   Each epoch may include any number of stages, each lasting anywhere from 2 to 10 million years. The last of the dinosaur fossils are found in the Maastrichtian stage of the Late Cretaceous. This is when all the non-bird dinosaurs died off.

Locked in the Rocks

These layers tell us the story of life. Because the rocks that contain the tale are kind of heavy, here's the abridged version.

The Laid-Back Life

The oldest, deepest layers, dating from the previous eon, which ended more than 540 million years ago, contain only the simplest forms of life: fossilized bacteria, algae, and fungus. These are the pre-Cambrian layers, formed on the floors of the prehistoric ocean when all life was in the sea. (The Cambrian layer is the first layer of the current eon, the Phanerozoic.) The fact that fossils from these ancient sea floors can be found in the mountains of today shows how much things can change in a billion years!

The pre-Cambrian days lasted much longer than all the other periods combined. In fact, most of our planet's history was pretty uneventful because during this whole first eon—almost nine-tenths of the earth's total existence—things happened really slowly. The oldest rocks formed as the hot, molten surface of the earth hardened, the first water began to form on the surface, and an atmosphere of unbreatheable gas and water vapor settled in on top of the rock and water. Finally, about a billion years ago, tiny bits of living scum developed and floated around in the ocean.

Eventually, at a crucial moment of the pre-Cambrian Period, this scum developed into blue-green algae, which began producing oxygen, setting the stage for when, far into the future, the first animals would slog their way out of the sea to a life on land.

So much for the pre-Cambrian layers. The next layers of rock tell the story of an ever-increasing variety and complexity of life: the first fish fossils are found in the Ordovician and Silurian layers; the first forests and amphibians appear in the Devonian layers. In the Carboniferous layers came the amniotes, creatures who could lay eggs on land. This was the Paleozoic Era, which was topped off with the Permian Period.

Dig This
Leonardo da Vinci was among those who noticed sea-floor fossils up in the mountains and reflected on the changing nature of things. Such fossils prompted similar reflections among people in ancient China.

Dig This
Blue-green algae lived in colonies that formed huge reefs. Many of these reefs have been fossilized in limestone and can be found all over the world. Geologists call these fossils **stromatolites**, from the Greek words *stroma*, meaning flat, and *lite*, meaning stone.

Definosaurus
Residue left from each of the periods of geologic time form in layers called **strata**. The interpretation of these layers is **stratigraphy**.

Dino Might

At the start of the next era, the Mesozoic, things really started coming alive. The amniotes divided into different groups. One group, the reptiles, would give rise to the dinosaurs. Another group, the synapsids, would give rise to the mammals. These two strands of evolutionary thread—mammals and dinosaurs—were woven simultaneously at the start of the Mesozoic Era. Events of this era are preserved in the Triassic, Jurassic, and Cretaceous layers, the time when the dinos lived.

The Triassic layer is full of more mammal than dino fossils, suggesting, of course, that more mammals existed at the time. This story changes in the Jurassic layer. Here most of the mammals disappear amid an explosion of dinosaur dominance! This is when the dinosaurs really take over, and the mammals that are left are small, timid critters who come out only at night for fear of the dominating dinos.

The tables were turned during the end of the Cretaceous Period and the beginning of the Tertiary. Here it is written in Cenozoic stone that the dinosaurs had all died out—or flown away as birds—leaving the mammals plenty of evolutionary space to let their hair down. Finally, in the last layer, the Quaternary, fossils of the earliest humans appear.

Fossil Fallacy

Traditionally, dinos have been seen as big, dumb, lumbering lizards who became extinct when they were finally outfoxed by the wilier mammals. This theory no longer holds water. Instead, wily and agile dinos like *Troodon* may have come close to wiping out our fur-bearing great-grandparents!

The Sediment Express

Here's your very own evolutionary train schedule, with all the stations where life has changed on its long ride to the present day.

Geologic Time Table

Millions of Years Ago	Era	Period	Evolutionary Event
		Quaternary	First humans
65	Cenozoic	Tertiary	Mammals dominate
		Cretaceous	Last non-bird dinosaurs
		Jurassic	First birds
			Dinosaurs dominate
			Pangaea breaks up
250	Mesozoic	Triassic	First dinos and mammals
		Permian	Great extinctions
		Carboniferous	First amniotes
		Devonian	First amphibians
		Silurian	First jawed fish
		Ordovician	Jawless fish only
544	Paleozoic	Cambrian	Sea creatures with shells
4,500	Cryptozoic	Pre-Cambrian	Bacteria and algae

This is the basic story told by the blankets of debris that cover the planet. These layers are known as geological *strata*, and the science of interpreting these layers is known as *stratigraphy*.

The Layered Look

As mentioned earlier, one important reason that the planet's old rock takes the form of successive, separate layers is that each layer contains fossils left by different life-forms. Old life-forms change, evolving into new species as they adapt to changing situations; or they fail to adapt and die out. Although the changing layers of rock provide a fairly clear record of these changes, they provide only mysterious and tantalizing hints of why these changes occurred.

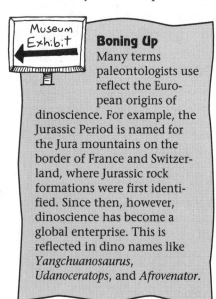

Boning Up

Many terms paleontologists use reflect the European origins of dinoscience. For example, the Jurassic Period is named for the Jura mountains on the border of France and Switzerland, where Jurassic rock formations were first identified. Since then, however, dinoscience has become a global enterprise. This is reflected in dino names like *Yangchuanosaurus*, *Udanoceratops*, and *Afrovenator*.

We'll talk about theories explaining how the dinos came on the scene and why they disappeared in Part 5. These theories, though, are highly speculative and controversial. In fact, it is unlikely that we will ever find one single, simple explanation for why or how a species evolves or becomes extinct.

These events may involve any number of interrelated factors including changes in climate, changes in the atmosphere, the availability of food, the spread of disease, and changing animal behavior. Any change may trigger other changes that may have further impact on the environment as a whole, leading to the kinds of global change that show up in the geologic layers. That's why paleontologists try to piece together the whole story of the prehistoric planet from outcroppings of sedimentary rock and from fossil deposits found all over the world.

The Dating Game

The study of stratigraphy tells us that big changes can happen pretty much all at once all over the world. This doesn't necessarily mean that sudden disasters, such as an asteroid hitting the planet, ruining the atmosphere, and causing all the dinos to suddenly drop dead, took place with each new period of time—although paleontologists explore just this sort of possibility.

It *does* mean that the little hand on the stratigraphic clock clicks just once every several million years or so. In other words, a change that may have taken 500,000 years may look sudden when seen as the clearly defined difference between two layers of rock.

No set correlation exists between the thickness of a layer of stone and the amount of time it took to form that layer. In fact, strata thickness varies from place to place. Regardless of the thickness of each layer, though, the sequence in which the layers form is the same wherever you go.

If You've Got the Fossils, We've Got the Time

Geologists have figured out this sequence, incorporating all the most important sedimentary rock formations around the world into a single coherent time scheme. Because the sequence of changing layers of rock is the same all over the world, it is possible to compare the ages of dinosaur fossils discovered on different continents. This kind of comparison is called *relative dating*. No, relative dating isn't incestuous social behavior that led to the extinction of the dinosaurs! It's a process for figuring out whether one fossil is older or younger than another.

Geologists try to be as precise as they can in their relative dating. To make accurate use of their stratigraphic stopwatches, paleo-geologists rely heavily on certain kinds of fossils as markers for comparing the age of other finds. If you want to know how a newly discovered fossil fits in with the overall geologic time scheme, it helps to find another fossil right below it (earlier), right above it (later), or at the same level (during), whose age is already known.

The fossils most useful for relative dating have two characteristics. First, they represent a species that occurred all over the world. This makes it easier to compare them to other fossils found everywhere. Second, they represent a species that lived for only a few million years before dying off. This allows for more dating precision.

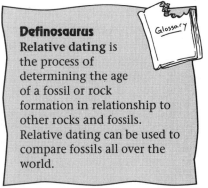

Definosaurus
Relative dating is the process of determining the age of a fossil or rock formation in relationship to other rocks and fossils. Relative dating can be used to compare fossils all over the world.

Fossilized pollen has proven especially useful for relative dating. It is found all over the world, and each species survives only a relatively short time before evolving into a new form. Thus we can often tell the age of a dino by looking at what made it sneeze!

Nuke the Dinos!

Relative dating does not tell us how old a fossil is in years but only how old it is in comparison with something else. No numbers are involved in relative dating, only words like old, older, and really old! To figure out the age in numbers of years of a rock or fossil, *absolute dating* is required.

Absolute dating can be used together with relative dating to get the fossil record in sync. The most effective method of absolute dating is called *radiometry*. This involves analysis of certain elements at the atomic level.

Believe it or not, many elements decay. No, a rotten rock doesn't smell bad, but some elements found in

Definosaurus
Determining the age of a fossil in terms of the number of years old it is requires **absolute dating**. The most useful method of absolute dating is **radiometry**, a technique for measuring minuscule amounts of radioactive elements in some rocks.

rock actually break down and fall apart at a steady rate. The rate at which these elements fall apart can be used to find the age of the rock.

Get a Half-Life

As you may remember if you've ever taken a chemistry class, all elements are made up of electrons, protons, and neutrons. The number of protons and electrons determines which element is which. A carbon atom, for example, has six protons and six electrons. A nitrogen atom has seven of each.

The number of neutrons in an element can vary. Variations in the number of neutrons within any single element are called *isotopes* of the element. What's more, some isotopes are more stable than others. Unstable isotopes are radioactive. In a radioactive isotope, a neutron may spontaneously explode into fragments. These fragments consist of a new proton, an electron, and an antineutrino. At the same time, gamma radiation is released.

When this happens, the element actually changes into a new element. The unstable isotope Carbon-14 has six protons and eight neutrons. When one of its neutrons falls apart, it picks up an extra proton from the fragments and turns into nitrogen.

The decay of unstable isotopes is a gradual process that occurs at different rates for different elements. The rate at which an isotope decays is its *half-life*. The half-life is the time it takes for half the unstable atoms of an isotope to decay. In fact, once it has taken a certain length of time for half of a certain amount of an isotope to decay, it will take the same amount of time for half of the remaining isotope to decay as well. The rate of decay, in other words, is steady.

Different isotopes have different half-lifes. Carbon-14, for example, has a half-life of 5,730 years. Isotopically speaking, this is a fairly short half-life, making Carbon-14 useful in dating recent fossils such as those left by early humans. More useful for dating dinos is Uranium-236, with its half-life of four-and-a-half billion years.

Definosaurus

Isotopes are atoms of a particular kind of element that have more neutrons than the element usually has. Some isotopes are unstable and give off energy, or decay into more stable atoms. The rate at which an isotope decays is the **half-life** of the isotope. The half-life is the length of time it takes for half of any amount of isotopes to decay. This rate of decay is constant regardless of the amount of isotopes.

Double Dating

As you can imagine, measuring elements and half-lifes one atom at a time can be tricky, requiring high-tech laboratories with sensitive—and expensive—equipment. It will be a while before tope-it-yourself dino-dating kits hit the market.

But even with the high-tech tope-timers, the dating game involves more than simply waiting for your fossil samples to come back from the lab with their birthdate stamped on them. As we mentioned, unstable isotopes—those useful in radiometric dating—are generally not found in sedimentary stone but in igneous rock, formed through volcanic activity, where fossils are few and far between.

This difficulty means that radiometry must be employed together with relative dating to place fossil finds in time. To date a fossil you find in your backyard, you may need to find some fossilized pollen along with it. To date this pollen, you may need to compare it to some pollen of the same species that was found in Australia near some volcanic rock that contains some Uranium-238 that is slowly, slowly turning into Lead-206.

Fossil Fallacy

Every travel-back-to-the-time-of-the-dinos movie has at least one big volcano getting ready to blurp bright-red pancake batter all over the set. From this you might think that there would be plenty of volcanic rock mixed among real-life dino fossils. Actually, there was not much volcanic activity during the Mesozoic, making absolute dating that much more difficult.

Catching the Drift

Fortunately for dino daters, the Mesozoic layers, in which dinosaur fossils are found, contain many of the same dead dinos whether you look in China, Africa, or Argentina. This is especially true of the Triassic and Early Jurassic dinos. During the Late Jurassic and Cretaceous periods, however, there's an increasing tendency for different dino kinds to clump together on different continents.

This makes perfect sense. During the early stages of the Mesozoic, dinos could make it by land from any part of the world to any other part. All the continents were one huge land mass known as *Pangaea*. Pangaea was formed during Permian times when the supercontinent *Laurasia* (consisting of present-day North America, Europe, and Asia) collided with *Gondwana* (made up of what we now know as South America, Africa, India, Australia, and Antarctica). Pangaea began breaking apart again into smaller continents during Jurassic times. Since the big break up, certain land-locked dinos started evolving on some continents but not on others.

Definosaurus

At the start of the Mesozoic Era, the earth's land was one huge continent known as **Pangaea**. Pangaea formed during the Permian Period at the end of the Paleozoic when **Gondwana**, a supercontinent made up of present-day South America, Africa, India, Australia, and Antarctica, collided with **Laurasia**, consisting of present-day North America, Europe, and Asia. The amassing and breaking up of supercontinents takes place due to the shifting of **tectonic plates**, the huge slabs of rock that make up the earth's crust and float on top of the molten rock beneath the surface.

Continental shifting occurs because the earth's crust isn't like a golf ball, with one seamless skin, but is made up of a number of slabs called *tectonic plates*. The tectonic plates aren't attached to each other (though they may collide and buckle together for a while), nor are they rooted in the earth. Instead, they float around on top of the molten rock that lies underneath.

In fact, the tectonic plates drift around from place to place, carried by the liquid rock underneath, which moves around in response to heat moving through it from the earth's core. This movement of the tectonic plates is called *continental drift*, and it continues today. We've been drifting farther out to sea at the rate of about an inch every year! We may even be on a collision course with China—who knows?

Continental Compasses

Geologists have uncovered some fascinating evidence to prove continental drift really has occurred, resulting in the present configuration of continents in the aftermath of the breakup of Pangaea, Gondwana, and Laurasia. This evidence is found in volcanic rocks containing little pieces of iron. This rock bubbled to the surface during the Mesozoic and Paleozoic eras. While it lay in its molten state, the iron was free to move within it so as to point towards the north pole like the needle of a compass. The rocks then cooled and froze the iron pieces in place.

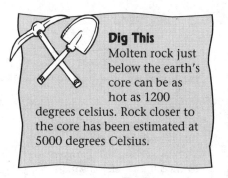

Dig This
Molten rock just below the earth's core can be as hot as 1200 degrees celsius. Rock closer to the core has been estimated at 5000 degrees Celsius.

The funny thing is, the iron pieces no longer point north but angle off in skewed directions. That's because not just the iron but the whole continent had shifted in relation to the north pole. By figuring out the ages of the various volcanic rocks containing pieces of iron, geologists have figured out the orientation of the continents at the time those rocks hardened into their present state.

Mesozoic Weather Report

Continental drift has led science to new approaches for explaining the world of the dinosaurs. Now that we're working with a totally different Mesozoic map, we may get a clearer picture of the lives of the dinos. The fact that the present continents were once clustered together into one landmass undoubtedly made a difference in climate. Air and ocean currents would have taken a completely different pattern, affecting temperature and rainfall all over the planet.

In fact, attempts to reconstruct the climate of dinodom suggest that climates were warmer and drier during the Triassic than today, with clear temperature differences from season to season. Mild temperatures continued in the Jurassic Period. The polar ice caps were small, and sea levels were high, with only slight shifts in temperature with the changing seasons. In the Cretaceous, polar ice expanded, and seasonal fluctuations increased again.

What these changes in the weather meant for the dinos is still a matter of speculation, but many dinoscientists think these climatic conditions may have played a part in the rise and fall of the dinosaurs.

The Least You Need to Know

> ➤ All over the world, layers of rock correspond to periods of geologic time.

> ➤ In general, the farther down from the surface a layer of rock is, the older it is.

> ➤ Rocks tell the story of the evolution and extinction of all known forms of prehistoric life.

> ➤ Paleo-geologists calculate the age of fossils and rocks through relative and absolute dating.

> ➤ Continental drift has altered the configuration of continents on the face of the planet throughout dinosaur times and ever since.

Chapter 3

Rising to the Occasion

In This Chapter

➤ Understanding evolution

➤ How species change

➤ What makes new changes work

➤ The downside of evolution

➤ Evolution as feel-good theory

➤ Key adaptive traits of the dinos

One of humanity's most important scientific discoveries is that living things evolve. Evolution has had profound effects, not just on the way scientists understand living things, but also on how people everywhere understand life. Few scientific concepts have been so fascinating for so long for so many people.

Dinosaurs fit into evolution, obviously, because they evolved. But they also contributed to the formation of the theory because dinosaur fossils began to get serious scientific attention in the years just before Charles Darwin came out with his theory of natural selection in 1859. Although Darwin doesn't talk about dinos in his famous book *The Origin of Species*, he certainly knew about them through fellow scientists like Sir Richard Owen, the first person to use the term "dinosaur" to describe an old set of bones.

Darwin drew on input from Owen and others in developing his scheme for how evolution worked. This was a good thing because the dinosaur fossil record was crying out for a new theory to explain it. Since Darwin's time, evolution has come a long way in explaining the rise of the dinos to Mesozoic dominance.

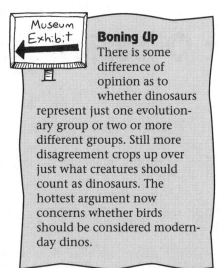

Boning Up
There is some difference of opinion as to whether dinosaurs represent just one evolutionary group or two or more different groups. Still more disagreement crops up over just what creatures should count as dinosaurs. The hottest argument now concerns whether birds should be considered modern-day dinos.

Boning Up
All scientists agree that evolution takes place, although there is some disagreement about how it works. A modification of Darwin's theory was offered in the 1970s by Niles Eldridge and Stephen Jay Gould, who described evolutionary change as "punctuated equilibria." In other words, it doesn't happen gradually, a little at a time within a species, as Darwin proposed, but all of a sudden between long intervals of stability.

Quick-Change Artists

Dinos are known for their variety. Hundreds of species have been discovered, representing branches of one of the bushiest family trees of all time. This shows that, for whatever reason, dinos evolved and adapted in many different ways to many different environments—all in a mere 160 million years.

In a sense, evolution is just a four-syllable word for change. Things change all the time in all sorts of ways for all sorts of reasons. Evolution refers specifically to changes in kinds of living things, known as species. Species, like everything else, change in all sorts of ways for all sorts of reasons.

The special thing about evolution as Darwin explained it is that individual creatures don't evolve. Evolution is the change from a group of individuals into a new group. It doesn't take place inside any single living thing but happens—sometimes—when living things reproduce.

Calling All Creatures

Perhaps you've played the game "telephone," as a kid or at a really wild party. Everyone sits in circle, and the first kid makes a "call" by whispering a message into the ear of the kid next to him. That kid whispers what she thinks she heard into the next kid's ear, and so on around the circle. By the end of the party line, the message has always changed to a crazy permutation of the original.

The original message may have "evolved" through a whole series of changes. None of the callers changed the message they "heard" before passing it on; changes only took place between callers, just when the message was being reproduced. Since Darwin's time, we have learned that the "messages" sent by a species to its descendants take the form of complex sequences of DNA. These are molecules that contain the code for how an organism—a living thing—will develop during its lifetime.

The fossil record shows the changing messages heard by living things as they evolved from the beginning of life itself: "be a fish, pass it on," "be an amphibian, pass it on," "be an amniote, pass it on," "be a mammal, pass it on".... Paleontologists want to trace the whole series of changes as they occur from caller to caller. These changes tend to occur in all living things. When they do, they are known as *variation*.

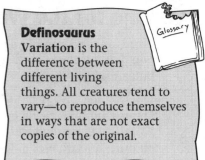

Definosaurus
Variation is the difference between different living things. All creatures tend to vary—to reproduce themselves in ways that are not exact copies of the original.

Try, Try Again

Evolution is a challenging concept. One aspect that can be especially hard to grasp is how random the whole thing seems. If it really works like a game of telephone, why aren't there species of three-headed purple orangutans flapping around with butterfly wings, sucking frogs and daffodils into their mouths with 20-foot tongues? The fossil record seems to have more meaning to it than a kid's game. Life seems intricately balanced and organized, as if it had all been carefully planned out ahead of time.

In fact, scientists believe that the life-forms that *seem* to result from careful planning actually take place pretty much by accident. Evolution occurs as the whole system of living things becomes temporarily disrupted before achieving a new balance. New species do not evolve to preserve ecological balance but as part of the process through which balance takes place. This process is basically a matter of trial and error.

Countless changes may take place in the mixed messages that come out of any species' gene pool that never get passed on to new generations. Only the messages that actually help a species survive get passed along. The rest get left by the evolutionary wayside. As a result, the purple orangutans get weeded out before they even become species.

Finding Out the Hard Way

Variations of a species don't know ahead of time whether they will be beneficial to the species. Each variation has to take its chances, and in most cases, variations don't help and don't get preserved in the gene pool.

The process of weeding out variants that don't work well is known as *natural selection*. Only under especially lucky circumstances does a successful change occur that can be passed along to a new species. This is called *adaption*. And you don't need us to tell you that when a whole species fails to adapt and dies out, it's called *extinction*.

Definosaurus
Selection happens when creatures with certain traits survive while other creatures with other traits die out. **Adaption** happens when a particular variation is selected to survive. **Extinction** means "R.I.P. species."

Change for the Worse; Change for the Better

Evolution can seem like a pretty nasty set of rules to live—or die—by! There's no consolation prize for losers in the game of life. Even worse, characteristics especially important to human beings—like moral goodness—don't guarantee our place as Mother Nature's favorites.

Even so, understanding evolution doesn't mean we have to be morally traumatized. After all, we're alive, aren't we? What's more, we share the planet with many wonderful creatures and wonderful fossils left by creatures that once lived. So what if we don't "deserve" this existence by virtue of our charm, good looks, or nice table manners?

Yes, it's too bad that we hunted the woolly mammoth and the dodo to extinction on the way to getting where we are today. And it's chilling to think that we are likely to die off ourselves at some point in the future. But none of this means it's bad to be alive. To the contrary, it shows how lucky we are. The evolutionary odds against us were staggering, but we made it!

Fossil Fallacy

Nature has its own ways of working things out, but that doesn't let human beings off the hook for taking care of ourselves—and each other. In fact, leaving things to "nature" can lead to disastrous results. In the late 19th and early 20th centuries, a popular philosophy known as "social Darwinism" recommended letting human nature run its competitive course. This philosophy tried to justify wealthy entrepreneurs' exploitation of low-income laborers in evolutionary terms, by looking at economic prosperity as if it were biological success. Since then, we have learned that fiscal fitness doesn't depend on preying on the workforce!

The Grim Reaper

A phrase that sometimes gets used to mean more or less the same thing as natural selection is "survival of the fittest." One suggestion behind the idea of survival of the fittest is that the different species are all in competition with one another for a limited amount of evolutionary space. A species cuts the mustard until some new species gets an inside edge and it can no longer compete successfully.

The idea of competition can lead people to paint a grim scenario about the evolutionary scheme of things: It's dog eat dog, eat or be eaten, use it or lose it, winner take all. What's even more depressing is that for every successful change, there may be any number of failures as each species tries to cover all its evolutionary bases. In fact, ever since the theory of natural selection was put forward, people have found it disturbing.

Opportunity Knocks

Competition among species, however, is only one, and perhaps not even the most important, influence on evolution. Even while creatures compete for available evolutionary space, they are also creating new space and adapting to fill it.

In other words, although species evolve to some extent through competition, they also evolve through *opportunism*. They are not simply forced to compete; they have the opportunity to adapt. Turtles, for example, are even older than dinosaurs. The fact that the dinos evolved was no skin off the turtles' noses, nor was the turtles' success a stumbling block for dinos. Dinos and turtles were never in serious competition but took the opportunity to evolve along different lines. They occupy different *niches*, or evolutionary spaces.

Dinoscientists are still trying to figure out the extent to which dinos evolved as a result of competition with other creatures and as a result of opportunism, adapting to fill niches that no other animals occupied. It seems likely that both of these evolutionary forces, competition and opportunism, worked together in the rise of the dinos.

Star Qualities

Many key adaptive features that helped make possible the rise of the dinos can be traced in the fossil record. The dinos descended from fish to amphibians to ancient lizards known as *thecodonts* before emerging as bona fide dinos. Along the way, they found themselves in competition with the *therapsids*, the early mammals.

Before we see our dino-stars appearing in their adaptive roles, here's the supporting cast of "A Mesozoic Night's Dream." You can also take a look at Appendix D for some even more detailed lists that show how all these creatures are related.

Cast of Characters

➤ **tetrapods** Four-legged land-lubbers, including practically everything that isn't a fish.

Boning Up
The English Victorian poet, Alfred Tennyson, was filled with despair as he pondered the fate of the dinos (referred to as "dragons") because he felt it showed that Nature was similarly unconcerned about human life. He asked, in his poetic masterpiece, *In Memoriam* (1849), would people,

Who loved, who suffered countless ills,
Who battled for the True, the Just,
Be blown about the desert dust,
Or seal'd within the iron hills?
No more? [Humanity is] A
Monster then, a dream,
A discord. Dragons of their prime,
That tore each other in their slime
Were mellow music matched with him. (56, 17-24)

Tennyson and other Victorians often looked with horror on what they regarded as the cruelty of nature.

Definosaurus
Opportunism is the idea that evolution takes place not just through competition but as a result of new space opening up for creatures to adapt their way into. The evolutionary spaces creatures occupy are called **niches**.

➤ **amphibia**   The first tetrapods, with all the makings of a land animal except for having to keep their eggs wet.

➤ **amniota**   Tetrapods that can lay eggs on land or even give life birth, thanks to a special membrane called the amnion.

➤ **thecodonts**   The grand-daddies of the dinosaurs.

➤ **therapsids**   The ancestors of all us mammals, they shared evolutionary space with the thecodonts and early dinos.

➤ **archosaurs**   Class of ruling reptiles, including the thecodonts, dinos, and modern-day crocodiles.

Land Ho!

Perhaps the most important dinosaur adaptation came long before the dinos themselves. This was when the first four-legged creatures came out of the water to occupy a whole new niche: land! These leggy land-rovers are known as *tetrapods*, and they're still around today. In fact, you're one of them—a proud descendant of the paleo-pioneers who made the uncharted trek onto dry land.

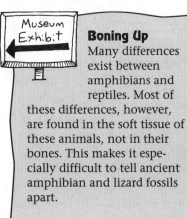

Dig This
Snakes are actually tetrapods. That is, they are descended from four-footed creatures but have lost their legs in the process of adapting to fit their particular niches.

All amphibians, reptiles, birds, and mammals are tetrapods—dinos, too. "Tetrapod" means four feet. The fossil record shows that the four feet of the first tetrapods adapted from fins. In birds and human beings, of course, the front "feet" have adapted even further, to become hands and wings.

Obviously, feet are better than fins for moving around on land. They became an especially successful adaptation. The first tetrapods to evolve feet were the *amphibians*, creatures like the salamanders who lay eggs in the water. They also evolved lungs in place of the gills fish use to breathe with and passed this feature along to the rest of the tetrapods.

Over Easy

Boning Up
Many differences exist between amphibians and reptiles. Most of these differences, however, are found in the soft tissue of these animals, not in their bones. This makes it especially difficult to tell ancient amphibian and lizard fossils apart.

Although amphibians have their skeletal structure and their lungs in common with other tetrapods, they differ in that they need to lay eggs in the water because they haven't developed the portable little biospheres reptiles, birds, and mammals use for developing their embryos. These non-amphibian tetrapods are called *amniotes* because their eggs are enclosed in a membrane called the amnion that keeps the embryo moist as it develops. Amniotes—including mammals, whose eggs remain in the mother's uterus until birth—can lay their eggs or give birth anywhere, allowing them to go still farther up on land.

So legs and eggs were key developments leading to the dino dynasty. But these features are not unique to dinos because all amniotes have them. Another useful adaption many—but not all—amniotes underwent is increased ability to walk or run. Here dinos really set the standard.

Standing Up for Saurians

Salamanders walk with their legs way out to the side. This is known as a sprawling posture. Most other tetrapods are either semi-erect—like crocodiles, whose thighs still stick out to the sides, but whose shins are nearly perpendicular to the ground—or fully erect, like horses, whose legs are completely underneath their bodies.

Some creatures, including certain dinosaurs, birds, and people, have taken posture one step further, walking or running around on just two feet. This is called *bipedalism*, a trait that frees up the forepaws for a whole new set of activities.

It isn't clear how bipedalism helped the first upright dinos adapt, however, because they tended not to use their arms for any specialized purpose. Even so, the dinosaur two-step may have been helpful for unknown reasons because it set them apart from other early tetrapods.

Needing Another Hole in the Head

In the days leading up to the dino dynasty, the planet was ruled by two kinds of beasts, the thecodonts and the therapsids. The thecodonts were founding members of the class known as *archosaurs*, which would come to include the dinos. The therapsids were in the process of becoming the first mammals.

In many ways, these two clans were similar. Both were four-legged, amniote foragers and predators of the plains and forests of the Permian and Triassic periods. In fact, it would be difficult to tell them apart except for an important difference in the structure of their skulls.

The therapsids and their descendants (known collectively as synapsids) have an extra hole in their skulls just behind each eye socket. This became a defining characteristic of the early mammals. The thecodonts go the therapsids one better; they have two extra

Boning Up

Studies have shown that upright posture, as found in dinosaurs but not in many lizards, makes it easier to breathe while running. Lizards with a sprawling gait can often move very quickly. The problem is, the side-to-side movement of their legs interferes with their lung capacity. As a result, they can't run fast for more than a few seconds at a time.

Definosaurus

The ability to walk on just two feet is **bipedalism**, a trait found in people, birds, and many dinos. This doesn't mean that people, like birds, may be descended from dinosaurs. In fact, bipedalism seems to have evolved separately in birds and in people.

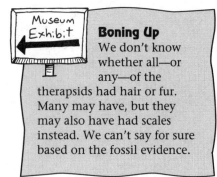

Boning Up
We don't know whether all—or any—of the therapsids had hair or fur. Many may have, but they may also have had scales instead. We can't say for sure based on the fossil evidence.

Dig This
Many thecodonts were big, growing to be 16 feet long. Dinos, though, were even bigger, reaching as many as 90 feet long!

holes in their skulls behind each eye socket, plus another hole in front of each eye.

How are these extra holes in the head an adaptive advantage? For one thing, it makes the skull weigh less. This may have made it easier for dinos to grow larger in size and to become bipedal. It's hard to walk around on two feet when your skull is too heavy to carry, especially if you grow to be as tall as a house!

For another thing, and contrary to what you might expect, the extra head-hole may actually have made thecodont noggins stronger, more like a well-designed scaffold than a hollow boulder. What's more, the head holes were ideal loops for attaching strong, ropey jaw muscles. As a result, certain dinos were able to develop huge, powerful jaws. In fact many meat-eating dinos had jaws that look disproportionately large compared to most predators of today.

This special thecodont feature did not prevent their rival therapsids from expanding into all the available niches of Pangaea. Throughout the Triassic, the therapsids had the upper hand over the outnumbered thecodonts. Early in the Jurassic Period, however, a drastic change took place.

Many Moons Ago

Therapsids started dropping like flies. Most species became extinct. Only a handful of tiny, nocturnal therapsids held on by a whisker to keep the mammal line alive during the dinosaur dynasty that was just beginning. Meanwhile, many thecodonts were changing, getting bigger and sleeker. One group in particular developed more streamlined hips. These were the first dinos, proudly displaying the distinctive dino butts that set them apart from the pseudo-saurs and wanna-be-raptors of the Mesozoic.

The Empire Strikes Back

Eventually, the new species on the block became the only name in big lizards. The thecodonts died off, and the mammals scurried into their burrows until nightfall. Meanwhile, the dino family tree branched off in all directions, variating into whole zoofuls of new species. The evolutionary term for this kind of branching off is *adaptive radiation*, a phenomenon that usually occurs immediately after a *mass extinction*. Mass extinctions involve the dying off of many species at or near the same time.

Mass extinction and adaptive radiation mark the end of an old dynasty and the beginning of a new one. These events took place not only at the beginning of the dino era, but at the end as well, when it became the mammals' turn to rule the planet.

Winners by Default?

What accounts for dino-dominance? Some think they out-competed the other species with the help of their adaptive advantages: upright posture, bipedalism, quickness, or bigger jaws. One especially hot theory is that the dinos may have been warm-blooded, hence, more perky than the colder, slower, thecodonts, while remaining fiercer predators than the fuzzy therapsids. Any or all of these features may have been enough to drive hundreds of rival species to extinction.

On the other hand, something else may have killed off the therapsids and thecodonts, leaving a big empty planet for the dinos to spread out in. An asteroid? A virus? A change in climate? A change in plant species? All these explanations are possible.

Definosaurus
When a number of new, interrelated species develop in a fairly short period of time, **adaptive radiation** takes place. Adaptive radiation tends to occur immediately after **mass extinction**, the ending of a different group of interrelated species.

The Least You Need to Know

➤ Evolution is change in the genetic composition of a species over time.

➤ Although it may seem to work by design, evolution is largely a matter of chance.

➤ Evolution has both a nasty and a generous side. These are natural selection and opportunism.

➤ Key dinosaur adaptions include skull structure and upright stance.

➤ Early dinos were in competition with the thecodonts, from whom they descended, and the early mammals known as the therapsids.

➤ It's not clear whether dinos drove their competitors to extinction or whether the thecodonts and therapsids died out as a result of some other cause.

Chapter 4

Sorting Out the Saurians

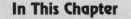

In This Chapter

➤ Naming and evolution

➤ Carl Linnaeus's system of names

➤ Tracing lines of descent

➤ How dinos are classified

➤ Why dino classification is tricky

Learning names is the first step in learning about people and things. The CB-radio custom of calling a name a "handle" makes perfect sense because names help us get a handle on what we're talking about.

Names can get complicated, though, when they are used as part of a system of classification. To really understand a systematized name, you have to learn the whole system. We can call a playing card a "seven of clubs," but that name doesn't mean anything unless we understand how the whole deck is arranged. And what about nested names, which include groups of other names and are included as part of a larger group?

Even though it's more difficult to learn a system than a name, once you learn the system, it's much easier to learn a whole bunch of names. It's especially worth taking the trouble to see how the dinosaurs get sorted out because dino-designations really are handles that scientists use for getting ahold of evolution.

Museum
Exhibit

Boning Up

With 300 known species of dinos, paleo-poll takers do more than give each kind a name. In addition, they cluster the kinds and name the clusters; then they cluster the clusters and name those, too. But there's more. Imagine clusters within clusters that not only help you keep the kinds straight but also tell you about a whole system of evolutionary relationships. This is what the system of dino names does.

Dig This

A few partial skeletons exist for what is probably the dinos' closest ancestor, a little critter called *Lagosuchus*. It's difficult to tell, though, partly because the skull of this animal has never been found.

The Name Game

Getting ahold of dinosaur names can be tricky, not only because of all the Greek and Latin scientists use, but also because paleontologists have recently been reshuffling the dino deck to improve the system.

Dino designations are applied with an eye toward showing how dinos have evolved and how they relate to one another. Saying "which dinos are which" is largely a matter of saying "which dinos are related to which other dinos."

Breeding Trouble

You might think that paleontologists, equipped with a workable model of evolution and a thorough knowledge of geologic periods and the fossil record, would have a fairly straightforward job of figuring out the right evolutionary sequences of dino descent.

In fact, nothing could be more difficult. We may figure out how to breed our own dinosaurs before we figure out how they evolved in the first place. One problem, of course, is the incomplete nature of the fossil record. All the evidence isn't in, but in the meantime, we still need to make sense of the evidence we have.

Another problem has to do with the nature of fossils. Aside from footprints, the rare skin impression, and the even rarer mummy, we're dependent on bones for what we know, and bones only tell part of the story of who begat whom. By the time paleontologists come on the scene, all the juicy parts are gone.

We can't be sure whether dinos had feathers, for example, or whether they were warm-blooded. Although we may yet find a fossil with feathers, or enough fossils without them to let us be fairly certain one way or another, we're unlikely to find a fossilized brachiosaur blood-pressure test.

Old Names, New Dinos

These problems make it harder to make sense of the fossil record. These are paltry concerns, though, next to the real conundrums of dinoscience. The first has to do with the sneaky way evolution works. It would be easy to trace the evolutionary steps from one species to another if these steps always moved in the same direction. The fact is, evolution frequently doubles back on itself, undoing and redoing adaptive characteristics—in effect, changing its mind or saying the same thing in two different ways.

The other big problem has to do with the antiquated terminology—not quite from the days of the dinosaurs but from the 18th century, anyway—for describing and categorizing life-forms. Although this terminology has been valuable in helping biologists organize the living things on the planet, it has become old-fashioned because it originated before people even knew about evolution.

As a result, paleontologists over the years have spent a lot of time trying to squeeze prehistoric creatures into modern-day categories. It's taken years for scientists to come to terms with the possibility that dinosaurs might not simply be a kind of reptile, but a whole new critter—a missing link to the birds.

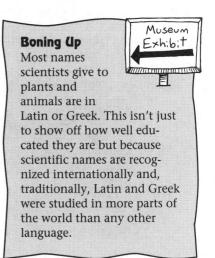

Boning Up
Most names scientists give to plants and animals are in Latin or Greek. This isn't just to show off how well educated they are but because scientific names are recognized internationally and, traditionally, Latin and Greek were studied in more parts of the world than any other language.

Made to Order

The science of classifying living things goes back to the pioneering work of Swedish naturalist Carl Linnaeus (1707–1778). Linnaeus was a botanist who noticed resemblances among different kinds of plants that seemed useful for keeping track of them. He made a big impact on science when he announced that all the plants in the world, including species that had yet to be discovered, could be classified in 1 of 26 groups based on their structural characteristics.

During Linnaeus's time, many parts of the world were just beginning to be explored by scientists. These scientist-explorers found plants and animals that people back in Europe had never heard of. Linnaeus introduced a naming system that made it easier to make sense of the new discoveries. Linnaeus's system was extended to apply to animals as well as plants and has become the standard system of biological classification.

The system works by dividing all living things into groups based on certain shared characteristics. These groups can be divided into smaller groups, or lumped together into bigger groups. Just as libraries keep track of books by sorting them into groups within groups based on their subject matter, the Linnaean system provides an overarching framework for organizing all living things.

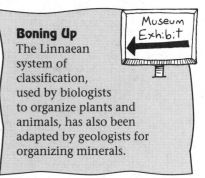

Boning Up
The Linnaean system of classification, used by biologists to organize plants and animals, has also been adapted by geologists for organizing minerals.

Life at Many Levels

The largest groups are known as *kingdoms*. Every living thing belongs to one of the five kingdoms: the plant kingdom, the animal kingdom, the fungus kingdom, the bacteria kingdom, and the protista kingdom, made up of little critters called *eukaryotes*.

Each kingdom is further divided into *phyla* (singular, *phylum*). Phylum is Greek for tribe. Since Linnaeus's time, phylum has become the basis for the word *phylogeny*, the study of the evolutionary history of living things.

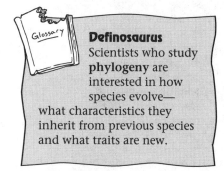

Definosaurus
Scientists who study **phylogeny** are interested in how species evolve— what characteristics they inherit from previous species and what traits are new.

The phyla are further divided into *class*, and then *order*, *family*, *genus*, and *species*. Species is the smallest grouping in the Linnaean system, although biologists sometimes refer to *subspecies* or *superspecies* for added flexibility.

Starting with species as the building blocks for the whole system, each group is made of many smaller groups. That is, a genus contains many different species, a family contains many different *genera* (plural for genus), and so on. As a result, each living thing can be grouped at each of the seven levels.

Creatures with Class

If the Linnaean system were a software program, each level would have a menu with links to each group in the next level. To get to "fish" from "house cat," you'd have to click back from cat (species) through genus, family, order, and class to phylum. From phylum you could click forward to fish. In other words, the order of fishes and the cat species are parts of the same phylum, the chordates. All chordates have backbones, and having a backbone is the closest phylogenetic trait a cat shares with a fish.

Here are all the classifying levels for another species of chordate, human beings:

➤ **animal kingdom**   Animals are known for having many cells and for moving around on their own steam. Plants get weeded out of this group.

➤ **chordate phylum**   Chordates have a spinal chord. Insects have to buzz off.

➤ **mammal class**   Mammals nurse their young. Reptiles get left out in the cold.

➤ **primate order**   Primates are mammals with grabby hands. The hoof and paw set drop the ball.

➤ **hominid family**   Hominids are primates with big brains. Strictly speaking, we are the only living members of this family. Extinct members include *Australopithicus* and *Paranthropus*. There is, however, a superfamily of hominoids that includes chimps, gorillas, and orangutans.

➤ ***homo* genus**   The homos include the extinct erectus, neanderthal, and habilis species, as well as us.

➤ ***sapiens* species**   That's you, me, and all our sapient siblings out there.

If the Name Fits...

Notice how big and flexible—as well as organized—the Linnaean system is. Any newly discovered species fits into place based on defining characteristics it shares with other species in its genus. If scientists discover a new whatsit with fur, grabby hands, and a swollen cerebrum, we'll know right where it goes—there with the hominids.

To prevent confusion, each species is identified by the name of its genus and its species together: *Homo sapiens*, *Tyrannosaurus rex*. This custom of identifying species is called *binomial nomenclature*, which is Latin for two-named naming.

Definosaurus
The scientific practice of identifying a creature by its genus and species name is called **binomial nomenclature**, from the Latin for two-named naming.

Glossary

Graduating Classes

The Linnaean system works great when we're able to observe living things and see for ourselves what characteristics they have. It gets tricky, though, when the critters we're looking at have been dead for more than 65 million years.

Part of the problem of applying the Linnaean system to dinosaurs is that Linnaeus did not have evolution in mind when he developed his scheme. Birds, reptiles, mammals, and amphibians were seen as totally separate classes. The idea that reptiles evolved from amphibians and that birds and mammals evolved from reptiles didn't occur to anyone until well into the next century. By that time, Linnaean classification had become universally accepted among scientists.

Back when dinosaurs were first recognized as a group, it was thought that they belonged to the reptile class and were made up of two distinct orders, the Saurischians (lizard butts) and the Ornithischians (bird butts). Reptiles, as everyone knows, are egg-layers with scales, not fur or feathers. Even though dinosaur scales had not been found, dinosaur teeth and bones had many characteristics in common with modern-day lizards, so dinos got classified as reptiles.

This makes sense in a way because dinos descended from reptiles. But then maybe we should also start calling mammals reptiles too because they are another branch of the reptile tree. And maybe we should call birds dinosaurs because birds may be as closely related to dinos as dinos are to reptiles.

Boning Up
The **Saurischians** are dinos named for their pelvises, which are shaped like a lizard's. The **Ornithischian** pelvises are shaped like those found in birds. Confusingly, birds are not descended from the Ornithischians but may well be descended from the Saurischians. Birdlike pelvises, then, are a convergent characteristic in birds and in bird-butted dinos.

Museum Exhibit

Best Clade Plans

Although Linnaeus didn't know about evolution, his system paved the way for Darwin and the other evolutionists. By looking at all living things in relation to one another and organizing them hierarchically, it became easier to see different species as descendants of other species.

As it happens, many Linnaean groups do, in fact, represent evolutionary groups. Of course it's not really such a bizarre coincidence that closely related animals often have shared characteristics that would lead people to lump them together as groups.

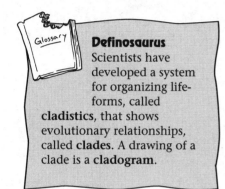

Definosaurus
Scientists have developed a system for organizing life-forms, called **cladistics**, that shows evolutionary relationships, called **clades**. A drawing of a clade is a **cladogram**.

Even so, Linnaean classification doesn't provide detailed evidence for evolutionary relationships, much less specify which groups are descended from which other groups. Because Linnaeus's system doesn't take evolution into account, scientists have developed a more evolution-minded way of organizing.

Today's scientists want to organize things in a way that reflects evolutionary relationships. Their new system is called *cladistics*, from the Greek word "clade," meaning branch. *Clades*, in fact, are kind of like family trees, only they are put together according to certain rules. A schematic of a clade is called a *cladogram*.

Cladogram of dinosaurs.

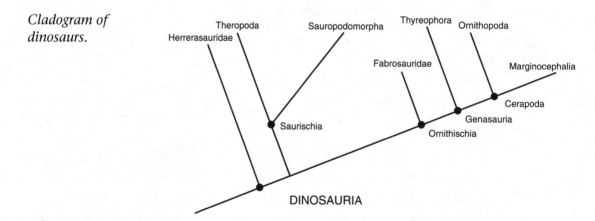

Nixing Mixing

Cladograms are attempts to establish which species or larger groupings descended from which other species or larger groupings. This is no easy task. Cladistics can get complicated, involving careful comparisons of hundreds of features. These features are noted in a cladogram as scientific evidence for the evolutionary relationships the cladogram represents.

In spite of all the hard work they put into cladistic analysis, scientists often disagree about dinosaur clades. Because different paleontologists interpret evidence differently, they sometimes come up with different evolutionary groupings. Although their groupings may differ, however, they try to base all their groups on evolutionary relationships.

One problem that produces cladistic boo-boos is mixing groups. Mixed groups, consisting of a lumping together of species that aren't directly related to one another, don't belong in a clade. Mixed groups are sometimes called *unnatural groups*. Only *natural groups*, groups based on evolutionary relationships, belong together in clades.

For some time now it's been thought that dinosaurs were a mixed group, made up of two separate branches—the Saurischians (lizard butts) and the Ornithischians (bird butts)—of a line of reptiles that weren't dinos themselves, the thecodonts. If this view is correct, it means that each group of dinos is more closely related to the thecodonts than they are to each other. This would make the category "dinosaur" a messy and confusing no-no for cladistic purposes.

Fortunately for those of us who would rather say "dinosaur" than "Saurischians-and-Ornithischians," there is strong evolutionary evidence that the dinos are, in fact, a close-knit family (or class, or superorder, or whatever). This is another way of saying the dinos form their own clade.

A Well-Turned Ankle

Dinos can be considered a natural group in part because they all have special features that their ancestors, the thecodonts, don't have. For one, dino ankle bones form a straight hinge, as opposed to the bent-ankle hinges of the thecodonts. What's more, dinos stand up straight and tall on their legs. If the two kinds of dinos, the bird butts and the lizard butts, evolved separately from the thecodonts, their special ankles and postures would have had to evolve twice—once for the LBs, and once again for the BBs.

This is certainly possible, but it seems more likely that these features evolved only once and were passed on to all the dinosaurs. For this reason, many scientists think that all dinosaurs were more closely related to each other than to any other groups.

Definosaurus
Glossary

A **natural group** is made up of creatures from a single line of descent. In contrast, an **unnatural group** includes creatures that did not evolve along the same lines. "Flying animals" is an unnatural group made up of insects, birds, and bats, three evolutionarily distinct groups. This grouping should not appear in a cladogram.

Boning Up
Museum Exhibit ←

Not only is there disagreement about whether dinos form a natural or an unnatural group, there also is disagreement among the naturalists about whether dinos form a superorder or a class. No, this isn't pointless bickering. Class status depends on the size, scope, and importance of dinos as a group. Should dinos stand as equals to the mighty mammals and revered reptiles, or should they be taken down half a notch?

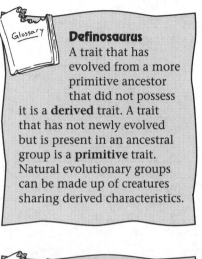

Definosaurus
A trait that has evolved from a more primitive ancestor that did not possess it is a **derived** trait. A trait that has not newly evolved but is present in an ancestral group is a **primitive** trait. Natural evolutionary groups can be made up of creatures sharing derived characteristics.

Definosaurus
Convergent evolution occurs when different groups evolve common traits independently of one another. When animals are lumped together on the basis of convergent traits, the result is an unnatural group.

If, as evidence now suggests, dinos are a natural group, then their ankle hinges are a newly *derived* characteristic that sets them apart from the thecodonts. A derived characteristic is one that has evolved from a more primitive ancestor that did not have that characteristic. In addition to newly derived dino traits are primitive characteristics the dinos shared with the thecodonts, including an extra hole in the skull in front of the eye sockets and larger hind feet than front feet. A *primitive* trait is one that has not yet disappeared through evolutionary change.

Converging with the Dinosaurs

Although cladists tend to assume that any given evolutionary characteristic is more likely to evolve only once rather than two or more times, some characteristics really do evolve more than once in two or more different species. As we mentioned in the last chapter, bipedalism evolved separately in dinos and in homos. In other words, humans and dinos took two evolutionary directions to get to a similar place. This is known as *convergent evolution*.

Although bipedalism is a convergent characteristic in dinosaurs and in people, the ability to walk on land is a characteristic humans and dinos both derived from the same ancestor. Land locomotion evolved only once—in amphibians who passed it along to all the rest of us tetrapods.

Because humans and dinos are only distantly related, it's pretty clear that bipedalism is a convergent characteristic in these species. Because land locomotion is a defining characteristic of all tetrapods (except those evolutionary backsliders, the marine mammals and reptiles), it's equally clear that homos and dinos derived this characteristic from the same place.

A clade of "bipeds" made up of humans and dinos is definitely out of its tree. A clade of tetrapods that includes humans and dinos, however, is iron-clad cladistics. Unfortunately, it isn't always this easy to tell the difference between derived and convergent traits, especially when looking at fossils of extinct species.

Just the Half of It

What's worse, some really extreme clado-masochists not only try to avoid mixed groups, they try to avoid incomplete groups as well. According to these hard-core cladists, every clade should include all the descendants of all the groups it contains. This has led some scientists to call for the abolishing of the thecodonts, the ancestors of the dinos.

Although dinos have traits thecos don't have, the defining traits of the thecos are shared by the dinos. This makes thecos a partial group.

Deriving Us Crazy

Because it's difficult to sayfor certain whether a given feature is derived or convergent, it's just as difficult to find two paleontologists who agree on how dinosaur clades should be organized. There's really a lot of sorting to do, and different experts do it differently, often using different names.

Fossil Fallacy

You might think that with all those Greek and Latin names to keep track of that dinoscientists would get confused—and you'd be right! The famous C.O. Marsh coined the terms "theropod" and "ornithopod" as names for different orders within the dino group. Theropod means beast-footed and was supposed to refer to the mammal-like feet of many plant-eating dinos. Ornithopod means bird-footed and makes excellent sense as a name for the three-toed, meat-eating dinos. Unfortunately, somewhere along the way, Marsh ended up tripping over his own two feet-names, and the designations became switched. To this day, the bird-footed dinos are called theropods ("beast-footed") and vice versa.

In Appendix D, you'll find outlines showing how dinosaurs are related according to cladistic studies endorsed by many paleontologists. Here we use an organization that makes good sense and that many folks basically agree on. But don't be surprised if you find others who do it differently!

The Least You Need to Know

➤ The Linnaean system of classification was developed before evolution was discovered.

➤ Linnaeus's system remains broadly useful but has been refined to reflect evolutionary knowledge.

➤ Cladistics is the mapping out of evolutionary relationships.

➤ Cladistics is tricky because it can be hard to distinguish natural and unnatural groups.

Part 2
The Lizard Butts

The lizard butts are the Saurischian dinosaurs, so called because they all have hip bones shaped like those of most modern-day lizards. Together, they make up a major dinosaur order. The lizards are further divided into two smaller groups, or infraorders: the theropods—meat-eaters such as T-rex with three toes—and the sauropods—plant-eaters such as "Brontosaurus" with long necks.

Horny Devils

In This Chapter

➤ The ceratosaurs, first of the theropods

➤ Why ceratos had horns

➤ The pack-hunting *Coelophysis*

➤ The fused feet of *Syntarsus*

➤ *Dilophosaurus*, the double-crested dino

➤ *Ceratosaurus* and its crowded neighborhood

Meat-eaters that have horns are a rarity in this or in any age. These days, horns are used by sheep, goats, and other herd animals mostly for friendly competition among themselves, less often for defense against predators (they'd rather run away than fight), and never for killing a next meal because they're vegetarians. Mammalian predators like lions and wolves don't need horns. They can wield their sharp claws and teeth with such precision that they can be used equally well for hunting or for just playing around.

This is not true of dinosaurs. Dinos have big jaws and teeth that must have been messy and reckless. A playful nip from a meat-eating dinosaur would have left a jagged, bloody wound that would be difficult not to take personally. The teeth and claws of predatious dinos are serious business. But, in addition to their killer qualities, some of the meat-eaters had a lighter, playful side.

These were the ceratosaurs, who had horns for knocking around in and crests for showing off, along with an arsenal of long, sharp teeth, cavernous jaws, and claws that were, well, sort of big, anyway. Ceratos were the only meat-eating dinos to develop these traits.

Pedigree Predators

The meat-eating theropods represent the biggest, most diverse order of dinos, and the ceratosaurs help make them that way. To many, the theropods are an especially interesting class of dinos. Not only are they meat-eaters, but many also closely resemble birds and are even bird ancestors.

The birdy traits exhibited by the theropods include light-weight, hollow bones. In birds, this feature enables them to fly. In theropod dinos, it increased their speed and helped them grow to a tremendous size.

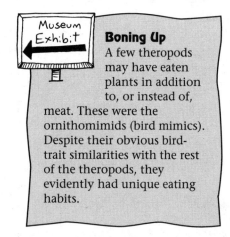

Boning Up
A few theropods may have eaten plants in addition to, or instead of, meat. These were the ornithomimids (bird mimics). Despite their obvious bird-trait similarities with the rest of the theropods, they evidently had unique eating habits.

Another bird characteristic of the theropods is their trademark three-toed foot. A typical theropod tootsie looks like it belonged to a pigeon on steroids.

Still another bird feature of theropods is their long, S-shaped neck. With this sort of stem for your head, you wouldn't have to rely so heavily on your arms and hands because you could grope under the sofa cushions for spare change with your nose! In fact, many theropods had underdeveloped forepaws, compensated for by their slinky necks.

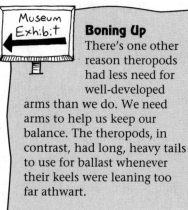

Boning Up
There's one other reason theropods had less need for well-developed arms than we do. We need arms to help us keep our balance. The theropods, in contrast, had long, heavy tails to use for ballast whenever their keels were leaning too far athwart.

The definitive theropod characteristic is bipedalism. Of course, many of the plant-eaters were bipedal, but then again, many veggie dinos fell back onto all fours. In contrast, all the theropods remained upright. This is the theropod clan, of which the ceratosaurs are the oldest branch.

A Growing Concern

Time was when no one realized how diverse the theropods were. They were divvied up into two groups, based on size. The bigger dinos, including T-rex, were called carnosaurs, and the small-but-deadlies were called coelurosaurs.

As it turns out, some of the dinos that were tossed into one group are closely related to some of the dinos tossed into the other group. These were the ceratosaurs. Paleontologists came to see that, in spite of their size differences, the ceratos were a group of dinos that had split off in its own direction from the theropod branch before the coeluros and carnos evolved.

Ceratosaurs are an older, more primitive group of dinos. They are known for their four-fingered forepaws, their arching, lightweight skulls, and the bony knobs and crests on their snouts and heads.

Horning In

Ceratos have been found in the western United States, Africa, and possibly even Antarctica. Ceratos survived throughout the Jurassic and, in the process, managed to acquire some formidable features. The conspicuous, short, bumpy horns on the ends of their noses are only the least dangerous of these. Cerato, in fact, means horn.

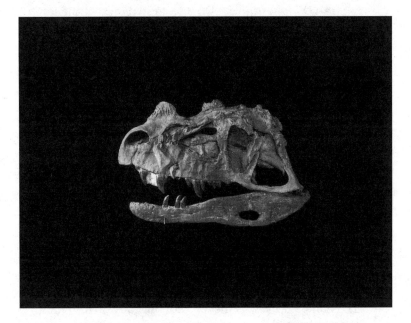

Skull of Ceratosaurus, *sporting its horn just behind the nostrils.*

(Department of Library Services, American Museum of Natural History; Neg. no.:2A21970; Photo.: Finnin)

More decorative than deadly, ceratos undoubtedly used their horns for display and for nosing in on one another's business, not for attacking prey. Along with, or instead of, the nasal horn, the cerato sibs had crests on their heads and bony ridges running down their backs.

Other notable features of the clan are their primitive, four-fingered hands (possibly useful in grabbing small prey and gobs of meat), their surprisingly lightweight skulls, and their fused foot bones, good for running fast.

Here are the main members of the ceratosaur family.

Boning Up
Ceratos are the only predacious dinos known to have horns, although other theropods, including *Allosaurus*, seem to have had short, bumpy ridges on their heads. Horns are more prominent and more common on the plant-eaters, most notably the ceratopsians.

Boning Up
Coelophysis lived through a time in prehistory when many other animals—namely all the thecodonts and some synapsids—went extinct. These animals may have been wiped out by dust kicked up by a huge meteor that rocked the planet in Triassic times. Then again, they might have been rendered obsolete by the superior hunting skills of the coels.

Boning Up
How the light- and heavy-skulled coels are related isn't known for sure. They could represent different types of the same species, or different species of the same family. Another possibility is that coels changed shape slightly as they went through different phases of life. The most likely explanation is that the different shapes and sizes go with different sexes. Coels had crests on their heads, which they probably used for attracting mates. Sexual display often goes with different size and shape between the sexes, as in many birds. The same may be true of the coels.

➤ *Ceratosaurus*   Twenty-foot-long predator with a horn on its nose and a chip on its shoulder. Filling a late-Jurassic role, it had to play understudy to the bigger, more common *Allosaurus*, with whom it shared the same niche.

➤ *Coelophysis*   A Middle- and Upper-Triassic dino well known thanks to the Ghost Ranch find consisting of hundreds of skeletons, this dino hunted in packs, killing prey up to five times its size.

➤ *Dilophosaurus*   Double-crested dino of the lower Jurassic who puzzles paleontologists with its big strong teeth and dainty jaws.

➤ *Syntarsus*   *Coelophysis*'s cousin from Zimbabwe, named for its fused foot bones that have morphed into a quick set of trotters.

Getting Coelophysical

Coelophysis is the oldest cerato. In fact, it is one of the earliest predacious dinos to evolve. Coels spelled trouble in red capital letters for the non-dino animals of the Mesozoic, both because they preyed on these animals and competed with them for evolutionary space. They lived for 15 million years through the Middle and Upper Triassic, flourishing in both desert and forest environments in what is now South Africa and the United States.

The name *Coelophysis* means "hollow body." This refers not to their insatiable appetite but to their light bone structure. In this, like many theropods, they resemble birds. Some dinoscientists suggest they had feathers and even plumes coming out the crests at the back of their heads.

Good Eaters

This paleo-predator had state-of-the-art hunting techniques at its disposal: speed, strong jaws, and sharp teeth. And just to be sure to get these traits in the right proportions, coels developed in two varieties, one with a short, heavy skull, and another with a long, lighter, slenderer skull.

What's more, their forepaws may have been adapted for grasping small prey or chunks of meat. As if this weren't enough, coels exhibit another characteristic that set them apart as the first really serious paleo-predators. They hunted in packs. This is evident from the fact that coel fossils have been found in groups. With their appearance on the Middle-Triassic horizon, big-game hunting was in season.

On top of these features, coel jaws are equipped with a particularly wicked set of food-processing attachments. In fact, thanks to their special set of teeth and snout, coels could hunt both large and small prey. At the end of a coel's snout is a slight crimp that seems intended to give it a better hold on the little beasts it nabs. Its teeth at this portion of its snout are cone-shaped, the better to spike you with, before tossing you back down its greedy throat.

Farther back in its jaws are teeth of a completely different shape, curving backward like sickles and serrated at the back edge for extra slicing ability. These teeth would have left a long, jagged wound. The snout is quite long in proportion to the rest of its body, and the head looks disproportionately large. In this feature, coels look forward to those other oversized dino noggins, the tyrannosaurs of the Cretaceous.

Different Strokes

The coel's teeth suggest a completely different approach to killing from most land predators of today, like tigers, wolves, and other hunters of the cat and dog clan. Cats' and dogs' teeth and jaws are built for precision. When these animals are ready to kill, they go straight for the throat and don't let go until their victim's dead. Only then is it dinner time. If they bite more than once, they're just playing around.

Coels did things differently, making big, sloppy, saw marks wherever their teeth landed. They took as many mouthfuls as necessary, possibly starting their meal before completely finishing their victim. They used these sharp, sickle-shaped teeth on larger animals. They may well have hunted even the big sauropods, converging in packs on plant-eaters up to 10 times their size.

Boning Up

Museum Exhibit

The first coel bones were discovered in the 1880s in New Mexico by dino hunter David Baldwin. The find was tantalizingly scanty—only a few vertebrae, pieces of ribs and pelvis, and some leg bones. Unfortunately, Baldwin worked alone, so the site, later known as Ghost Ranch, wasn't fully explored. Sixty-five years later, a team from the American Museum of Natural History rediscovered the site—and a good 25 coel skeletons in a mass grave. No one knows what killed so many dinos all at once. Thanks to this find, scientists can study coels in a range of age groups—hatchling to adult.

Dig This

Dinosaurs are notorious for having small brains. Some, however, have more gray matter than others. In general, the meat-eating theropods win out, brainwise, over the plant-eaters.

No Way to Treat Your Baby

Not that coels had anything against meat-eaters as food. In fact, *Coelophysis* fossils have been found with little baby *Coelophysis* bones inside. Although it has been suggested that these baby coels are embryos, *Coelophysis* is almost certainly an egg layer, and the babies' bones are too well developed not to have already hatched. This means that they had been eaten, possibly as a way of staking out territory on the part of an ambitious male, or possibly as a last resort during hard times.

Boning Up
Some dino-scientists have complained that there are too many separate genera of dinosaur that really should be classified as different species of the same genus. Of course, the opposite problem is not uncommon. Many new dinos have been wrongly classified as previously discovered species and genera.

A Small, Re-coelable Package

One of the more recently discovered ceratosaur species is the beagle-sized *Syntarsus*, known from fossils unearthed in Zimbabwe in 1969. Its name means "fused tarsal bone," in honor of the ossified ankles that help give it a streamlined stride. Like the coel, *Syntarsus* is small and may actually be a species of *Coelophysis*.

In fact, all the ceratos have fused ankle bones, as well as several fused vertebrae just above the hip. These features give them more stability when running, heightening the effect of the straight ankle hinges common to all dinosaurs.

Syntarsus would probably not have been able to pivot on one foot or change directions quickly while running. With its straight, narrow stride, it would have had to use its long, powerful tail to keep its balance.

Dilopho My Life

Another important ceratosaur was *Dilophosaurus*, one of the oldest of the big (well, medium-sized) meat-eaters. Dilopho is almost as old as *Coelophysis*, but survived only a fraction of the time the coels lived. Its characteristic double crest flared out a mere three million years or so into evolutionary history. In contrast, the coels survived almost 30 million years.

Put a Lid on It

The name, dilopho, means two-crested and in fact, dilopho's double crest is the jauntiest of the cerato headgear. It forms a V-shape over the snout and head, making it look a little bit like Yankee Doodle in his three-cornered cap. The first dilopho fossils to be discovered did not include this stylish chapeau. Only recently have we come to see how striking—visually as well as physically—these beasts must have been.

Fossil Fallacy

Dilophosaurus made a stunning screen debut in *Jurassic Park* as one of the more interesting-looking dinos. In fact, the screen version was the spitting image of the original—literally. In the film, the dilopho spews poison sludge all over Wayne Knight, who plays a devious and duplicitous computer programmer. Much as Peck may have earned his juicy just deserts, there is no fossil evidence to suggest that dilophos dispatched their prey in this manner. In fact, they were clearly equipped to kill in more conventional ways. The movie dilopho also had a neck frill, unlike fossilized dilophos.

Where's the Corkscrew?

Like other ceratos, dilopho had big teeth and a surprisingly light skull. Its snout, however, was abruptly tapered at the end, a feature that may have weakened its jaw strength. This taper may have made room for an especially long fang or tusk set into the lower jaw, allowing it to protrude from a closed mouth. Another possibility is that the tapered snout worked something like a set of tweezers for pulling little lizards and mammals out of holes or crevices.

The combination of a delicate jaw and big sharp teeth poses something of a puzzle. This combination of features seems to make as much sense as putting a big meat cleaver on a skinny little handle. When something gives, it might not be the meat!

Although dilopho jaws appear delicate, they may have been braced by strands of tough tissue that did not get preserved along with the fossils. Compounding the puzzle, however, is the uncertain strength and effectiveness of dilopho's forepaws.

Like many meat-eaters, dilopho had short, small front claws relative to the rest of its body. It's difficult to say how they were used and whether they made effective hunting or eating tools. They could probably grasp small animals and bronto cutlets, but then again, dilopho may have used them mostly just for picking its teeth after a big meal!

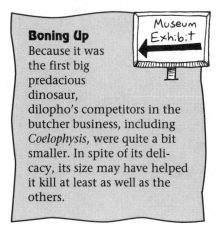

Boning Up
Because it was the first big predacious dinosaur, dilopho's competitors in the butcher business, including *Coelophysis*, were quite a bit smaller. In spite of its delicacy, its size may have helped it kill at least as well as the others.

Que Cerato Cerato

The namesake of all the ceratos is the *Ceratosaurus*, a critter who lived much later in the Jurassic than the others. The best-known species is *Ceratosaurus nasicornis*, which means "horny lizard with a horny nose." First brought to light in Arizona in 1884, it was wrongly identified as a megalosaur, another meat-eater of about the same size or larger. *Ceratosaurus* gets to be about 20 feet long.

Much larger than *Coelophysis*, *Ceratosaurus* was once classified in a separate group, the carnosaurs, before the many resemblances to its smaller, older sibling were recognized. As a larger, newer model of coel, *Ceratosaurus* was loaded with lethal features. The problem for the cerato, though, was that by the time it evolved in the Upper Jurassic, it had to compete with an even bigger dino, the *Allosaurus*.

Lovers or Fighters?

In fact, *Ceratosaurus* has been confused with *Allosaurus*. Some believed cerato was the male and allo was the female of the same *sexually dimorphic* species. (Sexual dimorphism is when the male and female of a species can be characterized by different size or shape.)

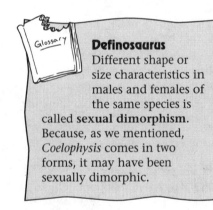

Definosaurus
Different shape or size characteristics in males and females of the same species is called **sexual dimorphism**. Because, as we mentioned, *Coelophysis* comes in two forms, it may have been sexually dimorphic.

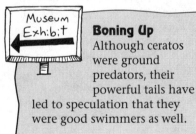

Boning Up
Although ceratos were ground predators, their powerful tails have led to speculation that they were good swimmers as well.

Ceratos and allos have since been identified as different species, but lumping them together was not such a far-fetched idea because allos and ceratos were neighbors and shared a similar lifestyle. Allos, though, are considerably more common and get to be a good deal larger.

Group Effort

Although hardly pipsqueaks at 20 feet long, ceratos may have had to gang up on some of their larger victims. Parallel trackways have been found and tentatively identified as cerato prints, suggesting that they may have joined forces.

This is especially logical because a major source of meat available to *Ceratosaurus* would have been filet of *Brachiosaurus*, a sauropod 85 feet tall! The ceratos would have had to use every millimeter of their long, sharp teeth to bring down a brachio, as well as all their speed to get out of the way as it fell!

One feature that distinguishes *Ceratosaurus* from all other dinos is the ridge of bony growths, called scutes, running along its spine. These may have added strength to the back-bones, providing a sturdier frame for the muscles. Similar, but more elaborate, growths are found among plant-eating dinos where they serve for protection or display.

The Least You Need to Know

➤ Theropods have many birdlike features, including hollow bones, three-toed feet, bipedal posture, and S-shaped necks.

➤ Ceratos, the most primitive group of theropods, used their horns for display and friendly competition.

➤ *Coelophysis* was among the earliest of the predatory dinos, and among the first dinos known to hunt in packs.

➤ *Dilophosaurus*, the oldest large theropod, had a distinctive double crest.

➤ *Syntarsus* is named for its fused ankle bones.

➤ *Ceratosaurus*, a Late-Jurassic dino, competed with the larger and more common *Allosaurus*.

Little Killers and Peckish Non-Predators

As you can tell from the title of this chapter, not all theropod dinosaurs were huge, hulking, and murderous. Many were small, agile, and murderous, including *Compsognathus*, the smallest dinosaur. What's more, not all theropods were big meat-eaters. The ornithomimids (bird mimics) may have preferred to fill up at the salad bar. The compies and bird mimics are just two subgroups of the theropods known as the coelurosaurs.

Many coelurosaurs hunted small game of the forest and desert regions of the prehistoric world. Others moved up the food chain, taking on creatures their own size and larger. Many evidently learned to hunt in packs, an adaptive strategy that gave them their choice of the Mesozoic meat supply, allowing them to feed on even their largest neighbors.

Other coelurosaurs, the bird mimics, seem to have learned to do without eating much meat. Equipped with beaks rather than teeth, they evidently foraged among the plants for food. In addition, they may have gobbled up small lizards, mammals, or insects.

The coelurosaurs existed from near the beginning of the dino days and survived far into the Jurassic Period. Most, however, died off before the last dino hurrah of the Cretaceous, when the trend was for predators to get bigger and bigger. But even as a tendency toward enormous size became the rule by Cretaceous times, a few little killers hung on and held their own in a world dominated by overgrown dinos.

Featherweights

Although all the theropod dinos are birdlike, the coelurosaurs are especially so, having light bones with many hollow spaces in them and skeletons that reveal many birdlike features. But, as the compies and ornithos demonstrate, there's more than one way to be like a bird.

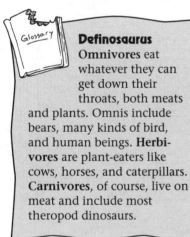

Definosaurus

Omnivores eat whatever they can get down their throats, both meats and plants. Omnis include bears, many kinds of bird, and human beings. **Herbivores** are plant-eaters like cows, horses, and caterpillars. **Carnivores**, of course, live on meat and include most theropod dinosaurs.

You Are What You Eat

Some birds of today, of course, are predators, including hawks, eagles, and owls, that hunt rodents and other small creatures. Although they couldn't fly, compies probably maintained a similar diet as these birds. They may also have joined forces in bringing down bigger quarry.

Strictly speaking, birds that live on insects and worms are predators too, although many insect-eating birds also eat other things as well, including seeds, berries, and green stuff. Birds like this are *omnivorous*, meaning that they eat plants and meat. Vegetarian species, in contrast, are *herbivorous*, whereas meat-eaters are *carnivorous*. The coelurosaurs known as ornithomimids were probably omnivores.

Coelurosaur All Stars

Here's a list of some of the more important coelurosaurs, not including the raptors, covered in the next chapter.

➤ *Procompsognathus* Less directly related to compies than the name implies, this rare and primitive Middle-Triassic dino was set apart from other theropods by its big hips.

➤ *Compsognathus* This Upper-Jurassic predator was the first to set off the bird controversy due to its similarities with the feathered *Archeopteryx*.

➤ *Ornitholestes* This small-game hunter of the Upper Jurassic had a small, horny growth at the end of its snout that may have been used for playful jousting with its cronies. More useful for hunting were its sharp teeth and grasping forepaws. Although the name means "bird robber," it now seems unlikely that birds formed a large portion of its diet.

➤ *Microvenator*   Its name means "little hunter," and it's rare to find such a small predator so far into the Cretaceous when size was in style. It is known only from an incomplete skeleton.

➤ *Ornithomimus*   Ostrichlike dino with peculiar, elongated forepaws.

Slated for Fame

Back in the mid-19th century, in the section of Germany known as Bavaria, printmakers used slabs of limestone from a nearby quarry. The fine-grained, sedimentary stone was perfect for etchings that could be used for prints. In a few of the slabs, however, Mother Nature stepped in ahead of the printmakers, carving some of the most remarkable shapes ever set in stone. A few of these were the famous early species of bird dubbed *Archeopteryx lithographia*. The name is based on the technique of lithograph printmaking.

Among these limestone lithographs was the first complete theropod skeleton ever found—the whole bag of bones in one small, tidy package. The find came to be known as *Compsognathus*, "pretty jawed," and compies have since become best-known favorites of all the diminutive dinos. In fact, compies are generally recognized as the smallest of all the dinosaurs.

Compies had very long necks and longer tails. Often, when they died, rigor mortis would set in and snap their necks back over their bodies like a dancer in Matisse's famous painting, *La Joie de Vivre*. But back when they had their heads on straight, they were long and lean like two-footed greyhounds, well equipped for running down scurrying little lizards and mammals. They also had jaws with double hinges—good for swallowing whole those extra-large morsels.

Non Compies Mentis

In spite of the high-quality fossils that have long been available for study, compies have generated considerable confusion. One compie skeleton was found with a

Dig This
Right from the beginning, Bavarian fossil finders recognized the combined aesthetic and scientific value of their discoveries. They sold them at high prices to state museums as well as to foreign scientists.

Boning Up
Convincing and lifelike motion-picture replicas of *Compsagnathus* appear in the Spielberg film, *The Lost World*. They appear cute and friendly, like cat-sized geckos on two feet, but prove to be tenacious, swarming predators who converge on their victims and take hundreds of tiny bites of flesh.

Museum Exhibit

lizard in its belly. This was wrongly identified as a compie embryo by the famous 19th-century dinoscientist Othniel Charles Marsh. Paleo-pundits of today agree the little bones were actually the compie's last meal.

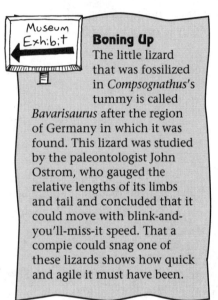

Boning Up

The little lizard that was fossilized in *Compsognathus*'s tummy is called *Bavarisaurus* after the region of Germany in which it was found. This lizard was studied by the paleontologist John Ostrom, who gauged the relative lengths of its limbs and tail and concluded that it could move with blink-and-you'll-miss-it speed. That a compie could snag one of these lizards shows how quick and agile it must have been.

Boning Up

Long after compies were first found in Germany, compie-like fossils appearing to have feathers were found in China. Since then, more compie kin have been found in Spain. These Spanish dinos left well-preserved skin impressions that clearly lack feathers. Thanks in part to these unfledged fossils, some dinoscientists say that the "feathers" on the Chinese fossils are really something else—scales, maybe, or the impressions of spilled guts. The debate rages on!

Another compie fossil was found with unusual, long strands of sediment around the forepaws. This fueled speculation that some compies were aquatic, with flippers rather than front feet. This theory, too, has since been debunked. Compies were certainly land predators. Their forepaws, however, remain something of a mystery. The bones of the claws are so tiny and delicate that it's hard to tell whether they have two front claws or three.

The biggest debate surrounding the nature of compie-kind, however, is also the focus for one of the most important unanswered questions about dinosaurs in general. This has to do with the relationship of dinos to birds.

Compies of a Feather?

The association between compies and early birds stems from when they were first discovered in Bavaria about 150 years ago. Found with the compies in the same limestone quarry were a number of fascinating feathered specimens from the same period—the Upper Jurassic. These compie contemporaries were the *Archeopteryx*—"ancient wings," creatures with tails like lizards but with many other features found only in birds. We'll get to archeopters in more detail in Chapter 15, but for now the most notable thing about them is their fossilized feathers.

Structurally, compies appear quite similar to the archie birds. In fact, an archeopter skeleton was even wrongly identified as a compie for a number of years. Among these similarities are especially birdlike ankles, three-toed birdy feet, and a ribcage that suggests compies possessed lungs with air ducts inside—an efficient and sophisticated feature many animals lack but birds have. As with many theropods, it's anybody's guess whether compies had feathers.

These and other characteristics led the 19th-century naturalist Thomas Huxley to argue that compies were bird to the bone—near and direct ancestors of the birds of today. Huxley's idea has been batted around ever since, and no clear unanimous decision has been reached. We'll look at this debate in more detail in Chapter 24. For now, it's nice to think that the little creatures who wake us up with their singing in springtime are really downy dinosaurs.

A Lost Art

One factor that makes it difficult for people to see compies as closely related to birds is their predatory lifestyle. As we have seen, they are quick small-game hunters, stalking smaller animals across grassy plains. To most people, this doesn't sound like a birdlike way to make a living, and few birds live this way.

Once, however, there were many predatory, ground-hunting birds, most of which have since died out. One that has survived is the secretary bird, about 4 to 4¹/₂ feet tall, from the plains of Africa. Dinoscientists point to this feathered, flightless, long-legged, quick, carnivorous creature to show how *Compsognathus* and other small coelurosaurs must have hunted.

Jurassic Jackal

Another little killer who lived a similar lifestyle at about the same time as *Compsognathus* was *Ornitholestes*, or "bird robber." This dino got its name because its light bones, powerful legs, and agility made it appear capable of leaping so quickly and so high as to snatch birds out of the air in midflight.

Unfortunately, this idea doesn't hold much water because birds are not now considered a staple protein source of bird robber. Instead, dinoscientists now think it hunted for lizards or scavenged—stealing meat that was killed by bigger dinos like *Allosaurus*.

Scavenging in this way would have made *Ornitholestes* something of a Jurassic jackal, relying on its quickness and agility to survive while letting others do the dirty work of killing.

The bird robber would have been able to snatch meat quickly with its jaws. These were larger and more powerful than those of other coelurosaurs. And to help it pick the meat off the bones it had two long fingers and one shorter one on each hand. The short finger turned inward and could have been used like a thumb for holding things.

> **Dig This**
> Forty-five million years after the dinos died out—just over 20 million years ago—lived a species of bird known as the terror bird. These creatures had wings with claws attached at the end, which they used for hunting small game. The terror birds occupied the same evolutionary space once filled by the coelurosaurs.

> **Boning Up**
> Evidently, *Ornitholestes* lived alongside a similar dinosaur known as *Coelurus*. *Coelurus* is less common than the bird robbers and is known only from partial skeletons. It may turn out that *Coelurus* and *Ornitholestes* are actually the same dinosaur. If this is so, then *Ornitholestes* will have to be renamed because the species was originally identified as *Coelurus*.

Six Dinos Dancing

Certain dinos seem to have evolved out of their way to become odd birds. These are the ornithomimids, the bird mimics, a group of coelurosaurs dug up out of Late Cretaceous rocks in the western U.S. and in Mongolia. These birdalikes evolved too late in time to be serious contenders for the title of bird ancestor. They developed their birdy ways separately.

As you can see from the following list, there are enough bird mimics to fill up half the verses of "The Twelve Days of Cretaceous Christmas."

➤ *Ornithomimus*   Bird mimic; the standard the whole bizarre group is measured against.

➤ *Struthiomimus*   Ostrich mimic; similar to *Ornithomimus* except in the proportion of its limbs.

➤ *Gallimimus*   Chicken mimic; these little dinos crossed the road just as the Cretaceous sky was falling.

➤ *Dromiceiomimus*   Emu mimic; what more needs to be said?

➤ *Garudimimus*   Here we move beyond real-life weirdness. Garuda was a mythical bird.

➤ *Deinocheirus*   "Terrible hand"; if bird mimics are Dr. Jekyll, *Deinocheiris* is Mr. Hyde.

Putting the Stretch in "Ostrich"

The main branch of the birdalikes is *Ornithomimus*. This dino is built like an ostrich, with a long, snaky neck; strong, bony back; big midsection; and long, skinny legs. Unlike the ostriches of today, however, the dino has long, gangly arms and forepaws. These reach almost to the ground, much to the bewilderment of paleontologists trying to figure out how they were used.

Another species of dinobird, called *Struthiomimus*, is built even more like an ostrich. In fact, *Struthiomimus* means "ostrich imitator." Struthios and ornithos are similar, differing mainly in the proportions of their limbs, which can range from long and skinny to longer and skinnier.

Their feet had the trademark theropod three toes, but with special flat, cleatlike pads on the bottoms. Turf toe would not have been a problem for these dinobirds. Like today's ostrich, they were excellent runners. Their footprints

Boning Up
Studies have shown that ostrich mimics had primitive elbows that would not have enabled them to bend their arms enough to fold them up out of the way as birds can do with their wings.

Dig This
A whole gaggle of *Gallimimus* thunders across the set of the film *Jurassic Park*, fleeing from a hungry T-rex. All but one got away!

indicate they could reach speeds of 30 miles per hour. It isn't known whether they ran to catch their food. In any case, they ran to escape being eaten themselves. Among the dinos likely to have preyed on the birdalikes was T-rex.

Care and Feeding

The bird mimics sport some peculiar features that have kept the dinoscientists guessing about what they ate and how they got their food. As theropods, the birdalikes are classified with the meat-eaters, and, in fact, they may have eaten meat. But all kinds of alternative suggestions have come forward, including insects, plants, crabs, eggs, and all of the above.

One big clue that birdalikes didn't typically wolf down red meat is the fact that they didn't have any teeth. Instead, they beaked their food into submission before swallowing. Whatever meat they ate had to be small enough to kill and swallow with their rounded beaks, and it's hard to picture them pecking any of their fellow dinos to death.

In fact, these paleo-peckers were attached to skulls that were extremely flexible, like those of some birds of today, allowing them use their beaks deftly to flatten and swallow whatever it was they managed to get into their mouths.

Have You Hugged Your Bird Mimic Today?

Their gangly arms are another peculiar feature that has paleontologists guessing about their eating habits. As if these goony birds weren't weird enough already, their forelimbs bear a close resemblance to those of a modern-day three-toed sloth! This has led to speculation that they might have used their hands for bending branches to nip off leaves and tender shoots.

In keeping with their spindly arms, the legs on the birdalikes are also skinny—in fact, like bird legs. This fact, together with the fact that a number of bird-mimic fossils have been found on sites that were once shores of ancient lakes, suggests that the dinobirds were waders, stalking the shallow waters in search of crabs and small fish. The shape of their beaks does not support this idea, though, because they are not long

Dig This
Dinobird beaks were made of a tough protein called keratin, the same stuff your finger- and toenails are made of. Like fingernails, the dino beaks grew back when they got worn down or broken.

Boning Up
Museum Exhibit
Still one more suggestion for what the birdalikes did with their hands is that they used them as rakes for uncovering and breaking open insect nests, much as anteaters and aardvarks do with their paws. The problem with this idea is that the dinobirds seem to have been poorly equipped to get the bugs in their beaks after they tore the nests apart.

and pointed or scoop-shaped like wading birds of today. Still, it is possible that they grabbed their aquatic prey with their sloth hands!

Caped Crusaders

Because they closely resemble ostriches, it seems likely that the dinobirds were land feeders just as ostriches are. This seems especially true because, like ostriches, they must have been good runners. It is possible that they used their arms for balance while running.

One imaginative (but not widely accepted) suggestion is that they may have been equipped with flaps of skin stretching between their arms and their bodies. These little capes may have supplied enough wind resistence to keep the birdalikes on an even keel at full throttle. This idea, however, is only speculative.

Still one more freakish characteristic of the birdalikes is that they had two sets of ribs, one over their chest and another over their belly. The belly ribs were smaller than the regular set, and floated, unattached to the spine. They probably served as protection for the stomach.

Dig This
Deinocheirus's arms now hang suspended in midair at the Paleobiology Institute of Warsaw, Poland. They are mounted, of course, in the about-to-grab-you position. Like many of the more famous and important fossils, casts have been made of these, which are on display at major museums around the world.

Arms Escalation

We know, its hard to think about belly ribs when you can't get those long, gangly arms out of your head! With so many possible uses, you probably want a pair for yourself. You may also be interested to know that they come in size Extra-Extra Gigantic, with no dinosaur attached.

Paleontologists discovered the fossil remains of a single set of giant birdalike claws, hands, arms, and shoulders, with no other bones around to attach them to. These huge chicken feet from hell are the only evidence left of *Deinocheirus*, "terrible hand," a breed of birdalike that stretches the weirdness of the whole group to enormous proportions.

The arms are each 8 feet long, and the claws are easily big enough to grab a full-grown person around the waist, except there aren't any thumbs, just three huge birdy claws all curving the same direction. The scary thing about terrible hand is not how dangerous it was, but that such a huge, weird thing could have evolved in the first place.

The Least You Need to Know

➤ Although as a rule, the predacious dinos evolved from small creatures to very big ones, a few coelurosaurs remained small and survived into the Cretaceous.

➤ *Compsognathus* sparked a debate about the relationship between dinos and birds almost as soon as it was discovered in the 1880s. This debate continues today.

➤ *Ornitholestes* may have used its quickness for stealing meat killed by larger predators.

➤ The ornithomimids closely resembled ostriches with long, gangly forearms.

➤ *Deinocheirus*, "terrible hand," is a bizarre species of ornithomimid known only from a huge pair of forearms, each measuring 8 feet.

Claws Célèbres

Here it is, folks. The raptor chapter.

The raptors are the hottest dinos going, medium-sized predators who have clawed their way to stellar status—and into the hearts and adrenal cortexes of rapt audiences everywhere. Thanks in part to careful handling and savvy promotion, they've garnered a reputation for brains as well as beastliness, agility as well as aggression.

Riding a wave of popularity 65 million years in the making, the raptors have become stars of books, movies, and cladograms. And they've done it in spite of a long prehistory of bucking all the trends. While other predacious dinos were getting bigger, they remained fleet and petite. While other predacious dinos flaunted their big flashy smiles, the raptors relied on nimble footwork.

Indeed, these beasts bring out the foot fetishist in every dinophile. Sporting toenails that have evolved into machetes, the raptors leapt feet first into the killing business as no bipedal predator has done before or since. As a result, they've begun to rival even T-rex for popular appeal among meat-eaters.

Jeepers Reapers

The raptors were a clan of coelurosaurs that survived for more than 50 million years, right up to the mass dino extinction at the end of the Cretaceous. They are known for the large, retractile, sickle-shaped claws on the second toes of their hind feet. These claws are much like those on cats of today.

Raptors, though, are not cat ancestors but are probably bird ancestors. The name raptor means "thief," and is applied to today's birds of prey as well as to our group of dinosaurs, formally known as the maniraptoriformes, or "shaped like hand thieves."

Tricks of the Trade

Raptors may have leapt into the air and slashed at their prey Bruce Lee style. Or they may have jumped onto the backs of bigger dinos, holding on with their front claws while using the deadly, sickle-shaped toeclaw to disembowel their dinner in mid-run. Ride 'em raptor!

They've taken the Rocky statue down from in front of the Philadelphia Museum of Art, but these bronze Deinonychus, created by artist Kent Ullberg, still stand as memorials to dinosaur determination in front of the Academy of Natural Sciences.

(Ewell Sale Stewart Library, The Academy of Natural Sciences of Philadelphia)

Anatomical studies of certain horned, four-footed plant-eaters have shown that if you were to sever their stomach muscles, they would fall over. (Isn't science amazing?) The raptors may in fact have taken advantage of the Achilles' tummies of their victims, many of whom had tough, armorlike growths on their backs.

The raptors have been compared with saber-toothed tigers for their ability to hunt big-game animals much bigger than they were. This is not only because of their special claws. The raptors were also excellent runners and leapers. What's more, they had big sharp teeth, and lots of them.

Still, the retractile sickle claw really sets them apart from the run-of-the-mill Mesozoic flesh-eaters. These claws were typically 3 inches long and often considerably larger.

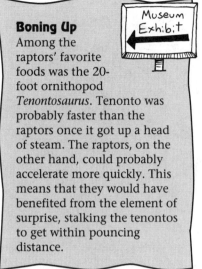

Boning Up
Among the raptors' favorite foods was the 20-foot ornithopod *Tenontosaurus*. Tenonto was probably faster than the raptors once it got up a head of steam. The raptors, on the other hand, could probably accelerate more quickly. This means that they would have benefited from the element of surprise, stalking the tenontos to get within pouncing distance.

Well-Adapted Raptors

To use their claws effectively, the raptors acquired special physical characteristics. For one, they had special hips with muscles that let them kick without jerking their long tails to one side. As a result, they were able keep their balance as they made sauropod sushi with their feet.

Because of their overgrown toenails, the raptors ran on just two of the three toes on each foot, keeping their sickles sticking straight up into the air. This doesn't seem to have slowed them down, though. The running toes were braced with extra layers of bone, and their tails were equipped with ossified tendons on the inside so that they could be held out rigidly behind them and used for balancing.

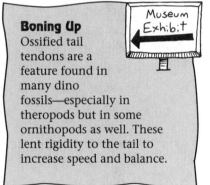

Boning Up
Ossified tail tendons are a feature found in many dino fossils—especially in theropods but in some ornithopods as well. These lent rigidity to the tail to increase speed and balance.

Pop Sickle Toes

Like many theropods, raptors had much in common with birds. In fact, raptor skeletons are especially birdlike, with delicate bones, narrow ankles, and long fingers and toes. Raptors have even been suggested as candidates for the ancestors of modern birds. One problem with this idea, though, is that ancient birds, known to have had feathers and to have been able to fly, had already been around for a long time before the raptors evolved.

Whether the raptors we know about are bird ancestors, they are the closest bird relations among all the dinosaurs. In fact, many dinoscientists now identify bird species both living and extinct as part of the raptor group.

Boning Up

Alfred Hitchcock's offbeat horror film *The Birds* (1963) shows flocks of the feathered set unaccountably attacking a California community. The fact that birds may be descended from dinos helps explain why the film is so scary. Hitchcock taps into the predacious impulses of the modern-day raptors, unknowingly recalling their evolutionary heritage.

It's possible, they say, that the raptors are near descendants of undiscovered dinos that *were* the ancestors of birds. One interesting suggestion is that raptors are derived from a pre-bird species that was actually able to fly but lost the ability themselves, adapting instead to a life on land.

This view, however, isn't widely accepted. If this is true, though, it means that the sickle claw may have evolved from a special perching toe used for climbing and holding onto branches. Many birds have sickle-shaped toes they use for climbing and perching. The idea is that the raptors came down out of the trees and figured out how to use their claws for climbing their way into the bodies of their victims.

Omnibus Claws

Sickle-clawed dinos come in various shapes and sizes. Here's a list, together with a notable non-sickle raptor, the *Oviraptor*.

➤ *Dromaeosaurus* (swift lizard)   With smaller claws and larger jaws than the other sickle-toed raptors, Dromaeo is a primitive, founding member of the raptor clan.

➤ *Deinonychus* (terrible claw)   This dino was an obscure and ignored pile of bones for more than 30 years until a better specimen was discovered in 1969, which reopened the bird-origin controversy.

➤ *Velociraptor* (speedy thief)   This overnight success is not only a movie star (*Jurassic Park* and *The Lost World*) but a basketball star too (the NBA's Toronto Raptors were established in 1993).

➤ *Troodon* (wounding tooth)   If dinos evolved into people, this would be their ancestor!

➤ *Oviraptor* (egg thief)   With a face only a mother could love, this dino is the exception to the rule of raptor panache.

➤ **Birds**   If birds are dinosaurs—and there's increasing evidence that they are—they belong with the raptors.

Wherefore Art Thou Dromaeo?

Velociraptor has become a star since appearing in *Jurassic Park*. Among its more appealing qualities—in addition to its relentless thirst for blood—are its sleek, streamlined physique, indicative of track-star speed; its exceptional intelligence, evinced by its large braincase; and, of course, its way-cool pedicure.

You've heard the big Hollywood success stories. Bogey, Marilyn, Pee Wee Herman. The rapid rise of *Velociraptor* fits the mold perfectly. Once known only as *Dromaeosaur*, the raptor made a modest living traveling around the western states as a small-time predator. Nobody who was anybody thought much about it.

It popped up a few times in the Gobi Desert. What it was doing in Mongolia is anyone's guess because it never talks about those days. It may have fallen in with some buddhasaurus monks and found inner peace. In any case, when it reappeared back in the states in the late '60s, it looked like a whole new dinosaur. The big shots started giving it a second look.

As so often happens, would-be stars that can't make it in the states go off to find themselves before hitting it big back home. Jim Morrison is an example. Well, this is just what happened with dromaeo. No one really knows what happened to it in the Gobi Desert, but it had clearly been through a lot. Then one day it turned up again back in the states. It was hanging out in Montana when Yale paleontologist John Ostrom came along. He took a good look and realized he had come across something special.

After the tests and photos, Ostrom decided dromaeo was ready for a whole new image—sleeker, meaner, faster, and with a hot new name and a hot new angle. Dromaeo's name became *Deinonychus* in keeping with a meaner, more macho look. Then came the hook that got everyone's attention: *Birds.* That's right; according to Ostrom, *Deinonychus* had bird in its blood. The news couldn't have been bigger if they'd said deino was second cousin to the Prince of Wales.

Boning Up
Velociraptor has proven to be major-league material with the establishment of the National Basketball Association expansion team the Toronto Raptors in 1993. Predacious rebounding and bipedal ball movement are definite adaptive advantages on the court!

Dig This
Although *Velociraptor* fossils are rare in North America where they were originally found, they have turned out to be fairly common in the Gobi Desert. We have yet to figure out why this is.

You know the rest of the story: photo shoots, promotions, wild parties, and of course the books and movies. It's rumored that soon they'll be laying a Cretaceous slab with a raptor fossil footprint in Hollywood Boulevard. And how 'bout those Toronto Raptors?

Fossil Fallacy

They say everyone looks bigger on-screen. In fact, the *Jurassic Park* raptors are two or three times bigger than the real McCoys. The movie similarly exaggerated raptorian brain power. Although the raptor's brain size indicates it may have been smarter than other dinos, it's unlikely that it would have been able to coordinate a group effort to systematically test an electric fence as they do in the movie.

Striking Poses

Years before *Velociraptor* became famous in movies, the fossil record released some *dino-mite* action stills of the speed demon. One fossil frames it in the process of doing what it does best, preying on another dino. This particular fossil, found in the Gobi Desert, shows the velocitous one going head to head with a *Protoceratops*.

Sandstone Standoff

We don't know how these creatures came to be locked into this pose by the surrounding sandstone. The two animals may have died separately, and their bodies may have been washed into position by flowing water. On the other hand, a sudden sandstorm may have swept in and suffocated the squabbling saurians in the midst of a fracas. In any case, the fossil really looks like the beasts were going at it at the moment they were buried.

The raptor has every appearance of being poised for action—extended claws, arched back, crouching legs, and outstretched tail. All four sets of the raptor's claws seem to be sunk into the bony face of the big plant-eater. Its long, rigid tail is swung back high over its head as if it were hanging on for the ride.

The raptor may have been going after the protocero's carotid artery when the two got sandblasted. Its sickle claw is resting deep in the place where its victim's neck would have been. If the two dinos were in fact fighting before becoming fossilized, the raptor may have attacked the much-bigger plant-eater out of pure audacious, predatious pugnacity. Another possibility is that the raptor was going after the protocero's eggs when Big Mama nosed her way into the fossilized facial.

Boning Up
Velociraptors probably did not prey on one another, although they may well have killed each other in fights over food, mates, or territory. It is likely, however, that they preyed on their near cousins, the *Oviraptors*.

Once Bitten

Another fossil that shows the speedster had exceptional fighting spirit is a mug shot, also recovered in Mongolia. This is a raptor skull that has two punctures put there, evidently, by a big set of teeth. The teethmarks correspond to the dental work of another raptor, so the skull fossil provides rare evidence of an interspecies skirmish.

There is no fossilized evidence of the bone healing. What's more, the marks suggest that the teeth bit through to the brain. This may have been a mortal wound, then, especially because the rest of the bitten raptor's bones are largely intact. The holes, in other words, were apparently not made in the process of scavenging an already-dead raptor.

Troo to Life

The raptor clan has sparked some of the most interesting speculation of all dinodom. This is especially true of *Troodon*, a more advanced dinosaur than the rest of the raptors. One of its improved features was its set of teeth: It had more than other raptors. These are curved backward and serrated along the back edge for more efficient flesh threshing. Although *Troodon* teeth are scary to think about, their eyes are really terrifying.

Reapers' Peepers

Troodons had especially big eye sockets that were set in the front of the skull, so they looked forward rather than out to the side. These characteristics, combined with some of the other raptor traits such as quickness, dexterity, and intelligence, have set some light bulbs going off in the heads of many dinoscientists.

Big eye sockets probably meant big eyes. Big eyes probably meant exceptional sight, possibly including good night vision. Good night vision probably meant nocturnal activity. Nocturnal activity definitely would have meant predation. Night predation would have meant hunting other nocturnal creatures. The most significant of these would have been mammals.

Mammals, as you may remember from Chapter 3, shared evolutionary space with the early reptiles at the beginning of the Triassic Period before the dinosaurs took over. When the dino dynasty got under way, however, the mammals got crowded out of the big niches, evolved to be much smaller and more furtive, and settled for the night shift when most of the big lizards left them alone.

This is how it was throughout the Jurassic and most of the Cretaceous. *Troodon* first made its appearance in the Late Cretaceous with its big, night-seeing eyes. Because these eyes were set forward in the skull, the night troopers would have had good binocular vision, allowing accurate depth perception in the dark—just the trick for getting a bead on the scurrying little furry things that came out at night.

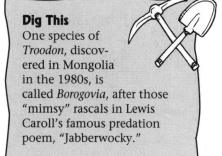

Dig This
To help process sensory input from its big eyes, *Troodon* had the largest brain for its size of any other dino. Its large brain would have increased its hunting abilities.

Dig This
One species of *Troodon*, discovered in Mongolia in the 1980s, is called *Borogovia*, after those "mimsy" rascals in Lewis Caroll's famous predation poem, "Jabberwocky."

Ding, Dong, the Dino's Dead!

The mammals held out against the "introosion" for just under 20 million years. How long could they have survived nocturnal predation from dinosaurs before lights out for good? Fortunately for us mammals, we'll never know. At the end of the Cretaceous, all the non-bird dinosaurs suddenly and mysteriously bit the dust. When this happened, the mammals came out of hiding like the Munchkins when Dorothy melted the Wicked Witch of the West, and it's been peace on Earth, good will toward mammals ever since.

Boning Up
Paleontologists aren't the only ones who like to imagine peoplelike dinosaurs. An episode of *Star Trek Voyager* featured an encounter with an intelligent species that turned out to be descended from the dinosaurs. It seems they survived the Cretaceous mass extinction and proceeded to evolve into some real nice folks—a bit conservative, though, as you might expect from a dinosaur. These humanoid dinos were descended from hadrosaurs, not raptors, and, according to the screenplay, were cold-blooded.

Dig This
The first known dino embryo ever found belonged to an *Oviraptor* and was discovered in Mongolia in 1993. The unborn dino was well-developed and still inside its egg when it became fossilized.

As we mentioned, this scenario is somewhat speculative because the troo-pers' big eyes do not necessarily mean they used their vision for nocturnal hunting. To know this for sure, dinoscientists would need to examine the actual eyeballs, and this is unlikely ever to happen.

Voted Most Likely to Succeed

But as long as we're speculating, why stop with the extinction of the mammals? Why not entertain the idea of how the dinos would have evolved if they had survived the Late-Cretaceous mass extinction?

This is just what certain dinoscientists have done, and they chose the *Troodon* for their mental experiment. They reasoned that its large brain and agile forepaws may have continued to develop, so that the troos of the future might have learned to use tools. As their brains grew larger, they would need straighter legs and a more upright upper body to support the added weight of their heads....

You guessed it! Lizard people! When the tabloids got wind of this flight of fossil fancy on the part of respected paleontologists, they reported that sapient saurians were alive and well and living in Terre Haute!

Egg on Its Face

Most families, even famous ones, have misfit members who go off on their own and refuse to uphold the image of the clan. The raptors, too, have a fossiled skeleton in the closet. This oddball is known as *Oviraptor*.

Oviraptor has a crest that looks like a mohawk haircut, a sawed-off beak with a serious underbite, and two and only two small, round teeth sticking right out of the roof of its mouth. Unlike the other raptors, its eyes look out on either side of its head, giving it the look of sort of a dim bulb.

Bad-Rap Raptor

Some paleontologists doubt it's even a real predator and suggest that it's specially adapted for eating some kind of plant we don't yet know about. Its beak, they say, isn't hooked like a predator's beak should be. What's more, its jaws evidently moved from side to side when it chewed.

Oviraptor means egg thief and, in fact, the first fossilized skeleton of the species to be discovered was found half on top of a nest full of eggs. These eggs were thought to belong to a *Protoceratops*. As a result, most agreed for years that *Oviraptor* kept to the egg business.

Recently, however, another *Oviraptor* skeleton was found on top of another nest. One of the eggs even had an *Oviraptor* embryo inside it. It turned out that this egg was the same as those in the nest where the first ovio fossil was found. These eggs were not protocero eggs but belonged to the ovio itself. It wasn't stealing the eggs but tending them, even incubating them like nesting birds of today. *Oviraptor*, then, has been misnamed. They should have called it *Funny-looking-nesting-dino-we're-still-learning-more-about-asaurus*.

The Least You Need to Know

➤ Raptors are known for the retractile, sickle-shaped claw sticking up out of the second toe of each hind foot.

➤ Raptors were closely related to birds.

➤ Raptors have become increasingly popular since the discovery of *Deinonychus* in 1969.

➤ The raptor *Troodon* may have evolved into a skilled nocturnal hunter of mammals.

➤ *Oviraptor* may have been misnamed because evidence of its egg stealing has been falsified.

Pumped-Up Predators

Many people think dinosaurs were big. They are correct. Dinosaurs included the biggest land animals ever. The biggest dinosaurs were the long-necked, sauropod plant-eaters. Many meat-eating dinosaurs, though, also got very big.

The biggest dinosaur predators were the tyrannosaurs, which could get to be 50 feet long and weighed 6 tons. By today's standards, this is humongous. The largest land predators of our day get nowhere near this big. By Mesozoic standards, though, this size is not really that earth-shaking. Many of the larger meat-eating dinosaurs, the carnosaurs, were in the same weight class, getting to be up to $5\frac{1}{2}$ tons and 45 feet long.

Think for a minute. If you were about to be eaten by a $5\frac{1}{2}$-ton carnosaur with jaws a yard long, 4-inch teeth, and 6-inch claws, would you be that much less scared than you would be of a 6-ton *Tyrannosaurus*?

In terms of geologic time, carnosaurs like *Allosaurus* and *Megalosaurus* paved the way for the tyrannosaurs by about 60 million years. What's more, the carnosaurs as a group exhibit many interesting adaptive traits, showing there's more than one way to skin a sauropod.

Swelled Fellows

Paleontologists have had a difficult time explaining the huge size of the dinosaurs. Some, like *Dilophosaurus*, got to be quite large fairly early on in the dinosaur dynasty, during the Early Jurassic Period. Since then, the trend among dinos was to keep getting bigger and bigger.

Living Large

The general rise in size may indicate a kind of evolutionary arms race between the dinosaur superpowers, the plant-eaters and the meat-eaters. The plant-eaters may have grown larger as an adaptive defense against the meat-eaters, which may in turn have grown larger to prey on the bigger plant-eaters.

Other factors were undoubtedly at work, too. As the Mesozoic Era continued, ice caps formed at the poles and the seas shrank. As a result, whole new areas of land appeared. The new energy resources—namely more plant life—may have been most easily exploited by bigger herbivores, the sauropods, allowing them to out-compete smaller species. Then predators may have evolved large sizes in turn to hunt the big leaf-eaters.

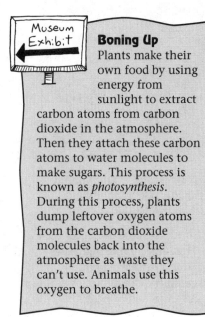

Boning Up
Plants make their own food by using energy from sunlight to extract carbon atoms from carbon dioxide in the atmosphere. Then they attach these carbon atoms to water molecules to make sugars. This process is known as *photosynthesis*. During this process, plants dump leftover oxygen atoms from the carbon dioxide molecules back into the atmosphere as waste they can't use. Animals use this oxygen to breathe.

Still another factor may have contributed to dinosaur supersizing. During the Mesozoic, the atmosphere was much higher in carbon dioxide than it is today. This may have enabled plants to grow more quickly and thickly than they do now. All this dino fodder may have meant salad days for the sauropods. And, again, the big carnosaurs evolved to eat the sauropods.

These may sound like plausible explanations. Actually, though, we don't really know what made many of the dinosaurs the biggest land animals ever on Earth. We do know that a group of meat-eating dinosaurs called the carnosaurs were among them. In addition to being the biggest meat-eaters, the carnosaurs are known for their short forelimbs and heavy skeletons.

Skin Deep

The only predacious dinosaur for which we have a good skin impression is the carnosaur called *Carnotaurus*. The skin was covered with small, fine scales, accented with rows of larger scales. Of course many dino-designers would sell their souls to know what patterns and colors dinosaurs came in, but we'll probably never find out.

Offensive Line

Here's the big starting line-up:

➤ *Allosaurus* (different lizard)   The most common of the carnosaurs, this dino has been found in large numbers in the western United States.

➤ *Spinosaurus* (spine lizard)   With a huge, fin-like, fan-shaped crest growing along its spine, this was one of the most stylish of predators.

➤ *Carnotaurus* (meat-eating bull)   This big critter gets its name from its bull-like appearance resulting from two horny crests that grew out of its forehead.

➤ *Baryonyx* (strong claw)   This big, crocodile-snouted predator may have lived mostly on fish.

➤ *Yangchuanosaurus* (lizard from Yang-ch'uan)   Known from a nearly complete skeleton found in China, this dino was a near cousin of *Allosaurus*.

➤ *Megalosaurus* (big lizard)   This is the first dinosaur to be named as a separate species, getting its moniker even before *Iguanodon*, whose bones were discovered first.

Dig This
The carnosaurs had a small pocket in their skulls most dinosaurs didn't have. This may have contained a gland for extracting excess salt from their blood, serving the same purpose kidneys serve. We eliminate salt through our kidneys by urinating. With salt glands, carnosaurs could have gotten rid of salt by simply sneezing it away, without losing water, a useful adaptation in arid climates.

Confronting the Other

In the 1940s, a paleontological expedition in Utah uncovered thousands of dinosaur bones from Late Jurassic rock, most of which belonged to carnosaurs. Outnumbering all the others were *Allosaurus* bones. In fact, some 45 allo skeletons were found, together with a good quantity of other predators and only a few plant-eaters. This bonebed is now known as the Cleveland-Lloyd dinosaur quarry, a protected national landmark.

Dig This
The Cleveland-Lloyd quarry has been nicknamed "the dinosaur department store" because so many museums "shop" there for fossils at a discount.

The quarry was an unusual discovery because fossils of meat-eating dinosaurs are rare in comparison with plant-eaters. Only about 3 percent of all the dinosaur fossils found are from meat-eaters.

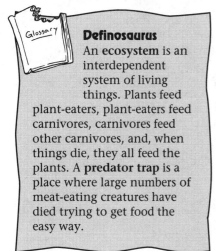

Definosaurus
An **ecosystem** is an interdependent system of living things. Plants feed plant-eaters, plant-eaters feed carnivores, carnivores feed other carnivores, and, when things die, they all feed the plants. A **predator trap** is a place where large numbers of meat-eating creatures have died trying to get food the easy way.

Balanced Dieters

In fact, in all highly developed *ecosystems* (systems of inter-dependent living things), including those of the Mesozoic, nonpredacious animals greatly outnumber predators. For ecological balance to be maintained, there can't be too many predators, or they will wipe out everything else. There have to be enough plant-eaters to keep the predators supplied with meat and to propagate their own species, so there must be many more of them than of the species that eat them.

The proportionately high numbers of *Allosaurus* bones in the Cleveland-Lloyd quarry resulted from special circumstances known to have occurred a few other times in prehistory. These conditions produce *predator traps*, natural environ-ments that lure predators to their deaths in large numbers.

No Free Lunch (an Allosaur Allegory)

What evidently happened at the Cleveland-Lloyd quarry one rainy, Late-Jurassic day is that a hapless sauropod got stuck in the mud. The mud must have been sticky, or deep, or both, because it couldn't get out. No matter how hard it churned with its huge legs, it only sank deeper.

Dig This
Another likely predator trap for dinosaurs was the Ghost Ranch site in New Mexico, where dozens of *Coelophysis* skeletons have been found (see Chapter 5). The most famous predator trap, though, didn't catch dinosaurs, but mammals. The La Brea tar pits in Los Angeles is the final resting place for extinct species of saber-toothed tigers, lions, and wolves.

Before it perished completely, when it was weak from struggling, a carnosaur came along, smelling an easy meal. "Don't try to eat me!" cried the pitiable plant-eater, "or you'll get stuck in the mud, too!" And, turning its long, snaky neck around to face the predator, gave it a most baleful look.

"That old trick's been around since the thecodonts," the carnosaur sneered. "I know a sitting-duck sauropod when I see one." And with that, the greedy meat-eater leapt into the mud and became as enmired as the creature it would have eaten.

The lesson of this story is clear: Look before you leap, let sinking sauropods lie, and any victim worth eating is worth hunting for yourself.

The story continues, however, because allosaurs are slow learners. Far from taking a lesson from the sad fate of the greedy allosaur, the next allosaur to come along made the same mistake. And so did the next and the next. Each would-be predator ended up as more bait for entrapping the next one. The end result was one of the biggest dinosaur bonebeds ever found.

Lightheaded

Although allosaurs may not have been able to learn from their mistakes, they were not thick-skulled. In fact, their lightweight skulls were an important adaption that helped them grow to their enormous height. Allos could spend less energy carrying their heads around, and more energy on important things like hunting and flirting.

In addition, light skulls increase jaw flexibility, a good thing if you're a gigantic predator that takes really big bites. An *Allosaurus* skull is more like a mesh basket than a bowl, with lots of hollow places where muscles can be attached and narrow supports that can move to accommodate a struggling mouthful without breaking.

Unfortunately, lightweight skulls tend to fall apart easily. As a result, allo skulls are rare in comparison with their other bones, which tend to be big and sturdy.

Allos may have used their large size not only in overpowering their prey but also for bullying smaller predators. It's possible that allos preferred fighting for meat killed by other animals to hunting their own prey. If so, this may help explain why so many allos were drawn to the predator trap at Cleveland-Lloyd.

An Allosaurus *hovers menacingly over the remains of a sauropod,* Apatosaurus.

(Department of Library Services, American Museum of Natural History; Neg. no.:35422; Photo.:Anderson)

Carno Chic

Although *Allosaurus* and most other carnosaurs looked like your typical huge, terrifying, predacious dinosaur, some carnosaurs stood out with some distinctive features. One is the

South American dinosaur, *Carnotaurus*, with horn-like crests that made it look like a bull with 4-inch fangs.

Two other unusual-looking carnosaurs are *Spinosaurus* and *Baryonyx*.

Sail of the Century

You've probably seen pictures of *Spinosaurus*, the dinosaur with an enormous sail running all along the length its spine. *Spinosaurus* bones were discovered in North African Cretaceous rocks. Its vertebrae (backbones) have long spindles growing out on top. In life, these spindles would have been wrapped in skin like the fin-bones of a fish, only these beasts lived on land.

On the other hand, that famous big-finned critter you've seen may not have been a dinosaur at all but *Dimetrodon*, an older, more primitive animal. *Dimetrodon* is a Paleozoic synapsid (synapsids started out as a group of lizard-like creatures that predated the dinos and later evolved into mammals). Both *Spinosaurus* and *Dimetrodon* have similar fins, even though they are not at all closely related.

The easiest way to tell the difference between dimo and spino is by looking past their fans and at their feet. Dimo has four on the floor; spino, like all predatory dinosaurs, has two in the blue.

> **Dig This**
> A partial skeleton of *Spinosaurus* indicates that this beast may have been the longest of all meat-eating dinos, including T-rex. If we add in the length of the missing vertebrae, it may have been 50 feet long. What's more, this particular spino skeleton may not have grown to be fully mature. (Upper and lower segments of vertebrae had not yet fused, which happens in full-grown spinos.) Thus some spinosaurs may have grown to be well over 50 feet long.

A Dinosaur's Biggest Fan

Spinosaurus' fan may have evolved to serve the same purposes for which humans use fans: temperature control and flirting. It may be hard to imagine a 4-ton carnosaur coyly waving a 6-foot fan like a Japanese geisha, trying to attract the attention of a potential lover, but that's the idea. The spino of the opposite sex takes notice of the fan and wants to see more.

Then again, the big sails may have served not to attract lovers but to repel rivals. Their fans may have made them look to other spinos—and maybe to other dinos too—even burlier and more threatening than they already were. Some dinosaur showdowns may have been decided by the biggest fan.

Another possibility, as we mentioned, has to do with temperature. Spinosaur fans may not only have cooled them down, but warmed them up as well. And if it did use the fan

> **Boning Up**
> Some living lizards also have fans on their backs, including the modern basilisk lizard. Basilisk lizards can grow to be more than 3 feet long and have fans that they can raise and lower, both to regulate their body temperature and to show off.

for cooling, it didn't try to make a breeze like we do with our fans. *Spinosaurs* did not have the characteristic S-shaped neck of the theropod dinosaurs, which would have enabled them to turn their heads back over their shoulders, so they couldn't shake their fans in their faces to cool off.

Instead, an overheated spino would have slipped into the shade or, if that weren't possible, simply turned its fin longways to the sun. The fin would cool more quickly than the rest of its big hot self. Blood could have flowed through the fin, become cool, and cooled the whole meat locker.

Dig This
Unfortunately, the best-known *Spinosaurus* fossils were destroyed during World War II. They were kept in a German museum that was damaged during bombing raids.

Just as the fin could have been used for cooling blood in the shade, it could have warmed the blood quickly in the sun. This view of spino fins as thermal control mechanisms supports the much-debated theory that dinosaurs were cold-blooded, with such low metabolism that they had to rely on the sun and shade, rather than food, for regulating their body temperature. For more on this debate, see Chapter 25.

Something Old, Something New

There's a new dinosaur on the Early Cretaceous block, discovered just over 10 years ago in England. It was evidently pretty strange looking. It was built much like the other carnosaurs, except that it had one extra-big claw on the pointer fingers of each of its forepaws. In honor of these claws, the dino was named *Baryonyx*, which means "strong claw" in Greek.

More striking than the claw, however, is its crocodile snout and jaws, which hold the most teeth of any known dinosaur. These special features were probably used for catching and eating fish. This idea is borne out by the partially digested fish scales found inside the baryo fossil. It probably did its fishing in shallow water because its limbs do not appear to be adapted for swimming.

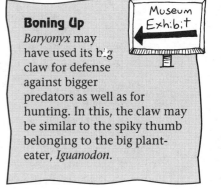

Boning Up
Baryonyx may have used its big claw for defense against bigger predators as well as for hunting. In this, the claw may be similar to the spiky thumb belonging to the big plant-eater, *Iguanodon*.

It may have been difficult, however, for such a large dinosaur to survive only on fish. *Baryonyx* may also have eaten smaller land animals. If so, it led an interesting double life, switching back and forth between hunting like a wolf and fishing like a crocodile.

Mega Mistakes

Boning Up

An unauthorized account of the theory that dinosaurs are ancestors of birds has it that the Victorian paleontologist T.H. Huxley was carving a turkey for Christmas dinner when he was struck by the similarity between the bird's leg bones and the *Megalosaurus* bones he'd been studying. Since Huxley proposed this theory, it has been hotly debated, rejected, and taken up again several times.

While *Baryonyx* is one of the more recently discovered dinosaurs, *Megalosaurus* is the first species to be identified and written up in a scientific paper, published in 1822. At that time it was known only from a lower jaw bone with some teeth in it. We still haven't found a complete *Megalosaurus* skeleton.

Not only have we known about megalos for a relatively long time, they were alive as a species for a relatively long time— more than 30 million years during the latter half of the Jurassic. In light of these facts, it's surprising—and frustrating—that there are no complete megalo skeletons.

Perhaps because megalo fossils are found in many Mesozoic layers, and because the name *Megalosaurus* has been familiar to fossil hunters for many human generations, many fossil odds and ends have been lumped into the megalosaur category. For almost two centuries now, almost any hard-to-identify scrap of dinosaur bone could seem like a megalosaur. This is especially true because megalo is a fairly nondescript sort of carnosaur.

Fossil Fallacy

Many so-called megalosaur offspring, siblings, cousins, and second cousins have been found consisting of incomplete skeletons. Although this is certainly confusing for paleontologists, the problem has produced some of the best names ever devised. You may want to hang onto this list of dubious megalosaurs for when it comes time to pick out names for your kids: there's *Unquillosaurus*, *Kelmayisaurus*, *Polyodontosaurus*, *Poicilopleuron*, *Laelaps*, *Zapsalis*, *Walgettosuchus*, *Tichosteus*, *Paronychodon*, and many more.

People who make drawings and reconstructions of megalosaurs have to model the missing parts on bones from other dinosaurs. This has resulted in misconceptions. For example, it has been drawn with *Spinosaurus* spines used as models, giving the impression that it had a big sail on its back.

The Least You Need to Know

➤ Carnosaurs are the largest land predators ever.

➤ A predator trap is where many hungry meat-eaters, such as *Allosaurus*, can get stuck.

➤ Carnosaurs have extremely lightweight skulls.

➤ *Spinosaurus* spines may have helped attract mates, threatened rivals, and regulated body temperature.

➤ *Baryonyx* combined fishing and hunting.

➤ *Megalosaurus* is the first dinosaur to be described in a scientific paper.

The Royals

Proudly upholding an august tradition dating back 75 million years, the tyrannosaurs are fossilized embodiments of a way of life that refuses to die off completely. At the height of their eight-million-year reign, they ruled with unquestioned authority and concentrated power that has never been paralleled by any other line of monarchs. It's no wonder, then, that we continue to look to them with awed respect, and it is, perhaps, forgivable that we find it difficult to restrain our sometimes impertinent curiosity.

Now that their glory has faded, these proud, somewhat conservative figureheads are understandably vexed by the clamoring attention they have received of late in the media. Inquiries about their physical stamina, their sex lives, and their resources for supporting themselves appear wholly unwelcome and are invariably met by a now-familiar and chilling grimace.

The royal line remains notoriously aloof. Only a dozen or so of its members have condescended to appear in public at all, and these have made only partial appearances. The rest have remained underground, scattered, and incognito, leaving the press and the public hungry for details. The peerage is hardly more forthcoming because, although some are slightly more accessible to the press, all remain loyally silent in deference to the tyrannosaur family.

But now, thanks to unprecedented largesse from the royals themselves and in cooperation with representatives of the academic community, which has long been working to establish connections among the firmest and most long-standing tyrannosaur constituents, the true story of the royals can be told in considerably more intimate detail. This story reveals a family that, although embattled, imperious, at times uncompromising, still has its tender side.

The King

Tyrannosaurus rex has long held great renown the world over as the biggest land predator to have lived. Recently, however, this position of eminence has been challenged by new fossil finds. One of these tyrannosaur cousins is *Giganotosaurus* (gigantic lizard) of Patagonia; another is *Carcharodontosaurus* (great white shark-toothed lizard) from the Sahara. The royal lineage is also the subject of recent debate. Many authorities claim the tyrannos are descended, not from the carnosaurs, as has traditionally been thought, but from the coelurosaurs.

His Royal Majesty, Tyrannosaurus rex.

(Department of Library Services, American Museum of Natural History; Neg. no.:35492; Photo.:Anderson)

Because no complete set of T-rex tail bones has been recovered, there is some room for dispute as to its actual length, but a full-grown T-rex could have spanned 50 feet in length and stood up to a height of 20 feet. With flesh on its bones, it may have weighed 6 tons.

A creature of such size would have lived a long time. It's been estimated that individuals of the species may have reached the reverend age of 100 years before bequeathing their state and their dominions to their heirs. Long live the king!

One T-rex skull is known to be 5 feet long. Tyrannos had the longest teeth of any dinosaur. They had extremely sturdy backbones and muscular necks. Although the superior strength and stature of T-rex is unquestionable, the way it used its power has been the subject of much speculation.

Head of State

Greatest of the royal accoutrements were the jaws, known to have been the strongest of any land predator's at any time. These jaws were attached to a solid and sturdy skull. In contrast to the light, flexible skull of *Allosaurus*, *Tyrannosaurus* skulls did not bend in response to pressure from the huge mouthfuls it took in. The teeth were also unusually sturdy and set deeply into their sockets.

This means that T-rex would not have played with its food to tire out its still-living prey before being swallowing it. Instead, jaws and head were strictly business, getting right to the point and leaving no room for contradiction.

The Body Politic

The better to support the royal noggin, the tyrannosaur spine was massive, bracing large, powerful neck and back muscles. The mighty neck could have been used for twisting off cart-sized bites of meat from the carcass of its prey—assuming, of course, that the carcass was indeed its prey.

Boning Up

The age of tyrannosaur fossils can be estimated by counting layers that form as the bones develop. Although no fossils left by 100-year-old tyrannosaurs have been found, we do know of fossils left by teenagers that were not yet mature. This shows that it took a fairly long time for tyrannosaurs to reach adulthood. A long childhood generally means an even longer adulthood, leading to the conclusion that tyrannos could have reached a ripe old age.

Boning Up

As with all royal families, there has been a good deal of squabbling over who is, and who isn't, a close blood-relation of T-rex. Some think there have been too many distinctions made among kinds of tyrannosaur. Some suggest, for example, that *Tarbosaurus* should be classified as a T-rex. In contrast, some elitists think the fossils currently identified as T-rex actually belong to two distinct varieties of tyrannosaur. This distinction is based on differences in size and skull structure that could reflect age or sex difference, or other variation within the species.

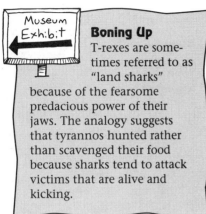

Boning Up

T-rexes are sometimes referred to as "land sharks" because of the fearsome predacious power of their jaws. The analogy suggests that tyrannos hunted rather than scavenged their food because sharks tend to attack victims that are alive and kicking.

The royals have long been criticized for their alleged inability to support their own voracious appetites in a seemly manner. They have been accused, for example, of burdening the commonwealth by taking a large percentage of the victims of their meat-eating subjects for themselves. In a further affront to the royal dignity, it has been suggested that rather than hunt for themselves, they stooped to scavenging. There is some circumstantial evidence in support of these claims, as well as a good deal of evidence to the contrary.

Whigs

Those who suspect the royals of scavenging point to their bottom-heavy physiques. Such prodigious posteriors, they say, argue against energetic predation. The royal forearms, moreover, are notoriously underdeveloped, and not at all suited for attack. In fact, a 6-ton tyranno has forearms no bigger than the arms of a 150-pound human being. These are equipped with only two claws each. Not only are these forearms clearly useless for hunting, there is considerable question about whether they were useful for anything at all.

Tories

Many observers have rallied to the defense of the monarch, insisting that the death-dealing capabilities of its jaws are self-evident. Furthermore, they say, although the hips are admittedly ponderous, the tyrannical ankles were long and unencumbered with heavy tissue—assuring signs indeed of uncommon agility in such a large and stately figure!

Further fossil evidence that *Tyrannosaurus* was light on its feet are the many trackways of theropod footprints that have been found. None of these include the snaky trail of a tail being dragged along the ground. Because the custom among human monarchs of having their trains carried by pages was unknown to the dinosaurs, we can only assume that T-rex was sprightly enough to keep its own tail proudly aloft while on progress through its realms.

Dig This

Stereoscopic vision also developed in those impressive dinosaur predators, the raptors, which evidently used their keen vision for hunting at night and for accurate grabbing with their claws.

Still more staunch rex defenders allude to the royal gaze and say, "Here is no strabismatic, walleyed, unfocussed face of a mere scavenger! The visage faces forward, thanks to the narrowness of the royal demeanor, allowing the ocular overlap necessary for stereoscopic sight and depth perception! Such visual acuity clearly bespeaks an accomplished predator." With vision such as this, even swiftly moving quarry may be accurately gnashed.

Taken together, these assets indicate that the tyrannosaurs' predatory prowess was truly worthy of the king of meat-eaters. One further point made by the more zealous rex loyalists is that the skull and jaws could have withstood and absorbed the force of a fast-moving victim. The point is that not only were the tyrannosaurs predators, but they also were singularly direct and efficient. Making a kill and taking a bite amounted to pretty much the same thing.

Olè!

Many dinophiles agree that the all-time stellar matchup of predator and prey is T-rex versus *Triceratops*. It seems likely that *Triceratops* would have supplied a significant source of food for the tyrannos, but it would not have been an easy victim with its powerful, compact body and three large horns.

T-rex may have had to rely on the element of surprise, stalking the tricero and attacking from behind to avoid being gored. Another tyrannosaur tactic may have been to frighten one or more triceros into running away. A T-rex could overtake a running *Triceratops* from behind and avoid a skewering.

If the *Triceratops* stood its ground, however, facing the tyranno head on with its horns, it had a good chance of surviving until another day. A tyrannosaur would have been unwilling to risk its life in combat just for a meal.

> **Dig This**
> Like some human kings of the past, some tyrannosaurs evidently overindulged their appetite for their favorite food. Tyranno fossils have been found that show signs of gout, a disease human beings can get from eating too much red meat. Tyrannos also suffered from osteoporosis and nasty arthritis. When your bones are as big as a T-rex's, your joints can really ache!

Hand Jive

We have mentioned that tyrannosaur forearms are underdeveloped in relation to the rest of the physique. Although a T-rex could bend its neck down to reach its forepaws with its snout, it could not reach the end of its nose with its claws while holding its head up straight. This deficiency has fostered speculation that tyrannosaur forearms were essentially useless.

Push Ups

Royal supporters have argued that the tyranno forearms were indeed indispensable appendages, if for no other purpose than to hoist the royal corpus from its prone resting position. Without its arms to brace itself, it would have had to lean on its nose to stand up. Everyone loyal to the rexes can take satisfaction that these modest two-clawed forearms rendered such an undignified recourse wholly unnecessary.

One more expedience furthered by the royal forepaws is of a somewhat delicate nature and might be better left unmentioned were there not a pressing need to silence rex's detractors. It seems that the tyrannicals may have indulged in forepaw-play, as it were.

Love Handles

As you may imagine, sexual encounters between consenting rexes must have been exciting for more than just the obvious reasons. Above and beyond the attraction two adults might feel toward one another, they must have been aware of the challenge of their undertaking. Such trysts undoubtedly would have presented no small degree of danger, given the size and proximity of the parties concerned.

Consider that the family jewels had to be tucked away beneath the tail for safekeeping. For two rexes to exchange compliments, one would be obliged to climb to a lofty height atop the other—indeed, just at that juncture of the tyrannical form where the ascent is steepest and most fraught with peril.

Present-day attempts to reconstruct the scene suggest that the ordinarily bipedal tyranno-saur may have become temporarily monopedal in its efforts to oblige its partner. This must have produced the risk of a long fall to the mounting rex, and of a heavy crushing to the one underneath.

Boning Up

If the card absolutely refuses to go in its slot, it may be snagged on something else in your computer. Specifically, the backplane of the sound card may be snagging the back of the computer.

Consider further that the tyrannosaur tail, effective though it must have been in maintaining balance under most circumstances, would, in the throes of tyrannosaur passion, have tended rather to frustrate than to serve that purpose for which it was otherwise so useful.

There can be little doubt, then, as to the value of the tyran-nosaur forearms, superfluous though they may have been ordinarily. When rexes commingled, the forearms ensured stability. For this reason alone, if for no other, they have earned our respect as helping hands to the royal succession.

The House of Tyranno

As absolute a monarch as rex was, it did not rule without the confidence and support of its retainers among its extended family.

➤ *Tyrannosaurus* (tyrant lizard)   Not all tyrannos were T-rexes, but all were big meat-eaters.

➤ *Albertosaurus* (lizard from Alberta)   Prince Albert has been the indispensable confidant of the King and presided over the Canadian province from which he takes his name.

➤ *Daspletosaurus* (frightful lizard)   Another Canadian tyranno, slightly smaller than *Tyrannosaurus*.

➤ *Tarbosaurus* (terror lizard)   Ruler of Late Cretaceous Mongolia, this oriental potentate is a mirror image of its western counterpart.

➤ *Nanotyrannus* (dwarf tyrant)   This tiny T. from Montana is actually a full-grown tyranno.

Prince Albert in a Can-adian Formation

Prince Albert is smaller and more primitive than *Tyrannosaurus*, having a longer, shallower snout, a lighter skull, and shorter teeth. Except for one skeleton found in Mongolia, all known specimens are North American. Its name stems from the fact that it is known chiefly from fossils found in Alberta, Canada. Some *Albertosaurus* specimens went by the name of *Gorgosaurus* (fierce lizard) before it was decided that the name alberto had priority.

It evolved earlier than T-rex and lasted longer as a species—about 20 million years in comparison to 8 million for T-rex. In the days before T-rex came of age, Prince Albert served dinodom as regent and later ceded the throne to its larger, more powerful nephew. Prince Albert was thoroughly upper crust, however, surviving right up until the Cretaceous mass extinction.

The Little Prince

Nanotyrannosaurus is a dwarf species of *Albertosaurus*, weighing a piddling half ton and spanning a mere 17 feet in length. Undersized as it was, it must have had a real Napoleon complex. The fossil record shows, however, that it was a rare species, so it evidently met with severe difficulties in its attempts to conquer the Cretaceous world.

We know nano was full grown, rather than a young tyranno, because many of the bones of its skull and spine are fused together. This happened at maturity. What we don't know is whether nano evolved to be small from giant-sized ancestors, or whether it was a more primitive ancestor of the larger tyrannos.

Dig This
There are a number of dinosaur dwarf species besides nanotyranno, including *Microceratops* (a mini frill-face), *Microhadrosaurus* (a dinky duckbill), *Micropachycephalosaurus* (a little thick-skulled dinosaur, and also the dino with the longest name), and *Microvenator* (a little killer).

What nano lacked in size it may have made up for in quickness and agility. As a result, it probably occupied a different niche than the big tyrannos. Instead, it may have competed for prey with the sickle claw raptors. Faced with these odds, it's no wonder that nanos were even more scarce than the none-too-common T-rexes.

All She Wrote

T-rex and the royal family of tyrannosaurs presided over the demise of the dinos. During their reign, all the non-bird dinosaurs died off. In fact, they have probably taken more than their fair share of the blame for the mass extinction that occurred at the end of the Cretaceous. Many critics attribute the fall of the house of tyranno, and of all dinodom, at least in part to the size of these predators, and of their prey, the enormous sauropods and duckbills that formed a good part of their meat supply.

The enormity of these beasts can be seen as an overspecialization. *Specialization* for dinosaurs is, in evolutionary terms, very much the same as it is for people in professional terms. It happens when a species develops unusual capabilities that allow it to live in a way that most other creatures can't.

Specialization allows a species to occupy a niche other species are unable to fill. It can be a problem, however, because it can make it more difficult for the species to adapt to changes in the environment. If the specialized niche disappears for whatever reason, the specialized species is liable to disappear with it.

Definosaurus

When used in an evolutionary sense, **specialization** occurs when a species adapts in unusual ways to occupy a niche that most other creatures cannot fill. An example of specialization in a living animal is the long sticky tongue of the anteater, allowing it to eat even more ants than a human more than twice its size!

The global conditions that allowed many kinds of dinosaur to evolve into their humongous forms may have been unusual because such big creatures had never lived on land before, and never have since. It seems possible, then, that the dinosaurs died off in part because so many had become so big, overachieving in a world that could not continue to support such supersized inhabitants.

There are problems with this view, though, because a good number of more ordinary-sized species—dino and non-dino—became extinct at the same time. It is uncertain to what extent the demise of smaller species may have been linked to the fall of the giants with which they shared the ecosystem. Although it is possible that size played a part in the end of the dinosaur dynasty, there were certainly other factors leading to the cataclysm. We'll say more about extinction in Chapter 26.

The Least You Need to Know

➤ T-rex has long been considered the largest land predator ever, with the most powerful jaws, and the biggest teeth.

➤ Contenders with T-rex for the title of largest land predator are *Giganotosaurus* and *Carcharodontosaurus*.

➤ Tyrannosaurs may have been scavengers as well as hunters.

➤ They may have used their underdeveloped forearms for getting up on their feet after lying down and for stability during sex.

➤ *Albertosaurus* is a smaller, more primitive tyrannosaur.

➤ *Nanotyrannus* is a dwarf species of tyrannosaur.

➤ The size of the tyrannosaurs may have contributed to the mass extinction at the end of the Cretaceous.

Big Browsers

As big as T-rex and the other meat-eaters were, they weren't the biggest dinosaurs. That honor goes to the plant-eating "Brontosaurus"-like dinos. These are the classic sauropodomorphs, the first things most people think of when they hear the word "dinosaur."

These long-necked, barrel-bodied behemoths include some of the oldest known dinosaurs. They branched off from the rest of the dinosaur clan early on, taking the concept of what it meant to be a dinosaur in a completely new direction. At this time, other dinosaurs tended to be bipedal, small, agile, and carnivorous. The browsers, though, had other ideas about how to get around, what to eat, and how big to be.

They were the first plant-eating dinosaurs and the first dinosaurs to walk on four feet. This way of life worked well for them, and they also lasted a long time, living throughout the entire span of non-bird dinosaur history—about 150 million years from the Mid-Triassic right up until the end of the Cretaceous.

In addition to being big, they were peaceful and spent their time minding their own leaf-eating business, unlike the predacious theropods. They were not simply walking steakhouses for the meat-eaters, however; they evolved an array of strategies for eating and for defending themselves against being eaten.

> **Dig This**
> The sauropods include not only the biggest known dinosaurs but the smallest as well. In fact, the smallest dinosaur skeleton ever discovered is a sauropod called *Mussosaurus* (mouse lizard). This is a baby dinosaur. The skeleton, found without a tail, is 8 inches long. It is estimated that it might have grown to be 10 feet long as an adult.

Mighty Morphs

There were two groups of big browsers: the *sauropods* (lizard-footed dinos) and the *prosauropods* (dinos that came before the lizard-footed dinos). Together these groups make up a larger group, known as sauropodomorphs (dinos shaped like lizard-footed dinos).

In fact, all the sauropodomorphs are shaped pretty much the same. This has caused problems over the years because many partial sauropodomorph skeletons and scattered bones have been found. These bits and pieces tend to get mixed up, causing confusion between the different names and characteristics. No wonder it's been difficult to keep track of all the bones. One sauropod, *Apatosaurus*, has more than 80 vertebrae in its tail alone!

With their big bodies and long necks, they are specially adapted for eating large quantities of leaves growing high in the tree tops. In spite of this basic similarity, though, they are a large and diverse group.

A Big, Long List of Big, Long Dinosaurs

Here's a list of some of the better-known browsers, not counting the really huge ones listed later in this chapter.

Prosauropods

➤ *Anchisaurus* (near lizard)   Gets its name from being a near descendant of the non-dinosaur reptiles.

➤ *Plateosaurus* (flat lizard)   Gets its name from its flat teeth.

➤ *Mussaurus* (mouse lizard)   The smallest dinosaur ever found. It's just a baby, 8 inches long.

➤ *Melanorosaurus* (black mountain lizard)   Was more sturdily built than the other prosauros.

Sauropods

➤ *Diplodocus* (double beamed)   Gets its name from the extra ridge on its vertebrae that added support to the neck and back.

➤ *Apatosaurus* (deceptive lizard)   Was hardly deceptive in life, but gets its name because its bones have been confused with those of other species.

➤ *Camarasaurus* (chambered lizard)   Had chambers in its vertebrae that made them lighter, as did many other sauropods.

➤ *Brachiosaurus* (arm lizard)   Unique among sauropods in having front legs that were longer than its back legs, hence its name.

➤ *Saltasaurus* (lizard from Salta, a province in Argentina)   Important because it had bony armor on its back to protect it from predators. Some of the other sauropods may have had this kind of protection too.

➤ "Brontosaurus" (thunder lizard)   Turned out to be the same critter as *Apatosaurus*, the official name. But because most people know the name bronto, it still gets used.

Feet on the Ground

The prosauropods were the first of the sauropodomorphs. They gave rise to the sauropods that followed. Although they look like sauropods in that they are four-footed and have long necks, their front legs are noticeably smaller than their hind legs. This suggests they descended from bipedal creatures. We mentioned that bipedal posture was an important innovation that helped set dinosaurs apart from other Mesozoic land animals. The browsers, though, got back down on all fours.

Boning Up
Not only the browsers, but all four-footed dinosaurs, including *Triceratops, Stegosaurus*, and *Ankylosaurus* are descended from bipedal creatures. In effect, these dinosaurs undid evolutionary work that had already been done, that of getting up on two feet.

Lofty Ambitions

The prosauropods, however, were evidently able to rear up on their hind feet to reach lofty branches with their snouts. This, together with their long necks, enabled them to live on edible plants that other creatures couldn't reach. By taking the high road to food, they led the way to an entire era of evolutionary success for the sauropods.

We can tell the prosauropods were not completely bipedal because their skeletons show the bulk of their weight would have been set too far forward for them to walk around upright all of the time. This shifting forward of body weight has to do with their leafy diet.

A Gutsy Approach

The sauropodomorphs probably ate ferns and the leaves of cycad trees, which were tall and palmlike. They also may have eaten the rather tough leaves and needles of evergreen trees. They did this despite their relatively small jaws by simply swallowing their food without much chewing.

The real work of grinding the green stuff was done in the stomach with the help of gastroliths, or gizzard stones. These are sharp, smallish pebbles swallowed specially to help with digestion. And you think your laxative tastes bad! The browsers may have kept the stones in their gastric mills until they became too smooth to be useful, and then chucked them up. With those necks, they had to come a long way.

The gastroliths enabled the big browsers to eat more than they could have otherwise. In fact, they probably had to spend almost all their waking hours eating. They had to eat more than meat-eaters because, pound for pound, a diet of meat is higher in calories than a plant diet. Meat can also be digested more quickly than plants. This means that plant-eaters not only had to eat a greater quantity of food than meat-eaters, they also had to carry it around inside their stomachs for a greater length of time. As a result, they needed bigger stomachs.

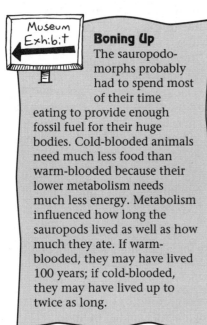

Boning Up

The sauropodo-morphs probably had to spend most of their time eating to provide enough fossil fuel for their huge bodies. Cold-blooded animals need much less food than warm-blooded because their lower metabolism needs much less energy. Metabolism influenced how long the sauropods lived as well as how much they ate. If warm-blooded, they may have lived 100 years; if cold-blooded, they may have lived up to twice as long.

Carrying those big guts around took a lot of energy. Fortunately, the skeletal structure of the sauropodomorphs adjusted to make the load easier to carry. Bipedal creatures like the meat-eating theropod dinosaurs carried their stomachs with their hips more or less underneath them, sort of like a basket. In contrast, the SPMs carried their stomachs slung from their spine like a big sack. This was an easier way to carry a big load, but it meant they had to move around on all fours.

As the sauropod clan evolved into bigger and bigger leaf-eaters, they developed bigger and bigger stomachs and stood more and more firmly on all four feet. In contrast to the early prosauropods, whose front feet were smaller than their hind feet, some later sauropods like *Brachiosaurus* had front legs that were even larger and sturdier than their hind legs.

Rubbernecking

This makes it that much less likely that they balanced on their back feet to reach the treetops. Instead, their necks evolved to an enormous length. Why stretch to reach something when you can just evolve a longer neck?

Many sauropods had huge, long, muscular necks, like a giraffe's only bigger. To move their necks around, they needed neck bones that were big and strong but also lightweight. In fact, they developed hollow spaces in their vertebrae called *pleurocoels* that enabled them to grow longer, stronger necks that weren't too heavy to be maneuvered.

In addition, some sauropod fossils have a deep groove running all through the vertebrae for encasing a strong, cable-like ligament that helped the sauropods move their necks and keep their heads upright while resting. It's no accident that Fred Flintstone used a Brontosaurus for a crane when he went to work. The sauropods are well-designed pieces of heavy machinery.

Safe and Saury

The big browsers' huge size would have made them difficult to kill. Even so, they were hunted by the theropod dinosaurs, which evolved to be pretty huge themselves. In addition to size, the sauropods had other means of protecting themselves.

Sauropods had one big claw on the inner toe of their forefeet. They may have used this to kick with in self-defense. Another weapon at their disposal was their long tails. These may have been useful as big, heavy whips. In addition, some sauropods, namely *Saltasaurus*, and possibly *Titanosaurus*, had bony armor on their backs for increased protection against predators.

One additional line of defense that may have been practiced by sauropods was traveling in herds. Herding would have provided protection, especially for the younger ones. Some fossilized trackways have been found that include many different sauropod prints in the same area. This may reflect herding. It isn't clear, though, whether all the browsers were there together at the same time. Also, bone beds including many sauropod skeletons have been discovered, but again, it isn't clear whether all the animals died together as a herd or whether their bones were swept together by moving water.

Boning Up

Museum Exhibit

The sauropods' long necks pose questions about their blood circulation. They must have had tremendously high blood pressure to overcome gravity enough to circulate blood to their brains. They may have had special muscles in their necks that helped push the blood up to their heads.

Definosaurus

Glossary

Many sauropods have hollow spaces in their vertebrae called **pleurocoels** that keep their skeletons light without weakening them too much. *Brachiosaurus* has pleurocoels not only in its vertebrae but in its ribs as well.

Boning Up

Museum Exhibit

Saltasaurus, the sauropod dinosaur known to have bony armor on its back, lived at the end of the Cretaceous and was one of the last sauropod species to evolve. The bony armor, then, may have been a defensive adaptation that evolved as a response to the Late Cretaceous predators, T-rex, and the other big carnosaurs.

103

Going Pro

As we mentioned, the first long-necked leaf-eaters were the prosauropods. They lived during the Late Triassic and Early Jurassic Eras. Two important kinds of prosauropod were *Plateosaurus* and *Anchisaurus*. *Anchisaurus* wasn't much bigger than a human being. In fact, the first *Anchisaurus* fossils, discovered in Germany in 1818, were thought to be human bones. *Plateosaurus* skeletons have also been found in Germany, in great quantities, in fact. The fact that so many of these fossils have been found in one place suggests that they may have been herding animals.

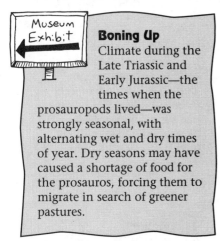

Boning Up
Climate during the Late Triassic and Early Jurassic—the times when the prosauropods lived—was strongly seasonal, with alternating wet and dry times of year. Dry seasons may have caused a shortage of food for the prosauros, forcing them to migrate in search of greener pastures.

Some think the German plateos were on a seasonal migration in search of green leafy stuff when they were killed as a herd all at once by some unknown catastrophe. Others think the bonebed grew gradually near a place where plateos lived year round. In either case, plateos are well known thanks to this site. So much so that plateo bones are sometimes used as models to fill in the missing pieces of other, less well-known species.

Stuck in the Middle

The prosauropods can be thought of in evolutionary terms as a transitionary group between the theropods and the sauropods. They had a number of characteristics that link them to the theropods that the sauropods didn't have, or had to a lesser degree.

As we mentioned, although they walked around on all fours most of the time, the prosauropods could also rear up into the trees to eat from the higher branches. In doing this, their hips functioned as fulcrums, enabling them to raise their bodies like the rising end of a see-saw, with their tails to counterbalance the weight on the other side. Some sauropods were able to get up on their hind legs too. It wasn't as easy for them, however, as for the prosauros.

While standing on two legs, the prosauropods could use their forepaws for manipulating branches. They could turn their hands inward and pull trees and branches toward them, a trick that later sauropods couldn't pull off. Even though the prosauropods could use their forepaws for hands, their wrists were "double-jointed," or hyperextended, so they could use their forepaws as easily as feet.

Boning Up
Some creatures of today are only partially bipedal, much as the prosauropods were. These include bears and apes.

Their partial bipedal ability and partial use of their forepaws as hands shows the prosauropods were more closely related to the theropod dinosaurs than the later sauropods were. In addition, the prosauros were more like the theropods in being more slender, agile, and small.

More to Chew On

On top of these similarities, there is an additional—but misleading—resemblance between the meat-eating theropods and the prosauros. Both kinds of dinosaur have serrated teeth. This trait has led to speculation that the prosauropods may have been meat-eaters, or were perhaps omnivorous. Actually, though, the serrations in theropod and prosauropod teeth are quite different, and most dinoscientists agree that prosauro teeth are fully adapted for eating plants.

Another plant-eating adaptation of the prosauropods is in the peculiar set of the jaw. Their jaw hinges are actually lower than their bottom set of teeth, allowing them to mash food more securely.

Drying Up

It has been well established that all the sauropodomorphs were adapted for eating leaves growing high on trees where other creatures couldn't reach them. Dinoscientists of today agree that sauropods were land creatures. This, however, has only become clear within the past 30 years or so.

Prior to that time, many thought that sauropods spent most of their lives under water. Quite a lot of evidence has been found in support of this view. Nevertheless, it's all wrong. Still, it's an interesting theory. Here's how it goes:

Dig This
Some of the first sauropod bones ever found were originally identified not as dinosaur bones but as a species of crocodile. This set a precedent for a whole series of mistaken ideas about sauropods and water.

A Theory That's All Wet

➤ Their relatively small jaws and delicate teeth don't seem up to the task of grinding enough leafy food to have kept them going. Water plants would have been more tender and easier to eat, as well as possibly more nutritious.

➤ Their huge bulk may have been too difficult to carry around on land. Underwater, however, their enormous bodies would have been buoyed up.

➤ Water may have provided safety from theropod predators.

➤ Their long necks may have been used as snorkels, enabling them to breathe even while standing at the bottom of a deep lake. This seems especially possible because many sauropods had nostrils on top of their heads above their eyes. In shallower water, they may have fed on surface plants by sweeping their long necks from side to side.

As attractive as this line of reasoning may be, a number of even more convincing arguments have been made to refute it. Here's a list of some of them:

Landing the Big Ones

➤ Even though they have small jaws and teeth, they had gastroliths—stomach stones—for grinding large amounts of leafy food plucked from the branches of trees.

➤ They had strong, pillar-like legs capable of carrying their bulk around on land, especially because their bones were lightweight. They also had padded heels like modern-day elephants for absorbing the wear and tear on the feet.

➤ Air breathed in at the surface of the water would have expanded greatly in their lungs many feet below the surface. This increase in atmospheric pressure would have been too much for their lungs to deal with.

➤ The fact that some sauropods had nostrils above their eyes remains something of a mystery, but does not prove they were aquatic. This weird nose position may have meant they had trunks, like an elephant, whose skull also has nostril holes above the eyes. Another possibility is that they developed special noses for making special noises, hooting or honking in particular ways to communicate with one another. Both of these ideas, though, are speculative. We really don't know why some sauropods breathed through the top of their heads.

Diplodocus skull. The holes for the nostrils are situated between the eyes on the top of the skull.
(Department of Library Services, American Museum of Natural History; Neg. no.:35052; Photo.:Anderson)

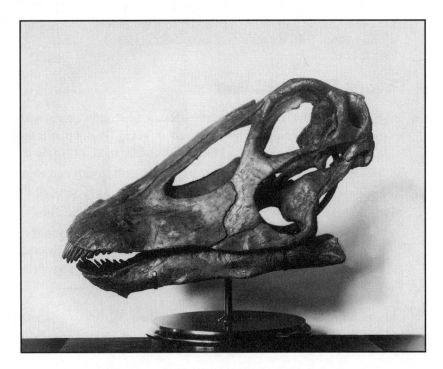

Big as Life

If sauropods communicated with one another, it could only have been in the simplest of fashions. Judging by the size of their brains, they can't have been very smart. A 60 foot *Apatosaurus* has a small head—only about the size of a horse's—in relation to its huge body. Not only that, but its brain was even small in comparison with its head—only about the size of a large walnut.

Some of these nutheads have made history as the biggest land animals ever. And here they are:

➤ *Seismosaurus* A contender for the longest known dinosaur with an estimated length of 120 feet from head to tail. Discovered in the mid-1980s in Utah as a nearly complete skeleton, it may have stood 18 feet tall not counting the neck and weighed 80 to 100 tons.

➤ *Supersaurus* Known from 8-foot-long shoulder blades, a 6-foot wide pelvis, 10-foot ribs, and $4^1/_2$-foot vertebrae. These fossils were discovered in Colorado in 1972. Depending on the unknown length of its tail, it could have been 140 feet long, the longest known dinosaur.

➤ *Ultrasaurus* Probably the tallest dinosaur at an estimated 55 feet as well as the heaviest at 100 tons. Discovered in 1979 in Colorado, it is known chiefly from a 9-foot long shoulder blade—the largest dinosaur bone ever discovered—and some 5-foot vertebrae.

> **Dig This**
> As yet no sauropod nests have been discovered, although we know they laid eggs. One peculiar fossil find in France includes sauropod eggs that were laid, not in a nest, but in a straight line, evidently while the egg layer was walking along!

The Least You Need to Know

➤ The sauropodomorphs were the biggest dinosaurs and the only ones to eat from the tops of tall trees.

➤ The prosauropods could stand on their hind feet to eat from the treetops, but they usually walked on all fours.

➤ The sauropod strategy of walking on all fours enabled them to have bigger stomachs for storing food.

➤ Many sauropods have hollow spaces in their bones that make their skeletons as light—and as large—as possible.

➤ Some sauropods had bony armor on their backs as a defense against predators.

➤ Sauropods had long been thought to live in water but are now known to have been land animals that lived a lifestyle comparable to today's elephants.

Part 3
The Bird Butts

The bird butts are the Ornithischian dinosaurs, so called because they have pelvises shaped like those of modern-day birds. The bird butts were not bird ancestors, but they developed bird-like hips along with new eating habits. They changed shape to make room for larger digestive tracts that could digest vegetation more effectively.

The bird butts are all vegetarians and acquired all kinds of unusual characteristics for eating, as well as for defending themselves against being eaten. These traits include teeth, armor, weapons, and adaptive social behaviors.

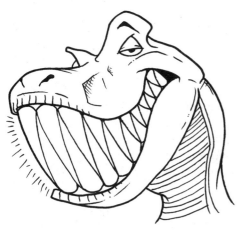

The Tooth Patrol

The Ornithischians were the grazing animals of the Mesozoic. They ranged from goat sized to trailer-truck sized. The smaller ones were fast as gazelles, and the bigger ones were not necessarily slow but may have been able to rumble along at a good clip. All of them made a living off low- or medium-growing vegetation, leaving the treetops to the sauropods.

Most of the larger ones had big, cauldron-like stomachs and long digestive tracts for turning the leaves and plants they ate into high-vitamin vegetable juice. As you may already know if you've ever eaten a half a ton of your favorite dish in a single sitting, having a lot of food in your stomach can slow you down. This is especially the case when the food takes a long time to digest, like grass, leaves, and other kinds of vegetation.

The fastest of the grazing Ornithischian dinosaurs were the ornithopods. They developed a new technique for digesting food quickly that let them get more nourishment out of food that spent less time weighing down their stomachs. The technique was chewing.

The Art of Chewing

To those of us who chew our food, it can be hard to imagine a time before chewing became a crucial food-processing activity. Many dinosaurs, however, didn't bother to chew much. The carnivorous theropods bolted down hunks of meat, which their stomach juices broke down into useable nutrients. The sauropods raked vegetation into their mouths and swallowed it in a big wad, called a *bolus*, to be ground up further by special gizzard stones. Neither group did much chewing.

It was the bird-butted Ornithischian dinosaurs that first used their teeth for more than simply killing and getting food into their mouths. They began the process of food grinding before swallowing, easing the strain on their digestive systems imposed by their coarse diet of vegetation. Because they didn't grow to be as large as the sauropods, and because they evidently didn't use gizzard stones, most of these plant-eaters couldn't rely solely on their digestive tracts.

Definosaurus
A **bolus** is a wad of vegetation that is swallowed without being chewed. Plant-eaters without highly developed teeth such as the sauropod dinosaurs swallowed boluses, leaving the task of grinding them to their digestive tracts.

So they developed specialized dental work for shredding the plants they ate. This was a gradual process. In fact, the chewing ability of many groups of Ornithischians improved as they evolved. We can see this process unfold with special clarity in the ornithopods (bird feet). (We mentioned in Chapter 4 that the accepted names "ornithopod" [bird footed] and "theropod" [beast footed] got switched by mistake, so the ornithopods actually didn't have birdlike feet as the name might lead you to expect.)

The ornithopods developed special teeth in adapting to live a special lifestyle—that of grazing. These dinosaurs fed off low growing vegetation, leaving the higher bushes and trees to the stegosaurs, and the very tallest trees to the sauropods.

Chew Chew Train

Here's a list of important ornithopod dinosaurs:

➤ *Heterodontosaurus* (different-toothed lizard)   A speedy, 3-foot long dinosaur that may have holed up in burrows every summer. It had three different kinds of teeth and chewed by grinding its lower teeth lengthwise across its uppers.

➤ *Hypsilophodon* (high-ridged tooth)   Once thought to live in trees but now believed to be one of the fastest running Ornithischian dinosaurs. In addition to teeth for grinding food, it had a horny beak for cropping vegetation.

➤ *Iguanodon* (iguana-toothed lizard)   One of the earliest known dinosaurs, equipped with a famous thumb spike. This dinosaur had teeth only along the sides of its jaws, relying on its beak for taking bites.

➤ *Hadrosaurs* (heavy lizards)   Duckbilled dinosaurs. Each one had hundreds of teeth. We'll get to them in more detail in the next chapter.

Always Room for More

Although chewing improved the ability of the bird-butted Ornithischians to digest plants, they developed another feature for this purpose that the lizard-butted Saurischian dinosaurs didn't have. This is the very feature that gives them the name bird butts—the shape of their hips.

In lizard-butted dinosaurs, the pelvis has an arch of bone called a *pubis* that points forward, lending stability to the hind quarters. This is a feature the Saurischian dinosaurs have in common with lizards. In the bird butts, the pubis sticks backward, the way it does in a bird's pelvis.

Having a pubis that points backward benefitted the bird butts by leaving additional room for a longer digestive tract. The bird-butted dinosaurs were more efficiently designed for digesting vegetation because of their specialized teeth and their specialized pelvises.

Definosaurus
The two main groups of dinosaurs, Saurischians and Ornithischians, are distinguished by the direction of the **pubis**, a bone arch in front of the pelvis. In Saurishchians, the pubis points forward; in Ornithischians, it points backward.

Messy Eaters

Most, but not all, of the Ornithischian dinosaurs had still another feature that the Saurischians didn't have—a very helpful feature to creatures that do a significant amount of chewing: cheeks. Chewing without cheeks is a little bit like beating eggs without a bowl. It gets messy and you waste a lot of food. Imagine an alligator trying to chew grass like a cow. It wouldn't work very well!

This is just the predicament faced by a group of Ornithischian dinosaurs known as fabrosaurs (named after the French paleontologist, Jean Henri Fabre). Although they developed specialized teeth for chewing vegetation, they didn't have cheeks for keeping the food in their mouths as they pulped it up.

Fabrosaurs are sometimes classified as ornithopod dinosaurs. They had many similarities with the smaller ornithos, the heterodonts, and the hypsilophodonts, including size, shape, and lifestyle. The fact that they didn't have cheeks, though, separates them and suggests they belong in their own group. In fact, the fabrosaurs are the only bird-butted dinosaurs that didn't have cheeks.

Boning Up
In spite of its many specializations, *Heterodontosaurus* was a fairly primitive dinosaur. In fact, it had a number of traits in common with the Saurischian prosauropod dinosaur, *Anchisaurus*, including a jaw hinge situated below the lower teeth and a special thumb claw. These similarities provide evidence that dinosaurs were a natural group (all more closely related to one another than to any non-dinosaur).

Boning Up
Scientists can tell whether an extinct animal had cheeks from its jaw bones. A creature that had cheeks has patterned scars left on its jawbone from where the cheek muscles were attached. The jawbones of plant-eating mammals of today have these scars. Reptiles of today, which eat without cheeks, do not have scarred jawbones. This tells us that cheeks evolved separately in mammals and in most Ornithischian dinosaurs.

The fabrosaurs must have been messy, inefficient eaters. Possibly as a result, they lost out to their cheeky competition, the ornithopod dinosaurs, and didn't survive past the Jurassic Period. They were more primitive than the ornithopods in a number of ways. They had five-fingered hands with claws on both front and back limbs, unlike the ornithopods, whose feet were more hooflike. Although the fabrosaurs had short arms in comparison to their back legs, their hands were large and strong, so they could evidently walk around on either two or four feet.

The fabrosaurs were 3- or 4-foot-long, fast-moving, vegetarian dinosaurs. In some respects they resembled rodents of today and may have lived in burrows. Some even think that they stayed in their burrows all during the dry season and came out during wet seasons when food was more plentiful. The best-known fabrosaur is *Lesothosaurus* (lizard from Lesotho).

Fangs for Everything

Similar to the fabrosaurs in many ways was *Heterodontosaurus* (different-toothed lizard). This dinosaur was much the same size and shape as the fabros and lived much the same kind of lifestyle, foraging among ferns and other low-growing plants, and possibly living in burrows. Heterodonts were different, however, not only in having cheeks but also in having a more specialized set of teeth.

Near the end of the snout, *Heterodontosaurus* had sharp, square-topped teeth for clipping and cropping. Closer to the back of the jaws, it had flat-topped teeth for grinding. Between the grinders and the croppers, some heterodonts had long fangs. These may have been useful for slicing especially thick and tough plant fibers, and possibly for defense against predators.

Heterodont fangs may also have been used for display while flirting or threatening rivals of the same species. It's likely that the heterodonts that had fangs and those that didn't were of the opposite sex.

The Tooth-Fairy Files

All dinosaurs had a special knack for growing teeth. Whenever a dinosaur lost a tooth, or wore one out, another grew back. In fact, predacious dinosaurs occasionally left teeth in the corpses of their victims. This sometimes provides clear evidence of which animals meat-eaters preyed upon. Plant-eating dinosaurs could replace their teeth, too. In fact, it has been argued that *Heterodontosaurus* had a special way of doing this—all at once, rather than one at a time.

Heterodontosaurus seems to have had a specially aligned row of teeth along the sides of its jaw. These teeth didn't chomp up and down on each other to grind food. Instead, the whole lower row moved back and forth lengthwise against the upper row.

Because of the way these teeth grind against each other, having just one missing tooth could jam the chewing motion of the others. This means that growing one tooth at a time would disrupt chewing. To keep the whole set in good working order, *Heterodontosaurus* would have needed to replace all its teeth at once.

Evidence that heterodonts did, in fact, replace their teeth all at once stems from the fact that their jaws have been found in which the teeth are all at about the same stage of wear, whether nearly new or nearly worn out.

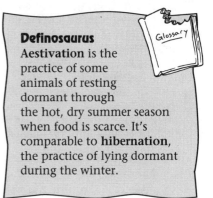

Boning Up
The lengthwise grinding motion of *Heterodontosaurus'* jaws can be compared to the chewing style of today's elephants and rodents, creatures that also eat lots of tough, fibrous vegetation.

Made in the Shade

Of course, growing a whole set of teeth takes time. Meanwhile, not a lot of eating can go on. To deal with the problem of not being able to eat while they grew new teeth, heterodonts may have lain dormant in their burrows. They could have done this during the hot, dry season when there may not have been much food to eat anyway.

The practice of lying dormant during the summer is called *aestivation*. This is just like *hibernation*, or wintertime dormancy, in that both behaviors are ways of conserving energy during times when food is scarce. Aestivation is also a way to beat the heat, whereas hibernation means coming in from the cold. It seems likely that heterodonts aestivated because they lived in warm climates with sharp seasonal changes in temperature and rainfall.

Definosaurus
Aestivation is the practice of some animals of resting dormant through the hot, dry summer season when food is scarce. It's comparable to **hibernation**, the practice of lying dormant during the winter.

Sleek and Slender Hypsies

Slightly bigger than *Heterodontosaurus* was *Hypsilophodon* (high-ridged tooth), an ornithopod dinosaur that got to be about 5 feet long. Hypsies had teeth that overlapped one another, forming an array especially designed for mincing leaves and plants. They became more numerous than the heterodonts and the fabrosaurs, possibly because of their efficient chewing equipment.

> **Dig This**
> Fossilized nests that belonged to the hypsies have been found. These nests show signs of repeated use, indicating that the hypsies returned to roost in the same nests year after year.

Chew Run Run

Hypsies may have been the fastest of all the bird-butted dinosaurs, with long, powerful hind legs for running. They are sometimes compared to modern gazelles and evidently lived a similar lifestyle of browsing for foliage and speeding away from predators. They had hard, beaklike snouts for cropping plants. Some species of *Hypsilophodon* had teeth at the tip of the snout, but others did not. These hypsies had to rely on their horny beaks.

Shaking the Trees

> **Dig This**
> One intriguing *Hypsilophodon* fossil shows a serious broken leg bone that healed, indicating that the hypsie was able to survive without full use of its running ability. This find has led to speculation that the injured hypsie was somehow cared for by its cohorts until it was nursed back to health.

Although hypsies are known today for their speed, scientists used to think that they lived in trees. They had long toes, and it was thought that the first toeclaw pointed backwards, enabling them to perch securely on branches by curling their back claw around for stability. It was thought as well that the tail would be useful in balancing and holding on to branches.

What's more, scientists identified what they thought were similarities between hypsie arm and foot bones and bones belonging to the Australian tree kangaroo, a present-day arboreal creature that has a shape similar to *Hypsilophodon*.

Scientists have since come to believe that life in the trees would not have suited *Hypsilophodon*. We know its first toe points forward like the other toes. What's more, the similarities between hypsies and tree kangaroos are superficial. A closer look at the bones reveals hypsies were especially well adapted for running around on the ground.

The Illustrious Iggies

Hypsies were a bit larger than heterodonts, and *Iguanodons* were much larger still. These ornithopods got to be 25 feet long. They are important in the history of dinosaur discoveries as one of the first ever found. They were the second dinosaurs to be named. They were also among the most widespread of all dinosaurs. Iggy fossils have been recovered on every continent except Antarctica.

Whereas *Hypsilophodonts* are comparable to modern-day gazelles, *Iguanodons* can be compared to horses. They were fast but strong as well. Many iggy skeletons have been found together in Belgium, suggesting that they may have traveled in herds. Like some hypsies, iggies had horny beaks for cropping vegetation. Although they had no teeth at the end of these beaks, they had numerous teeth at the sides of their jaws for grinding food.

Fossil Fallacy

An *Iguanodon* skull was discovered that had a round opening in the lower jaw. This opening was taken for evidence that the iggy had a big, grabby tongue for pulling leaves and stems into its mouth. This trait was thought to be in keeping with its browsing lifestyle. It was later found, however, that the opening was a hole in the jaw bone that formed by accident.

Action Figures

Iguanodons may have been able to run on two feet as well as all fours. Although their hind legs are considerably longer than their front legs, their hands are strong enough to have supported their weight.

When *Iguanodon* fossils were first discovered early in the 19th century, they made a big splash because so few dinosaur fossils had been found at that point. Scientists rushed to speculate about what they must have looked like. Unfortunately though, they had only a few bones to go on because no complete skeletons had been found. They believed that iggies were big, bulky, slow crawling reptiles. Huge sculptures were made of them squatting on all fours like hippos.

It wasn't until more than 50 years later, in 1878, that the first complete iggy skeletons were found. These showed them to be more upright and less ponderous. They have become recognized as fast runners and are often pictured standing on just two feet. Lately, however, some scientists have been putting their front feet back on the ground, saying they are built for traveling on four legs.

All Thumbs

Although their speed, large size, and herding behavior may all have been effective defenses against predators, iggies had a weapon to use as a last resort when attacked. This is a big spike located on the thumbs of their front paws. To use this spike, they would have reared up on their hind legs. In this position they could have stood 15 feet tall, face to face with many of the large carnosaurs of the day.

The thumb spike may have been especially effective because, as we mentioned in Chapters 8 and 9, many carnosaurs had extremely short arms. A pugilistic *Iguanodon* may have been able to poke painful holes in the powerful neck of a big predator, swinging into it sideways to avoid getting bitten.

The Least You Need to Know

➤ The bird-butted dinosaurs developed special teeth and special pelvis bones for processing vegetation more efficiently.

➤ The ornithopods were grazing dinosaurs, eating vegetation that grew close to the ground.

➤ The fabrosaurs were similar to the ornithopods in many ways, but they lacked cheeks.

➤ *Heterodontosaurus* may have gone into hiding during the hot, dry season.

➤ *Hypsilophodon* was once thought to live in trees but is now considered to have been the fastest runner of all Ornithischian dinosaurs.

➤ *Iguanodon* had a strong, bony spike for a thumb, which it may have used in self-defense—gouging the necks of carnosaur predators.

Dinoducks

Mother nature seems to have let her imagination run wild when she made duckbilled hadrosaur (bulky lizard) dinosaurs. These creatures looked, sounded, and acted like no other beast on Earth. They often grew to be 30 feet long and 15 feet tall, and could grow to be much larger. They had large, variously shaped beaks, webbed fingers, and long, high-but-narrow tails that could flap from side to side. They had rough, pebbly-textured skin and hooflike three-toed feet. Many had large, sometimes elaborate crests on their heads. These took a variety of shapes and were, in all likelihood, brightly and variously colored.

Many uses have been proposed for these conspicuous crests. Most scientists agree that, for one thing, they were used for communication, both because they were visually striking and could attract the attention of other duckbills and because they were attached to the nasal passages and could have made various honks and hoots. The duckbills may have made noise to identify themselves to one another and to signal when danger was near.

In fact, duckbills were probably the most social of all dinosaurs. In addition to their ability to signal each other, they may also have actively raised their young. Evidence suggests that junior duckbills remained in the nest for quite some time after hatching, perhaps long enough to pick up the signals they would need to use in later life.

Dig This
The first North American dinosaur ever identified was a duckbill known as *Hadrosaurus*, found in New Jersey.

The Grazer's Edge

In ecological terms, duckbilled dinosaurs didn't live like ducks but were big, herding grazers. They wandered around on land, keeping their heads low to the ground as they foraged for food. You might not have guessed that they lived this way because their beaks make them look more like buffleheads than like buffaloes. In fact, it's taken scientists many years of guessing and changing their minds to come to the conclusion that they lived on land and not in the water.

Skull of the crested duckbill, Parasaurolophus.

(Department of Library Services, American Museum of Natural History; Neg. no.:2A21968; Photo.:Finnin)

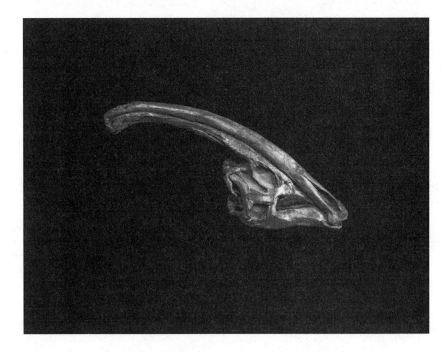

Fortunately, there are a number of especially informative fossils left by the duckbills, including some mummies—fossils with impressions of skin still preserved with the bones. These hadrosaur mummies are unique among dinosaur fossils. In addition to these mummies, there are a number of good skeletons of many different kinds of duckbills.

To Each Its Own

One theory about duckbills that has been revised over the years is the notion that they ate foliage from low tree branches by rearing up on their hind feet and stabilizing themselves with their tails, like kangaroos. We now believe they were built for browsing on all fours with their heads down. This view is based on the way their skeletons are shaped. It actually would have been difficult for the duckbills to look up.

They may have eaten any number of plants, even tough fibrous ones. Vegetation recovered in the stomach area of the mummy fossils includes evergreen needles, seeds, twigs, and leaves. They may also have eaten a whole new kind of plant that evolved for the first time during the Cretaceous: flowering plants.

Different species of duckbill may have preferred to eat different kinds of vegetation. This possibility is reflected in the fact that different species of duckbill had differently shaped bills. These bills may have evolved into particular shapes for the purpose of plucking certain kinds of vegetation.

Batteries Included

In general, though, duckbills could have eaten just about whatever plants they wanted. Although their beaks were broad like a duck's, they were actually hard and sharp—more like a tortoise's than a duck's—and could have been used for slicing through all kinds of vegetation. In addition, they had hundreds of teeth for grinding food.

Most animals have a single row of teeth on their upper and lower jaws. Duckbills had sets of teeth called *batteries* that were several rows deep. These would have grated against each other like the teeth of a coarse file or rasp. Not only did duckbills have an impressive number of teeth, but they also were able to replace them as often as necessary, so they had, in effect, an infinite supply waiting to come in. This was fortunate for them because their teeth evidently wore out quickly.

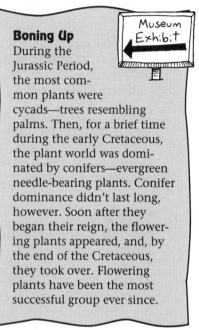

Boning Up
During the Jurassic Period, the most common plants were cycads—trees resembling palms. Then, for a brief time during the early Cretaceous, the plant world was dominated by conifers—evergreen needle-bearing plants. Conifer dominance didn't last long, however. Soon after they began their reign, the flowering plants appeared, and, by the end of the Cretaceous, they took over. Flowering plants have been the most successful group ever since.

Definosaurus
Any group of similar things used together for a single purpose can be called a **battery**. This term applies well to the many cheek teeth that grew several rows deep in the jaws of duckbilled dinosaurs. Some of the larger duckbills had close to 1,000 teeth!

Weak Evidence

The hard beaks and numerous teeth of the duckbills strongly suggest that they were grazers, capable of chewing just about anything that grew out of the ground. Unfortunately, this is not the impression given by the first duckbill jaws to have been studied, back in the mid-19th century. This important early fossil was broken and worn with time. The teeth in it were loose-fitting and fell out easily.

The weak condition of this particular fossil led to the belief that duckbill jaws in general were weak. Creatures with such weak jaws were considered incapable of grazing on land. As a result, as well as because of their ducklike appearance, scientists believed the duckbills spent most of their time in the water, eating soft, tender water plants.

Because of their long hind legs, they appeared to be waders, like modern-day cranes. They also seemed capable of swimming with the help of their powerful, paddlelike tails. This view was bolstered in 1908 when mummies of a duckbill named *Anatosaurus* were discovered. The skin tissue preserved over the fingers of these animals indicate that they had webbed forefeet.

Fossil Fallacy

It is ironic that a duckbill mummy would have been taken as evidence that duckbills were aquatic because, for a mummy to become fossilized, the skin must become dried out. Mummies of aquatic creatures, then, are extremely unlikely. Duckbill mummies actually supplied further evidence that they lived on land—the plants preserved in their stomachs.

From the Mummy's Tummy

Scientists today do not rule out the idea that the duckbills were capable of swimming. It has even been suggested that they may have retreated to water to escape from predators. This seems unlikely, however, because many now think predacious dinos were fine swimmers that could propel themselves through water with their tails like crocodiles. In any case, it seems clear that duckbills were much better adapted for feeding on land than on the shore or in the water as had been thought for years.

Evidence for a land lifestyle includes not only their hard beaks and teeth batteries and the fossilized plants found in the stomach area of the mummy but also their hind feet, which are not like paddles, but hooves, suitable for plodding over the turf.

Duckbill Do's and Don'ts

Although the duckbills all had similarly shaped bodies, they could be wildly different from one another from the neck up. The most striking feature of many duckbilled dinosaurs was their elaborate crests, many of which looked like way-out hairdos. Not all duckbills had them, though. Here's a list of some of the better-known duckbills.

➤ *Hadrosaurus* (bulky lizard)   A crestless dino, discovered in New Jersey. This was the first dinosaur to be found and identified in North America.

➤ *Anatosaurus* (duck lizard)   The best-known crestless duckbill, thanks to a mummified skeleton found in 1908.

➤ *Corythosaurus* (helmet lizard)   Had a crest shaped like a big mohawk hairdo.

➤ *Saurolophus* (lizard crest)   Had a crest shaped like a single horn sticking out backwards from the top of its head.

➤ *Lambeosaurus* (Lambe's lizard)   Had a crest that looked like a huge pompadour haircut.

➤ *Tsintaosaurus* (Tsintao lizard)   A Chinese duckbill with a crest like a horn sticking forward out of its head, making it look like a unicorn.

➤ *Parasaurolophus* (similar lizard crest)   May have a name that sounds like a serious disease, but it also had a one of the coolest crests, shaped like a giant boomerang.

➤ *Maiasaura* (good mother lizard)   Named because it is known to have cared for its babies, based on the discovery of a nest of fossilized young ones.

> **Dig This**
> The duckbill with the biggest crest was *Parasaurolophus*, which had a 6-foot long boomerang do.

Honk If You Like Duckbills

Duckbill crests were partiallyhollow, forming an extension of their nasal passages. This means that they could act as resonating chambers for whatever noises the duckbills might have made. These noises may have been useful for signaling.

Even the duckbills without crests had large and unique nasal passages in their beaks, so they, too, could make interesting whonking noises. The crests found on some duckbills are really extensions of their special beaks, which all duckbills had. This means that all of them may have relied on audible signals for communicating.

> **Dig This**
> Scientists have attempted to re-create the sound made by some crested duckbills with the help of a computer. One result was a monotonous, moaning roar. Perhaps, though, the duckbills could vary the tone and pitch of the sound with their throats and diaphragms, the way people do when we talk and sing.

Evidence of the Senses

Further evidence that the duckbills signaled one another by making special noises is the fact that duckbill fossils have been found that include tiny, thin, resonating bones in the ear. This suggests that the duckbills had a keen, well-developed sense of hearing. Perhaps they could hear and distinguish one another across long distances.

Duckbill crests may have served as visual display as well as audio signaling. The shape and size of these crests varies not only with species but also depends on the age of individuals within the same species and, most likely, on sex as well. This variation may have been useful to the duckbills for identification purposes.

The fact that the shape of the crests did not always simply follow the contours of the hollow chamber inside but may be padded by bony tissue, suggests that the crests may have served a special visual function. Their colors as well as their shapes may have provided further variation, allowing the duckbills to tell each other apart more easily. This possibility is borne out by the fact that duckbills probably had well-developed eyesight, evident from their large eyesockets.

Dig This
Many duckbills once thought to belong to a number of different species have been combined into just a few. Many skeletons assigned to different species based on the shapes and sizes of their crests are actually, in all likelihood, exhibiting variation based on age and sex differences within species.

To go with their keen eyes and ears, the duckbills may have had an excellent sense of smell. After all, their crests were basically elaborate extensions of their sinuses. With these serious sinuses, they may have had an extremely keen smelling ability.

Still one additional purpose the crests might have served is shielding the duckbills' faces as they ran through the underbrush. Because they tended to graze with their heads down, they must also have run this way too, and their crests may have absorbed much of the shock from whatever branches they ran into.

Sitting Duckbills

All these various possible uses for their crests may have worked together to compensate for the apparent inability of the duckbills to defend themselves from predators. In fact, duckbills seem to have none of the defenses used by other plant-eaters.

➤ Although the duckbills were not slow moving, they were not particularly speedy either. Their cousins, the heterodonts and hypsilophosaurs were much faster. Although these smaller dinosaurs used speed to escape attack, the duckbills could have been overtaken by many predacious dinosaurs.

➤ Although the duckbills were quite large, the carnosaurs that lived alongside them during the late Cretaceous were even bigger, so size was not an effective defense as it was for the sauropod dinosaurs.

➤ The duckbills evidently had no physical weapons—no fangs like the heterodonts; no thumb spike like *Iguanodon*; no long, whipper-snapping tail like the sauropods, ankylosaurs, and stegosaurs; and no long, pointy horns like *Triceratops*. They didn't even have any body armor like *Skutellosaurus* and the ankylosaurs.

From all this, you might think that these defenseless dinosaurs were sitting duckbills in the presence of the huge, flesh-eating carnosaurs that patrolled the Late Cretaceous. It's possible, however, that they evolved a unique early warning system that enabled them to get away before their hunters even knew of their existence.

Boning Up
As dinosaurs that flourished during the Mid- to Late Cretaceous, duckbills would have had to contend with the largest and most fearsome predators ever—the big carnosaurs, including T-rex and *Albertosaurus*.

Buffalo Soldiers

This early warning system may have involved the cooperation of whole groups of duckbills. In other words, the duckbills may have developed complex social behaviors that helped them deal with predators.

The duckbills probably spent most of their time foraging in herds like buffaloes. There may even have been sentry duckbills stationed on the outskirts of the herd that would have been aware of nearby predators before the rest of the group. With their sharp eyes, acute hearing, and keen sense of smell, they may have been able to provide sufficient advance warning of danger.

Boning Up
Many herding animals of today are extremely responsive to distress signals given off by one of the herd. As a result, they are prone to stampede. The duckbills may well have been stampeding creatures too.

After hearing or smelling a predator at a distance (which they may have been able to do, especially if the meat-eater hadn't learned to stalk the herd from downwind where it would not be detected as easily), the sentry duckbills could have given loud hooting signals—amplified by their beaks and crests—to the rest of the group. These signals may have alerted the rest not only to the danger but also to the direction it was coming from. At this point, the herd could have galloped to safety. Of course, this scenario is speculative. We can't know for sure whether the duckbills dealt with predators in this way.

It's possible that they had a highly developed ability to communicate with one another; they were too numerous not to have resisted predators somehow, and we know of no other defenses or evasive strategies they may have used. There is additional evidence, along with the evidence of their sensitive earbones, large eyesockets, and resonant crests, that the duckbills were social.

Bringing Up Baby

In 1978, several nests were found on the plains of Montana of a new species of duckbill called *Maiasaura*. These were all situated in one large area, easily within shouting distance of one another. This in itself suggests that duckbills relied on one another to some extent, at least while laying eggs.

Boning Up
Babies of many species have evolved an adaptive trait that helps them get the care they need from their parents. This trait is a combination of disproportionately rounded heads and big eyes that make them look like adorable versions of adults. Babies, in other words, evolved to look cute for an adaptive purpose.

Definosaurus
Altricial creatures are helpless at birth and need to be tended until they're strong enough to care for themselves. **Precocial** creatures can take care of themselves as soon as they hatch.

What was still more revealing about the nesting site was the fact that some of the nests contained not only eggs, but baby dinosaurs. Some of the babies seemed to be about a month old. They even had teeth that were beginning to show signs of wear from eating plants.

These babies certainly would not have been hanging around the nest so long after they were born unless a bigger dinosaur was taking care of them. In fact, a partial skeleton of an adult of the same species was found nearby, which belonged to just one of what must have been a whole community of *Maiasaura* duckbills.

The fact the babies stayed in the nest up to a month after hatching means that they were not ready to fend for themselves at birth but required care and feeding. This gradual process of becoming ready to go out into the world is called *altricial* development. Altricial creatures are helpless at birth and need to become stronger, and perhaps learn how to take care of themselves, before they can be left alone.

Altricial creatures are much more likely to be capable of complicated social behaviors than *precocial* creatures, those born ready to fend for themselves. This is because during the time they are being tended by adults, they are also bonding with them and learning from them. As altricial creatures become physically strong after birth, they may also become attuned to the actions of those that tend them.

We'll never know for sure what family life was like for the maiasaurs and the other duckbills. We'll never know whether it involved hierarchical relationships based on age or sex, whether young duckbills developed skills and awareness by playing with one another, or whether their nasal signals were complicated enough to communicate such things as fear or contentment. We do know enough about the duckbills, though, to think that such things might have been possible.

The Least You Need to Know

➤ Duckbills lived a lifestyle similar to that of modern-day buffaloes.

➤ Duckbills had hundreds of teeth, which they used for grating vegetation.

➤ Duckbills may have used their crests as resonating chambers for vocal signaling.

➤ Duckbills evidently had keen eyesight, hearing, and sense of smell.

➤ Duckbills seem to have been highly social creatures.

➤ Duckbills cared for their young.

All the Frills

Among the most striking and familiar dinosaurs are the ceratopsians (horny faces), including *Triceratops* (three-horned face) with its long horns, beaked jaws, and long skull ending in a big frill flaring out the back of its head. It must have looked something like a rhinoceros wearing a Halloween mask with devil's horns.

These big, herding dinosaurs were built low to the ground for grazing on all fours. With their squat, powerful builds they were probably capable of rumbling along at about 20 miles per hour, but running was not their specialty. Their powerful legs, shoulders, and necks enabled them to use their big horns for threatening one another and for fighting predators.

In fact, they are often depicted defending themselves against one or more large carnosaurs such as T-rex or *Albertosaurus*, looking gamely and with determination into the menacing eyes of the meat-eaters. The frillheads were peace-loving but scrappy contenders in one of the classic matchups of all natural history.

This was, judging from the number and variety of frillhead fossils that have been found, a matchup in which they came away with their fair share of victories.

Skull in the Family

The frill family was one of the biggest of all dinosaur families and lasted about 35 million years to the end of the Cretaceous. They ranged in size from about that of today's pig to twice that of a modern-day rhinoceros. In addition to their large, powerful bodies, they had disproportionately large skulls.

The skull of Triceratops.
(David Bennett)

Swelled Heads

In fact, this family produced some of the most impressive skulls of all time—the largest skulls of any land animal. The longest of all was more than 9 feet long, belonging to a frillhead known as *Torosaurus* (piercing lizard). Others have been found that are 4 feet wide. These skulls were useful for display, defense, and providing leverage for the frillheads' powerful jaws.

Fossil Fallacy

When the first *Triceratops* horns were found in North America, they were misidentified as belonging to an extinct species of buffalo.

The extended frillhead family, known as marginocephalosaurs (edgehead lizards), included some interesting members in addition to the frillheads themselves. One of these was *Psittacosaurus* (parrot lizard), named because its hooked beak resembled the one on Long John Silver's pet bird. Another related group of dinosaurs were the thick-skulled, dome-headed pachycephalosaurs. Although all these creatures looked different from one another, they were related and shared the characteristic of having specially adapted skulls.

Frills and Fringes

Here's a list of some of the more important frillheads, together with members of their extended family.

➤ *Psittacosaurus* (parrot lizard)   6 or 7 feet long and has been found in Asia.

➤ *Protoceratops* (first-horned face)   Had the famous frill but not the horns. It was one of the smaller frillheads.

➤ *Triceratops* (three-horned face)   The best-known ceratopsian as well as the biggest, reaching 25 feet in length and 9 feet in height.

➤ *Styracosaurus* (spiked lizard)   Had a frill edged with six spikes in addition to a single horn growing out of its nose.

➤ *Chasmosaurus* (opening lizard)   Named for the big windows in its frill. It has left fossilized skin impressions that show it was covered with big round scales.

➤ *Torosaurus* (piercing lizard)   Not the biggest frillhead but had the biggest frill.

➤ *Pachycephalosaurs* (thick-headed lizards)   Not frillheads but goatlike dome-headed cousins that used their thick skulls in head-butting contests.

No Frills and the Biggest Frills

Psittacosaurus, the parrot-beaked dinosaur, appears to be an evolutionary midway point between the small and swift ornithopods and the heavier horned and beaked ceratopsians. This paleo-polly developed the same kind of beak the frillheads had but didn't have the frill or the horns.

Instead, it had a ridge at the back of its skull. This provided leverage for the jaw muscles, which could exert considerable force on anything it held in its sharp, hard beak. In fact, this skull ridge started a trend that was taken up and exaggerated by the frillheads.

Dig This
One of the smallest dinosaur skeletons ever found belong to a baby *Psittacosaurus*, measuring just a few inches long.

Feeding the Frill

Boning Up
The grazing dinosaurs of the Cretaceous, including the frillheads, duckbills, and ankylosaurs, were so successful that they pushed ferns and conifers, which dominated the plant kingdom, to the verge of extinction. Plants remained alive by adapting a radical strategy of growing very quickly in a short time before the grazers could eat them as seedlings. These fast-growing plants are known as **angiosperms**, or flowering plants. Angiosperms have ruled the plant kingdom since the Cretaceous Period, thanks to the grazing dinosaurs.

The frillheads had extremely powerful jaws, with long, heavy muscles attached at the other end to their big frills. The frills evolved, at least in part, to anchor the big jaw muscles so they could put more force on the beak and teeth. In fact, the frillheads had the largest jaw muscles of all plant-eating dinosaurs.

Like the duckbilled dinosaurs, the frillheads had no teeth in the beaky part of their jaws but had batteries of cheek teeth. But whereas the duckbills used their teeth for grating, the frillheads used theirs for slicing. The beak, teeth, jaw muscles, and bony frill all worked together like a big pair of shears for slicing vegetation.

This method of chewing was not as thorough and efficient as the grinding approach taken by the duckbills. The frillheads compensated for this, though, by having big stomachs and long digestive tracts. After mincing their food with their scissorlike teeth, they cooked down the pulp in their big round guts.

The frillheads shared this digesting strategy with the other big, low-built four legged grazers of the Late Cretaceous, the ankylosaurs. The ankies were even shorter and squatter than the frillheads. Of course what really distinguished the frillheads from other dinosaurs was, yes, their frills.

The Frill of It All

Many frillhead frills were not made of solid bone but had windows in them, covered with skin. The windows made the frills lighter and easier to carry around and also gave the powerful jaw muscles something to latch onto.

The largest frillhead, however, that belonging to *Triceratops*, had no frill windows. Instead, trike skulls are solid bone. This helps explain why, even though trikes are the biggest frillheads, their frills are not the biggest frills. This also explains why so many fossils of trike skulls have been found. They are so solidly built that many of them have withstood the effects of 65 million years.

Although the frills were evidently useful for stabilizing the big, strong jaws, the jaw muscles alone do not account for the enormous size of the frills, or for the fact that many of them were studded with horns and bony knobs and took a variety of shapes. The frills had additional uses, including display and, to a limited extent, defense.

Frill shape appears to be different in male and female frillheads. This suggests the frills were also used for attracting mates. They may have been brandished to threaten rivals. It's possible that frill size helped establish hierarchies among ceratopsians.

In some frillheads, the frills probably worked together with long, sharp horns in showdowns between rivals of the same species. It's unlikely that the horns were used for fights to the finish between members of the same species, but they may have been used in sparring. Rather than trying to gore each other, rival ceratopsians may have locked horns—literally—before pushing and shoving to establish dominance. The frills may have provided some protection in this kind of tussling, deflecting horn thrusts and scratches away from the neck.

Sustaining the Frill

The neck and shoulders of the frillheads were powerful. This is clear from large fossils of these bones, even though it's also clear that the frillheads descended from bipedal dinosaurs. The front legs were much shorter than the hind legs. They were big and strong, however, with hooves rather than hands on the forefeet.

These strong legs and shoulders helped support the big skull. Additional support came from a specially adapted neck bone in which the first three vertebrae were fused into one bone. The massive, front-heavy design of the frillheads was not just a lot of extra weight to carry around but provided effective defense against predators.

The Frill of Victory

The dinosaur ecosystem of the Late Cretaceous pitted the frillheads against the world's largest predators, the tyrannosaurs, including *Daspletosaurus*, *Albertosaurus*, and T-rex. The fossil record indicates they held their own in the matchup, apparently for two main reasons: their long, sharp horns, and their ability to cooperate.

The frillheads were herding animals and undoubtedly clumped together when predators approached. It's

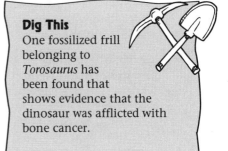

Dig This
One fossilized frill belonging to *Torosaurus* has been found that shows evidence that the dinosaur was afflicted with bone cancer.

Boning Up
The "horns" you see on fossilized frillheads displayed in museums are actually not the whole horns, but just the bony part known as the *horn core*. In life, horn cores were covered with actual horn, which would have extended their length considerably (horn cores alone can be 4 feet long), as well as making them sharper. The same can be said of frillhead beaks, which also were covered with horny material.

Dig This
One rare species of frillhead called *Pachyrhinoceros* (thick nose) has a thick, heavy ridge of bony material running along its snout instead of a horn. Only two of these creatures have been found. It's possible that this is actually not a separate species, but a frillhead with a disease.

likely that the meat-eaters stalked the outskirts of the herd hoping to surprise a straggler, especially one that was sick, old, or not yet fully developed. They would have preferred attacking quarry that would not put up much of a fight.

The big frillheads may have protected their babies by keeping between them and any predators. Unable to outrun the meat-eaters, they would face their assailants head on, perhaps standing shoulder to shoulder to make it as difficult as possible for a hungry killer to get to their vulnerable backsides. Head on, the long horns of a full-grown frillhead or two would have intimidated even the largest meat-eater.

Proto Types

The full-blown frills and horns of the latest ceratopsian dinosaurs evolved gradually. Fossils of an early group of frillheads have been recovered that represent an intermediate step along the way. This frillhead, known as *Protoceratops*, looks pretty much like the later ceratopsians except for a few significant differences.

The Frill Is Just Beginning

Protos were much smaller—about the size of a pig—than their later siblings and had smaller frills. What's more, instead of the three horns of *Triceratops*, some protos had no horn at all, whereas others had only a single horny bump at the end of the nose, which may have distinguished males and females. The protos also had lighter skulls than the later frillheads.

In addition, the later ceratopsians had a second layer of bone reinforcing the top of the skull that protos did not have. This skull had to be especially strong to withstand the force of the jaw muscles and support the weight of the big horns. With shorter frills, smaller jaws, and no horns, *Protoceratops* could do without the extra-thick skull that other frillheads developed.

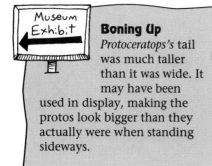

Boning Up
Protoceratops's tail was much taller than it was wide. It may have been used in display, making the protos look bigger than they actually were when standing sideways.

Although protos were smaller versions of the later frillheads, they had tails that were proportionately longer. This longer tail is a reminder left over from the frillheads' bipedal ancestors. Bipedal dinosaurs had long tails that they used for balance, a feature that became unnecessary for the big, squat, four-footed frillheads.

The ceratopsians, though, developed shorter tails only gradually, and we can see this process in comparing the relative tail lengths of protos and later frillheads. The protos may have been able to get up on their hind feet because their center of gravity is relatively far back. It is doubtful that the later frillheads could have done this easily, if at all.

Pteranodon sternbergi.

Allosaurus and Dryosaurus.

Stegosaurus stenops.

Sinosauropteryx prima.

Mononykus olecranus.

T-rex and Tricerotops.

Monolophosaurus jiangi.

Tylosaurus proriger.

Camarasaurus lentus.

Dilophosaurus wetherli.

The Frill of Discovery

Protoceratops is a significant species in the study of dinosaur science because of important remains found in the 1920s in Mongolia's Gobi Desert of an entire colony of this creature. This was the first dinosaur to have yielded fossil skeletons of a full range of age groups from babies to adults. What's more, the first dinosaur eggs ever found were proto eggs.

Even the eggs showed different stages of development from unformed embryos to babies just about to hatch. These eggs were about the size of baking potatoes and were found in nests that had been dug in the sand. Some fossilized nests contained newborn hatchlings rather than eggs.

This nesting colony proved conclusively that dinosaurs did, in fact, lay eggs as scientists expected, and that some dinosaurs lived in herds. The *Protoceratops* finds in Mongolia also helped fill in a big gap in the evolution of frillhead dinosaurs. In fact, the same expedition that uncovered the Mongolian protos also discovered another ancestor of the frillheads, *Psittacosaurus*.

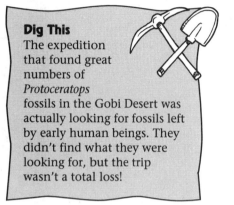

Dig This
The expedition that found great numbers of *Protoceratops* fossils in the Gobi Desert was actually looking for fossils left by early human beings. They didn't find what they were looking for, but the trip wasn't a total loss!

Thick Skulled

While the frillheads were developing special traits for their particular kind of herding lifestyle, their cousins, the pachycephalosaurs, were developing another set of traits for a different sort of herding existence. Like the frillheads, the packies developed a unique and interesting skull that reveals clues about their social behavior and approach to defending themselves from predators.

Packies are bipedal, beaked dinosaurs that range in size from 6 to 26 feet long. In the shape of their bodies and in their feeding habits, they resemble the ornithopods—beaked and hoofed dinosaurs that foraged for vegetation in groups and, whenever possible, ran away from predators. In addition, however, the packies had high, dome-shaped skulls made of solid bone that could grow up to 8 inches thick.

Their domed heads give their fossilized skulls an almost human appearance, like the bald heads of Benedictine monks or the helmeted heads of ancient Greek soldiers. Unlike human heads, however, packy heads are almost all bone and no brain.

Skull of the pachycephalosaur, Stegoceras.

(Department of Library Services, American Museum of Natural History; Neg. no.:2A21976; Photo.:Finnin)

Brotherhood of Boneheads

Here's a list of a few members of the fraternal order of pachycephalosaurs.

➤ *Homalocephale* (level head)   One of a group of packies whose domeheads were less thick and pronounced than the others. Homalos grew to be about 10 feet long.

➤ *Stygimoloch* (devil from the river Styx)   One of the most interesting-looking and cleverly named dinosaurs. It had elaborate knobs and long horny growths surrounding its high dome, which gave it a devilish appearance. Its horns, combined with the fact that it was found in the Montana formation known as Hell Creek, led its discoverers to name it after the mythical river Styx that bordered Hades, the ancient Greek underworld.

➤ *Stegoceras* (covered horn; the name shouldn't be confused with the more famous *Stegosaurus*—covered lizard—belonging to a different family)   One of the smaller packies, growing to be only about 6 feet long.

➤ *Pachycephalosaurus* (thick-headed lizard)   A big, 26-foot packy with a skull three times as long and three times as thick as that of *Stegoceras*.

Packy-ing a Whallop

Around the base of the dome, many packies had hornlike studs and bony knobs. These outgrowths must have been chiefly ornamental, though they may have added some extra protection as well. The bubble-shaped headbones, however, were undoubtedly used as serious weapons, possibly against predators as well as against other packy rivals.

Packies have been compared to rams and goats—creatures of today that take part in head-butting contests as a way of establishing herd hierarchies. Unlike ramhorns and goathorns, however, packy boneheads did not flare out into a flat surface that would have distributed the force of the blow throughout a wide area. Instead, when packies hit heads, a tremendous amount of force may have been concentrated at one small point of contact.

As a result, unlike sheep and goats, they may not have gone after one another head on, probably inflicting glancing blows instead. To absorb this kind of punishment, the backbones of packies were more closely interlocked than those of most other vertebrates. This evidently kept them from twisting, so that the shock of a blow could be absorbed evenly by the whole spine.

Although they probably used glancing blows in head-butting contests among themselves, they may well have collided head-on with predators, inflicting blows

Boning Up
Packy fossils are rare. The skeletons that have been found are worn and disjointed, suggesting that they had been washed away and deposited by water rather than buried immediately. This shows that packies may have lived in mountainous regions where they were unlikely to have been fossilized.

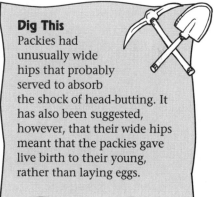

Dig This
Packies had unusually wide hips that probably served to absorb the shock of head-butting. It has also been suggested, however, that their wide hips meant that the packies gave live birth to their young, rather than laying eggs.

to the knees or the teeth. When riled, a packie may have been able to build up a big head of steam in a fairly short space and deliver crippling blows to any predators unlucky enough to be caught flat-footed.

The Least You Need to Know

- ➤ Ceratopsians have the largest skulls of any land animals.
- ➤ *Psittacosaurus* was a frill-less ancestor of the frillheads.
- ➤ Their frills helped stabilize the ceratopsians' powerful jaws and may have been used in display.
- ➤ The horns on many frillheads were effective defense against predators.
- ➤ A nesting colony of *Protoceratops*, an early frillhead, was discovered in the Gobi Desert in the 1920s.
- ➤ Pachycephalosaurs have thick skulls used for head-butting contests.

Of Arms and the Dinosaur

Some dinosaurs seem well equipped for medieval jousting tournaments, with elaborate ornamental and defensive armor as well as Gothic-style weapons attached to the end of their tails. These are the thyreophorans (shielded dinosaurs), a group that includes the spiky, plated stegosaurs (covered lizards), and the bumpy, knobby ankylosaurs (fused lizards).

Sir Stego is not known for brains, and its showy armor doesn't seem like it would be much use in a fight, but when challenged it had a nasty backlash in the form of a tail equipped with deadly spikes. Sir Anky was not the swiftest dinosaur, and its most effective defense may have been just sitting there under its bumpy, bony armor, but it also packed a wallop in the form of a heavy tail club.

These dinosaurs traveled the land far and wide, performing feats of derring-do during the fabled Jurassic and Cretaceous times when evil, carnivorous dragons troubled the realm.

Plates du Jour

Definosaurus
Osteoderms are bones that are not attached to the skeleton but lie embedded in the skin. Osteoderms include *Stegosaurus* plates and *Ankylosaurus* armor.

One way of thinking about the armored dinosaurs is as creatures with part of their skeleton on the outside of their bodies. Their armor is essentially bones, called *osteoderms*, that are not connected to the rest of the skeleton but are embedded in the skin.

The most obvious example of dinosaur armor ironically may not have been used for defensive purposes. These are the famous plates sticking up from the spine of *Stegosaurus* and the other stegosaurids. These do not seem to have been especially useful as shields because, however they were arranged, they still left large areas of exposed flesh within easy reach of hungry predators.

Sir Stegosaurus *in full battle regalia. Significant features include the small head, the row of plates along the spine, the tail spikes, and the long hind legs.*

(Department of Library Services, American Museum of Natural History; Neg. no.:313965B; Photo.:Beckett)

Suiting Up

For many years, in fact, there have been discussions about how the plates were situated. The first scientists who examined stegosaur fossils believed that the plates were shields that rested flat over the stego's back like shingles on a roof. Further questions arose over whether the plates were arranged in pairs running down the spine or were more spread out and staggered.

Everyone these days pretty much agrees that the plates stuck straight up and were not paired, but spread out as they run down the spine. This conclusion depends mostly on the assumption that the plates were less useful for defense than for temperature control.

Hot and Cold Warriors

Much like the sail running along the spine of the carnosaur *Spinosaurus*, plates evidently helped stegosaurs cool down and warm up. Each plate is full of lots of hollow places for blood vessels to travel through. As blood passed through the plates, it would be heated or cooled depending on whether the plates were spread out in the sun to warm or held to the wind to cool off. After returning from the plates, the blood would have heated or cooled the rest of the stegosaur.

Most agree that temperature regulation was the primary use of the plates, although some continue to think they served a defensive purpose as well, or were used as display. It has even been suggested that *Stegosaurus* could have moved the plates from side to side like flippers in the event of an attack by a predator. This view seems doubtful, however, simply because so much vulnerable flesh would have remained unprotected.

> **Dig This**
> To find what arrangement of plates would be most efficient for temperature regulation, scientists conducted an experiment with a model stego in a wind tunnel. Temperature changes were recorded with the plates in various positions. Staggered, rather than paired, plates seemed to result in the largest temperature change.

Heads and Tails

Fortunately for the stegosaurs, they had more effective weapons than their plates. These were their powerful tails, equipped with four, or sometimes eight, long, horn-covered spikes pointing up, out, and back from the end. Each spike was 3 or 4 feet long—long enough to inflict a fatal wound. Predacious dinosaurs would have done well to avoid stepping on this 20-foot scorpion.

Rear-Guard Maneuvers

Stegosaurus tails were all the more dangerous because they were flexible as well as strong. In contrast, many dinosaurs had stiff, bony rods in their tails, making them useful in balancing and easy to keep from dragging along the ground. The stegosaurs had less need of this kind of stability, though. Instead, their tails were snaky and muscular, so they could be used with speed and control, as well as force.

> **Dig This**
> Some stegosaurs, including *Kentrosaurus* (but not *Stegosaurus*), have additional spikes sticking backwards out of their hips. You may have sat on a nail at some point in your life. Imagine having a nail sit on you!

141

Unlike the frillheaded ceratopsians, which were most vulnerable to attack from behind, the stegosaurs were more vulnerable from the front. This weakness, however, may not have been as serious as you might think. This is because of the special way stegosaurs were put together.

Old Swivel Hips

The stegosaurs walked around on all fours even though, like all four-footed dinosaurs, they were descended from bipedal (two-footed) ancestors. This is evident in the fact that stegos have especially long hind legs compared to their forelegs. It's easy to tell the stegos walked on four feet, however, because their front legs are thick as tree stumps and are obviously better suited for walking than for anything else.

With their long hind legs, the stegos' weight was shifted well toward their back ends. This enabled them to pivot very quickly on their hind feet, pushing themselves around with their stocky forelegs. This means that a carnosaur could be looking a stego in the face one second, deciding how big a first bite to take, and then suddenly get a hard slap in the head with a set of yard-long spikes.

Evidently, the stegos could wheel around on a dime with their long hind pivot legs, slinging their tail spikes into their enemies with whiplash momentum. This, however, was probably the only thing they could do quickly. Otherwise, they seem to have plodded along at a rather leisurely pace.

Boning Up

Stegosaur hind limbs are so much longer than their forelimbs that this would have posed a problem for stegos running at high speeds: their front legs wouldn't have been able to keep up with their back legs. The likeliest way for them to avoid this problem would have been simply not to move very fast.

> Museum Exhibit ⬅

Slow Going

One sign that the stegos were slow movers is the fact that their thighs were longer than their shins. This suggests they moved with a plodding gait. Another indication was their need to carry food around inside them for a long time to digest it.

Stegosaur teeth were small and rudimentary, useful only for superficial shredding. The real work of breaking down the tough vegetation they ate was left to their big, barrel-shaped guts. They may have used gizzard stones to help this process along, much as the sauropods did.

No Brainers

Stegos are famous for having had tiny brains—about the size of a golf ball, in fact. That's not much gray matter when you consider how big the rest of the animal was (about 20 feet long, as we said). What does this say about their behavior and way of life? We don't know. It's safe to say stegos didn't spend their time working out problems in quantum mechanics, but beyond that, it's anybody's guess whether stegos were really dumber than the average dinosaur.

Stegosaurus's shrunken cerebrum gave rise to an interesting myth about their anatomy: that they had a second brain in their tails that helped control the rear portion of the animal. This idea was extremely popular for a while, although it has since been thoroughly discredited. The only evidence for this theory, aside from the smallness of the brain inside the skull was the fact that the stegosaur spinal column was especially wide just above and behind the hips. This is true, however, of many large animals. There may have been *room* for another brain farther down the spinal chord, but that's not a very good reason to believe there *was* one.

Stegos International

By far the most numerous stegosaur fossils belong to the species called *Stegosaurus*. Most of these have been found in North America. There were some other significant stegos, though, including *Kentrosaurus* (spiked lizard), known from fossils found in Tanzania. Kent was a small stego, only about 8 feet long, having plates that were somewhat spike-shaped. Another stego of note was *Tuojiangosaurus*, from Mongolia. Its plates were somewhat cone-shaped.

Things That Go Bump

The state of the art of dinosaur armor is best represented by the thyreophorans known as ankylosaurs. Ankies were about the same size as stegos, and sometimes larger, growing up to 30 feet long, but they carried themselves closer to the ground. They had beaks with a single row of unspecialized cheek teeth.

What really set the ankies apart, however, was their hard, bony covering. Most ankylos were covered with armor made of bony studs set right into their skin. Covered with bumps, they look something like dinosaur versions of the "Fantastic Four" comic-book character, The Thing.

Armored Transport

These armor plates were various sizes and situated in patterns that wouldn't restrict the ankies' flexibility too much—not that they would have practiced yoga anyway; they were built like tanks. They may have been fairly slow moving but were not crawlers. The

Boning Up
Almost all *Stegosaurus* species died out by the Middle Cretaceous. They may have lost out to the ankylosaurs, which became more numerous as stego numbers dwindled. One stegosaur species, however, known as *Dravidosaurus*, made it all the way to the end of the Cretaceous. Dravido fossils have been found only in India, where no anky fossils have been recovered. At some point during the Cretaceous Period, India broke off from the supercontinent of Gondwana and became an island. The dravidos may have survived because the island had no ankies to compete with.

Dig This
Ankie walking speed has been estimated at about 3 miles per hour based on trackway measurements. Top running speed may have been only 6 miles per hour. That's a brisk walk for a human.

structure of their legs and hips, as well as fossilized trackways left by ankies, indicate that they walked with their legs directly underneath them.

Joining the Club

In addition to their armor, ankies had tails tipped with heavy bone clubs. These clubs were made of big lumps of armor that fused with one another and with the last three vertebrae in the tail. Ankie clubs were as big as, or bigger than, your head.

Ankie tails tended to have less armor covering them, or smaller plates of armor, than on the rest of the body. This allowed the ankies the flexibility to swing their clubs at attackers. Like stegosaurs, ankies had muscles running the entire length of their tails for greater power and control. In addition, ankies had powerful hips for carrying the tails—evidently they didn't drag their tails along the ground.

Ankies do not appear to have been able to pivot while wielding their tail weapons the way stegosaurs could. Instead, they had to rely on their armor to protect them until a predator came within tail's reach before taking a swing.

Alternative Ending

Not all ankies had tail clubs. A special variety of ankie, known as nodosaurs (knotty lizards), had clubless tails. These dinosaurs had to rely entirely on their body armor to protect them. In fact, nodosaurs tended to be even more fully covered with armor than other ankies, with armor-covered heads and armor reaching to the tip of the tail. They also had narrower skulls than other ankies.

Fossil Fallacy

Nodosaurs were among the first dinosaurs to be discovered. Two kinds, found during the late 19th century, were wrongly thought to be meat-eaters and consequently are known today by names that suggest they are predators. These names are *Sarcolestes* (flesh robber) and *Struthiosaurus* (ostrich lizard).

Armored Regiment

Here's a list of some of the more important nodosaurs and ankylosaurs.

➤ *Scelidosaurus* (limb lizard)   Only tentatively classified as an ankylosaur. This is a primitive armored dinosaur of the Early Jurassic with no tail club. It is known from a partial skeleton found in England.

➤ *Nodosaurus* (nodular lizard)   Covered in bands of armor of alternating large and small size knobs. Like other nodosaurs, its armor may have been fringed with spikes around its sides and shoulders.

➤ *Panoplosaurus* (fully armored lizard)   One of the few nodosaurs to survive to the end of the Cretaceous Period.

➤ *Edmontonia* (from the Edmonton rock formation)   Another Late Cretaceous nodosaur with particularly long spikes coming out of its sides and shoulders.

➤ *Ankylosaurus* (fused lizard)   Known from fossils found in North America and was one of the last ankies to evolve, surviving to the end of the Cretaceous.

➤ *Euoplocephalus* (true armored head)   One of the largest ankies, weighing about 2 tons. It had hornlike spikes sticking out the back of its head. It also had sheets of bone on the skin covering its head providing extra protection for the skull.

➤ *Pinacosaurus* (plank lizard)   One of the smaller and skinnier ankies at 16 feet long.

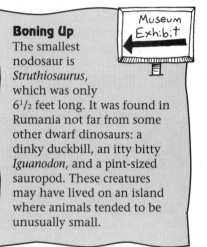

Boning Up
The smallest nodosaur is *Struthiosaurus*, which was only 6¹/₂ feet long. It was found in Rumania not far from some other dwarf dinosaurs: a dinky duckbill, an itty bitty *Iguanodon*, and a pint-sized sauropod. These creatures may have lived on an island where animals tended to be unusually small.

Peaceful Protest

It seems likely that, apart from the tail club wielded by non-nodosaur ankies, these dinosaurs defended themselves through non-violent resistance. In the presence of a predator, they may have hunkered down under their armored backs and sides with their limbs tucked in and their vulnerable stomachs underneath them. In this position, they may have withstood the claws and teeth of predacious dinosaurs without batting an eye.

In fact, the ankies were so thoroughly covered with armor that even their eyelids seem to have been reinforced with bone. An ankie under assault may have been impervious to all the scratchings and gnashings a hungry predator could dish out.

The fringe of spikes many ankies had growing from their sides and shoulders may have prevented big carnosaurs from digging their jaws in underneath them and flipping them over where their unprotected bellies would have been exposed. What's more, if a meat-eater did try to flip them over, they may have extended their powerful legs out the other side like Olympic wrestlers avoiding a fall, giving themselves a still broader, more stable base.

Thus, like tortoises and armadillos of today, which protect themselves by curling up into impregnable armored balls, the ankies must have been tough nuts for meat-eaters to crack. In fact, it would have been the predators that risked getting cracked with the heavy tail club.

Sharp Rebuttals

It is possible, however, that some of the ankies had more aggressive means of defending themselves in addition to their tail clubs. When riled, they may have been able to charge their attackers with their heads down and dig into the enemy with their shoulder spikes. This strategy would only have been effective at short range, however, where sudden bursts of energy may have caught the more agile meat-eaters by surprise.

Breathing Easy

Dig This
Casts of the inside of anky skulls indicate that, although their brains are not especially large, the region of the brain responsible for smelling was well developed. This provides evidence that the convoluted sinuses of the ankies provided them with a keen sense of smell.

The ankies evolved one other curious feature. Like many mammals of today, they had palates separating their nasal passages from their mouths. Why, of all dinosaurs, the ankies evolved this particular feature is uncertain. It is a trait possessed by many warm-blooded creatures, allowing them to chew food efficiently while breathing, but it provides only indirect evidence that ankies were warm-blooded too.

It does seem likely that their palates would have allowed them to breathe more easily while chewing than they otherwise could have done. They also would have given them longer nasal passages, which would have served to warm and humidify the air they breathed, as well as help them smell. Even so, ankies make poor candidates for warm-bloodedness among dinosaurs. Because they were so slow-moving, they wouldn't have needed a high metabolism.

The Least You Need to Know

➤ Thyreophoran body armor is made of bone that is not attached to the internal skeleton.

➤ Stegosaur plates were evidently used for temperature regulation and display rather than defense.

➤ Stegos could pivot on their hind feet to wield their tail spikes.

➤ The notion that stegosaurs had two brains is only a myth. Each stego had only one golf-ball–sized brain.

➤ Ankylosaurs' backs and heads were covered with armor.

➤ Nodosaurs did not have tail clubs.

➤ Ankies defended themselves by hiding under their armor.

Part 4
They Also Ran, Crawled, Flew, and Swam

While dinosaurs dominated the Mesozoic Period, they were not the only interesting creatures alive. In addition to the birds (who are dinosaurs anyway) were flying lizards (the pteradactyls), swimming lizards, non-dinosaur land lizards, and the first mammals. Many of these species became extinct along with the non-bird dinosaurs, but many have descendants that are still around today.

Chapter 15

First in Flight

From the earthbound perspective of land animals like us, the ability to fly can seem like an absolute miracle. It's difficult even to imagine using your body to lift yourself off the ground and maneuver from place to place just by pushing against the air. From an evolutionary standpoint, though, flying isn't such a big deal.

In fact, the ability to fly evolved not just once, but a number of times: in bugs, in birds, in bats, and in pterodactyls and the other pterosaurs (winged lizards). These creatures didn't inherit the ability to fly from one another; each group picked it up on its own. How this happened is uncertain. It's interesting, though, that it happened twice during the time when dinosaurs lived.

These flying things are further evidence that Mother Nature was pushing the evolutionary envelope during the Mesozoic Era. This is especially true because pterosaurs and the first birds not only learned to fly, they also learned to fill a variety of new evolutionary niches.

Lizards Aloft

Flight in reptiles has been confusing and controversial because it was such an unexpected discovery for scientists to make. Because scientists used modern animals as their frame of reference, the idea of flying reptiles seemed to belong with mythology rather than paleontology. Another source of confusion was the fact that flying takes different forms in different species.

Flying Leaps

In addition to the various critters that learned to fly by flapping their wings, a number of animals, including squirrels and certain lizards, have developed the ability to glide, jumping off a perching place into the air, spreading themselves out, and sailing off to the ground or to a new perch. Scientists are still in dispute about whether gliding provides the evolutionary jumping off point for the origins of actual flight in birds and in pterosaurs. Some say birds and pteros were gliders before they developed the ability to control their flight with their wings.

We know of lizards that were capable of gliding during the Triassic Period. One of these is named *Icarosaurus,* after Icarus, the mythic Grecian boy whose father made him wings out of wax. When Icarus flew too close to the sun, his wings melted, and he fell to his death. *Icarosaurus* fell too, in the sense that the species didn't survive for very long.

Icarosaurus was a unique creature in the history of flight. Its "wings" were actually bony extensions of its ribs sticking out on either side and covered with a membrane of skin. Although these wings could be used for gliding, they couldn't be flapped.

In fact, *Icarosaurus* and the other Triassic gliding lizards did not evolve into full-fledged flyers but seem to have died out. The pterosaurs, who had flappable wings with advanced flight capability evolved from a different group of animals during Upper Triassic times.

What Goes Up

The pterosaurs are closely related to the dinosaurs but are not dinosaurs themselves. Like dinosaurs, they had an upright, bipedal posture and straight ankle joints, but they evolved the ability to fly millions of years before birds came along. We don't know just what creatures the pterosaurs are descended from, but ptero ancestors were probably much the same sort of small, agile reptiles that dinosaurs descended from. One candidate is the small, quick, pre-dinosaurian predator known as *Lagosuchus* (rabbit crocodile).

Although they were the first vertebrates to become full-scale flapping flyers, it wasn't in the ptero cards for them to pass along their achievement. They went extinct at the end of the Cretaceous Period, along with all the remaining non-bird dinosaurs, and the planet has not seen wing-flapping reptiles since. It seems likely that birds took over the skies, out-competing the pteros in their airborne lifestyle.

Flighty Notions

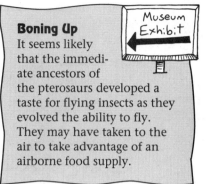

Boning Up
It seems likely that the immediate ancestors of the pterosaurs developed a taste for flying insects as they evolved the ability to fly. They may have taken to the air to take advantage of an airborne food supply.

Because flying reptiles haven't been seen for 65 million years, the fossil evidence of pterosaurs, first discovered in the 19th century, flew in the face of what most people believed about reptiles. It seemed too much to believe that lizards could actually fly by flapping their wings. At first many believed that their wings were really big fins used for swimming.

Even after facing up to the idea that pteros belonged in the air, most scientists believed that the pteros were simply gliders, a view that has prevailed until only recently. More careful analysis of the fossils and skeletal anatomy of these ancient flying lizards has revealed that most pteros were active fliers that could flap their wings much like modern birds. Their wings appear to have been narrower than originally thought and did not extend down to their feet (like a bat's wings do). Their wings also appear to have been stiffer than the soft skin found in bats' wings and may have been reinforced with long, thin fibers in the wing's surface.

Fossil Fallacy

The view that pterosaurs were gliders rather than flyers helped generate an interesting—if mistaken—theory about their extinction. The theory says that changes in climate at the end of the Cretaceous resulted in stronger winds and more extreme air currents that proved to be too much for the pteros to deal with. As a result, they couldn't survive.

Walk This Way

Still another controversy about the pteros concerns what these animals did when they were on the ground. One older idea, the "bat model," maintains that the pteros shuffled around on all fours like bats. (Because the forelimbs of bats are wings rather than legs, bats can only walk in a sprawling position, and very clumsily at that.)

Another more recent idea, the "bird model," says that the pteros walked upright on their hind limbs like birds, with their wings folded up at their sides. The bird model for ptero walking, however, is controversial. The earliest pteros had long tails that could be used to counterbalance the front end of the animal, thus it seems reasonable that these pteros could have walked on their hind limbs. The later (and bigger) pteros like *Pteranodon*, however, had no tails for balancing and thus would have been very front-heavy if they had tried to walk on just their hind legs.

Still other scientists say that the whole debate is a lot of hot air, and that the pteros fit neither the bat model nor the bird model but had a way of walking all their own! After all, these animals lived for some 150 million years, so however they may have walked certainly worked for them.

In fact, trackways have been found that some scientists believe were made by walking pteros. These trackways have been named *Pteraichnus* (wing trace) and, if made by pteros, reveal that these animals walked on all fours with the first three fingers of their forelimbs on the ground and with the fourth finger (which carries the wing) folded backwards and upwards.

Which Way Is Up?

Different pteros had different ways of using the sky as a base of operations. Many were evidently water hunters, plummeting out of the air or diving from the water's surface in search of fish and other sea creatures. Others were probably insect eaters. Still others may have lived a hawklike existence, swooping down on small game.

Ptero-Dynamics

Pteros ranged in size from that of a sparrow to that of an airplane. Pterosaur wings evolved as modifications of their hands in which the fourth finger is extremely elongated and acts as a frame for the wing membrane. The other three fingers stuck out separately part-way down the wing and may have been used for grabbing or scratching.

Pterosaurs tended to have large or long beaks, and many had teeth as well. Some had big crests sticking out behind their heads that helped counterbalance the weight of their beaks. Most pteros had extremely lightweight bones with many

Boning Up

Most pterosaur fossils have been recovered from rocks formed at the bottom or the edge of what once was the ocean. In spite of their bones' fragile structure, they were preserved by being buried quickly in ocean sediment. Most pteros are thought to have lived by the sea, like ocean birds of today. Inland pteros, however, may have been just as numerous and diverse but became fossilized only rarely because quick burial on land was less likely than by the sea.

Dig This

Since the beginning of the 20th century, some scientists suspected that pteros were warm-blooded, and that they would have needed some kind of insulation to prevent them from losing too much body heat while flying. Finally, in 1970, a well-preserved ptero fossil was found that seemed to show traces of fur covering the body. This creature was named *Sordes pilosus*, which means "hairy devil."

hollow places inside. Exceptions were the heavier diving pteros that plunged into the water after fish. Diving pteros had webbed feet for swimming.

Many think pterosaurs were warm-blooded; some or all of them may have been covered with fuzz to keep them warm. On the diving pteros, this fuzz may have been oily to repel water so as to enable them to get airborne from straight out of the sea.

Pteros seem to have had well-developed brains. The shape of the inside of their skulls suggests that they had well-developed sight, but not a well-developed sense of smell. This is what you might expect in an animal that spent most of its time up in the air.

The Leathernecks

Here's a list of some significant pterosaurs.

- ➤ *Eudimorphodon* (true two-shaped teeth)   An early, primitive, gull-sized pterosaur that had peglike teeth as well as sharper cutting teeth. It had a long tail but no crest on its head.

- ➤ *Pterodactylus* (wing finger)   One of the first pteros to be discovered. The name also refers to a whole group of short-tailed pterosaurs.

- ➤ *Rhamphorhynchus* (narrow beak)   Had a long beak with sharp teeth, a long tail, but no crest. It also had a large breastplate where powerful flight muscles were attached. This was evidently a fish-eating ptero because fish remains have been found where its stomach used to be.

- ➤ *Pteranodon* (winged but toothless)   The largest group of pterosaurs. It had a large bony crest counterbalancing its long, toothless beak and only a very short tail.

- ➤ *Dimorphodon* (two-shaped teeth)   Had an unusually deep, rounded skull for a pterosaur. It may have eaten insects and small animals. It had a tail but no skull crest.

- ➤ *Pterodaustro* (southern wing)   Known from fossils found in Argentina. This ptero has a long, weird-looking beak filled with hundreds of long, needle-shaped teeth, evidently designed for combing plankton or little sea creatures from the surface of the water.

- ➤ *Quetzalcoatlus* (named for Quetzalcoatl, an Aztec god who took the form of a feathered serpent)   The largest known pterosaur, a kind of *Pteranodon* with a wing span of 50 feet.

Early Birds

The next creatures to evolve the ability to fly did so only about 50 million years after the pterosaurs. These were the birds, which, from what we can tell, first took to the air late in the Jurassic Period. Unlike the pterosaurs, the birds got off the ground with the help of a unique adaption that only birds have: feathers.

Lizard Feathers

The first feathers were probably modified scales. These were probably not used for flight but insulation. It is likely that they served the purpose, initially, of preserving body heat, and only later became specially adapted for flying. Incidentally, they also became adapted for repelling water in swimming birds, a trait that helps them float easily.

Boning Up

Feathers continue to serve the dual purpose of flight and insulation in modern birds. In fact, different feathers are specialized as fluffy, downy feathers for insulation, and flat, rigid feathers for flight. In flight feathers, the feathery parts coming out of the shaft are called barbs, which are connected to one another by even smaller barbs, called barbules, into a kind of lightweight latticework.

Definosaurus

The **arboreal** theory of the origin of flight holds that wings evolved for gliding in creatures that climbed trees. The **cursorial** theory holds that flight evolved in creatures that ran on the ground.

Up a Tree

We don't know how the first birds actually started flying, but there are two strong theories. One idea is that they started as gliding animals that lived in trees. Feathers and wings developed as a way of breaking their fall and eventually became fully useful in flight.

One weakness of this theory is that we don't have much evidence that the bird ancestors—by many accounts the theropod dinosaurs—were tree-climbers. The theropods were meat-eaters, and most of their food supply lived on the ground, so they may not have had much reason to climb trees.

Nevertheless, this remains a viable theory, known as the *arboreal* (tree) theory. The other theory is the *cursorial* (running) theory, which says birds developed the ability to fly from ancestors who ran around on the ground.

See How They Run

Wings may have evolved from the long fingers of creatures that used their hands to grab small animals they wanted to eat. It's also possible that wings were initially useful in maintaining balance in fast-running creatures.

Still another idea about the earliest use of wings has it that the ancestors of birds hunted insects and used their feathery arms collecting their dinner, catching them or simply sweeping them within snapping distance of their snouts.

The most likely candidates for bird ancestors were, in fact, fast-running predators—the maniraptor dinosaurs. Still, no one has found any of them with arms that seem especially winglike, although the difference between early wings and ordinary arms may be hard to see in fossil skeletons because the first birds also had claws sticking out of their wings.

Old Birds

There are a number of candidates for the first known bird, including a partial Late Triassic skeleton known as *Protoavis* (first bird) that is now widely thought to have been a non-bird dinosaur. The odds-on favorite as first known bird is *Archaeopteryx*, a well-known, well-preserved early bird from the Bavarian limestone quarries. *Archaeopteryx* is definitely a bird because a number of good fossil skeletons clearly include feather impressions.

At the same time, it looks a good deal like a small theropod dinosaur. In fact, one archaeopter skeleton was misidentified for many years as belonging to *Compsognathus*. Archie's dinosaurlike qualities include its sharp teeth, claws not only on its feet but on its wings, and its long, bony tail.

Archaeopteryx differs from modern birds in having these dinosaur traits—teeth, tail, and claws. These features provided added weight that would only make flight more difficult for today's birds. Modern birds also have a well-developed breastbone with strong flying muscles attached. Archies don't have this, although many pterosaurs did.

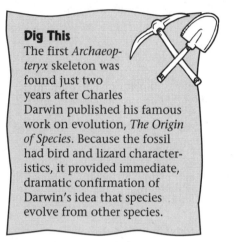

Dig This
The first *Archaeopteryx* skeleton was found just two years after Charles Darwin published his famous work on evolution, *The Origin of Species*. Because the fossil had bird and lizard characteristics, it provided immediate, dramatic confirmation of Darwin's idea that species evolve from other species.

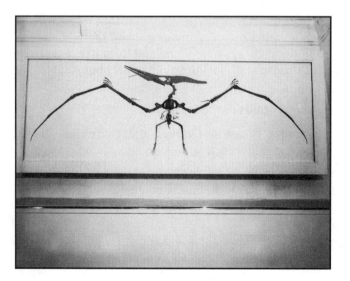

Archaeopteryx *skeleton preserved in Bavarian limestone—this is one of the most famous and controversial fossils ever found.*

(Department of Library Services, American Museum of Natural History; Neg. no.:2A23737; Photo.:Beckett)

Time Warp

Boning Up

Although a few good skeletons of Mesozoic birds have been found (namely the limestone *Archaeopteryx* fossils), there may be big holes in the fossil record as far as early birds are concerned. This may stem from a skeletal feature that enables birds to fly—their delicate, extra lightweight bones. Filled with hollow spaces to make them lighter, they were especially fragile and undoubtedly disintegrated more easily than heavier bones.

Archaeopteryx is clearly a primitive bird that may not have been a particularly competent flyer. Not long after the archies emerged in the Late Jurassic, however, birds evolved that were better equipped for the wild blue yonder, as well as highly specialized to live a variety of lifestyles. These birds become evident in the fossil record in the Early Cretaceous.

The next known species of birds to develop after *Archaeopteryx* are, in evolutionary terms, so much more advanced, it suggests that the archies may not have been a bird ancestor but could have been a primitive offshoot of the bird line instead. If this is true, *Archaeopteryx* lived side by side with more advanced bird species that we don't know about, and these birds, rather than the archies, gave rise to modern birds.

On the other hand, it's possible that archies were modern bird ancestors and that bird evolution proceeded extremely quickly over the next 15 million years. Scientists may need to discover more early bird fossils before they are able to decide this question either way.

Scattered Flock

The birds of the Early Cretaceous varied considerably in size and lifestyle. Some were small and evidently perched in trees. Others were larger and lived like seagulls near the shore, hunting fish. Others, of various sizes, lost the ability to fly but hunted small game on the ground.

Here's a list of some important early birds of the Mesozoic.

➤ *Archaeopteryx* (ancient wing)   The earliest known bird, combining a number of bird and dinosaur features.

➤ *Sinornis* (Chinese bird)   One of the oldest birds (from the Early Cretaceous) apart from *Archaeopteryx*, had teeth and a short, birdlike tail and, unlike *Archaeopteryx*, could fold its wings tightly across its back. Its claws were evidently adapted for perching in branches of trees.

➤ *Baptornis* (dipping bird)   Also from the Early Cretaceous, had teeth and only small nubs for wings. It couldn't fly but was a diver instead, paddling after fish with webbed feet.

➤ *Enantiornis* (opposite bird, so called because it has an opposable claw for perching)   A sparrow-sized bird of the Late Cretaceous. It was a good flyer and good percher.

Enantiornis is a single genus but also gives its name to all the sparrow-sized, perching bird species of the Late Cretaceous. Fossils of these birds have been found all over the world.

➤ *Hesperornis* (western bird)   A flightless diving bird like *Baptornis*. Because it was adapted for diving, its bones were heavier than bones of flying birds. Like *Enantiornis*, *Hesperornis* gives its name to a whole group of similar birds—divers with teeth and webbed feet.

➤ *Ichthyornis* (fish bird)   A bird that looked and lived like a modern sea gull. It was a strong flyer but may have scavenged the coastline as well as hunted for fish from the surface of the sea.

➤ *Mononykus* (single claw)   Probably a flightless ground bird of the Late Cretaceous. It had short, thick wings that looked more like claws sticking straight out from its body. Each claw is actually made of fused wing bones. It was a good runner that may have occupied a desert environment. One of its birdlike characteristics is its large breastbone, which many birds use to brace their flight muscles. In many ways, however, *Mononykus* looked like a dinosaur, with strong legs and a long tail.

Big Birds

Birds, unlike (other) dinosaurs, survived beyond the Cretaceous Period when many creatures, including (non-bird) dinosaurs, became extinct. Not only did birds survive, but they continued to evolve in a number of different directions. Today birds live almost everywhere except for underneath the ocean—cities, deserts, forests, plains, mountains, beaches, and arctic regions.

Some even expanded to fill the space left by the departed dinosaurs. In fact, a mere seven million years after the end-Cretaceous mass extinction, a group of running, flightless birds known as *ratites* evolved that grew to be as much as 9 feet tall.

The Least You Need to Know

➤ Flight has evolved a number of separate times in different creatures including bugs, birds, bats, and pterosaurs.

➤ The long-standing view that pterosaurs were primarily gliders has recently been revised. Most scientists think they were capable of powered flight.

➤ Pterosaurs are closely related to dinosaurs and probably had similar ancestors.

➤ Feathers serve as insulation as well as for flight.

➤ Birds are the only creatures to have evolved feathers for flight. Some maniraptoran dinosaurs may have also had feathers but only for insulation.

➤ The oldest known bird is *Archaeopteryx*.

Chapter 16

Surf and Turf

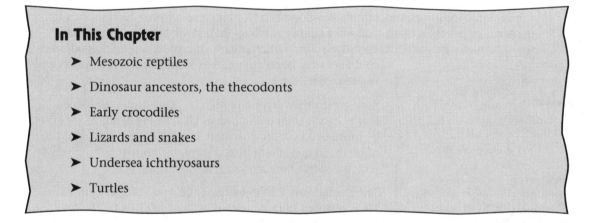

In This Chapter

- ➤ Mesozoic reptiles
- ➤ Dinosaur ancestors, the thecodonts
- ➤ Early crocodiles
- ➤ Lizards and snakes
- ➤ Undersea ichthyosaurs
- ➤ Turtles

Have you ever wished you could fill your swimming pool with snakes, lizards, crocodiles, turtles—all your favorite reptiles—and just jump right in? Sure you have! Well, this chapter is the next best thing: It includes all these reptiles that are alive today, as well as some that have been extinct since the Cretaceous Period.

Individual specimens of some of these would take up your whole pool. Others would feel more at home in the sandbox or up in the trees. In fact, the Mesozoic reptiles managed to fill up whole ecosystems.

Reading about the rest of the reptiles—the non-dinosaur varieties—should help you get a better sense of how the dinosaurs made a space for themselves during their years on earth. It could also help you think differently about some of the oldest creatures still living.

Older Than the Dinosaurs

Biological classification is arranged so that every group of living things is part of a larger group. Thus, dilophosauruses are ceratosaurs are theropods are lizard butts are dinosaurs. And dinosaurs are part of a bigger group known as archosaurs (ruling lizards). The archosaur umbrella covers not only dinosaurs but also pterosaurs, crocodiles, and the group of creatures that gave rise to all of these groups, the thecodonts (socket-toothed).

Big Influences

The thecodonts were crocodile-like reptiles who set themselves apart from other lizards of the Permian and Triassic periods in a number of ways. These features worked together to allow the thecodonts to grow quite large in comparison with the land creatures that came before them. The thecodonts passed this capacity for size along to their descendants: the dinosaurs and, to a lesser extent, the crocodiles.

As their name indicates, thecodonts developed teeth that were set into deep sockets in their jaws, rather than teeth that were simply fused to their jaw bones as other lizards had. This made their teeth especially sturdy, which meant that meat-eating thecodonts could go after larger prey rather than settling for insects and smaller vertebrates.

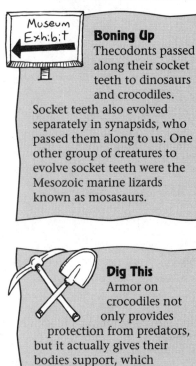

Boning Up

Thecodonts passed along their socket teeth to dinosaurs and crocodiles. Socket teeth also evolved separately in synapsids, who passed them along to us. One other group of creatures to evolve socket teeth were the Mesozoic marine lizards known as mosasaurs.

Dig This

Armor on crocodiles not only provides protection from predators, but it actually gives their bodies support, which improves the crocs' ability to walk around on land.

Along with their strong teeth, the thecodonts developed bigger heads than other lizards had. These heads tended to be more or less crocodile-shaped, with long snouts and lots of teeth. In fact, many thecodonts are known as "suchids," which is what the Greeks call crocodiles.

The thecodonts also developed hip and shoulder joints that allowed them both to stick their legs straight out to their sides and also to walk with their legs underneath them. This enabled them to keep their bellies higher off the ground than other lizards tended to. It also meant that they could carry more bulk than they could by dragging their bellies on the ground. To help them carry more weight, thecodonts developed stronger ankle joints that could withstand more pressure while walking and running. These improvements in posture and ankle design were carried even further by the dinosaurs.

As they developed their abilities to prey more effectively on larger creatures, the thecodonts also developed traits that helped them resist being eaten themselves. One of these traits is the improved mobility they enjoyed because of the design of their ankle and hip joints, which we just discussed. Thecodonts also increased their survival rate by growing to large sizes and acquiring tough, even armor-like skin on their backs. The thecodonts bequeathed this armor to the dinosaurs and to the crocodiles.

God Suchids

Take a look at this list of some notable thecodonts:

➤ *Proterosuchus* (before crocodile)   Among the first thecodonts to appear during the Lower Triassic Period. Unlike later thecos and crocs, which developed a more upright stance, Proterosuchus walked with its legs sprawled out to the side.

➤ *Erythrosuchus* (red crocodile, so called because the first fossil specimens found had red stains on them)   The largest land animal of the Lower Triassic Period, reaching lengths of more than 16 feet. Like modern crocodiles, the Erythrosuchus may have spent much, but not all, of its time in the water.

➤ *Ornithosuchus* (bird crocodile)   A smaller theco of the Upper Triassic Period that may have been capable of rearing up and running on its hind legs, despite its crocodile shape. Its skull and jaws closely resemble those of a small T-rex.

➤ *Aetosaurus* (eagle lizard)   An Upper Triassic theco that, unlike almost all others, appears to have eaten plants rather than meat. It had a relatively short skull and leaf-shaped teeth.

➤ *Lagosuchus* (rabbit crocodile)   A small and quick theco from the Middle Triassic Period, may be the closest relative yet found both to the dinosaurs and to the pterosaurs. It ran on two long and slender legs.

Quite a While, Crocodile

Crocodiles are the only living archosaurs, and they've been around for more than 200 million years. During this time, all kinds of different crocs have appeared and have adapted more or less for life on land as well as in the water. The basic pattern, though, remains pretty much the same and helps account for their impressive longevity as a group.

True to Form

Since the very beginnings of crocodile kind, crocs have adhered to pretty much the same lifestyle and body plan. They can move around on land or in water, they're big, they're sneaky, and they'll eat just about whatever they can catch, from frogs and fish to human beings, regardless of whether they killed it themselves or whether it was already dead.

Within these tried and true parameters, though, crocs have taken many different shapes. Some Jurassic crocodiles were completely aquatic, with flippers instead of feet. Other aquatic forms retained their feet but developed very slender, needle-like snouts good for catching fish but not land animals. These needle-nosed crocs include Jurassic varieties as well as gharials, a species currently found in India.

While some crocs have become better adapted to water, others have become especially well-adapted to land. In fact, some of the first crocodiles of the Triassic Period had long, slender legs for running—some were even bipedal.

Hard to Swallow

Crocs today are certainly capable of hunting on land, but they tend not to come far out of the water. In fact, these reptiles are especially good at sneaking up on birds or land animals who come near the water by hiding beneath the surface. Because crocs have eyes on the very tops of their heads, they can keep their entire bodies submerged while still getting a good bead on their quarry on the shore.

Crocs are unusual among reptiles in being stealthy hunters. One trait that helps them hunt by sneaking up on prey is their exceptionally good hearing ability. Crocs hear better than other reptiles—and almost as well as birds and mammals.

Though crocs are adept at grabbing hold of their prey, they can be messy eaters, especially if they've caught something too big to swallow whole. In the case of a land animal, crocs may have to drag it underwater and hold it until it drowns. Then, because their teeth are good for stabbing but not for cutting, they may have to shake and wrench the body from side to side until they can break or tear off a piece they can swallow. All this requires an extremely sturdy skull with powerful neck and jaw muscles, traits inherited from their thecodont ancestors.

The largest crocodile on record—the *Deinosuchus* (terrible croc)—dates to the Cretaceous Period. Known from a partial skull measuring 6 feet long, the living animal may have been as long as 50 feet from snout to tail—and may well have fed on dinosaurs.

Tropical Crocs

Crocodiles today are restricted to warm, swampy locations. During the Mesozoic Period, however—and especially during the Cretaceous Period—these animals were more widespread. This may be because a greater variety of crocs existed back then, which enabled them to inhabit various environments. Another explanation is that climates were milder during the Cretaceous Period than they are today, which gave these cold-blooded creatures more room to maneuver.

Who's a Lizard?

Ever since dinosaurs were first identified, it's been fashionable to speak of them as "big lizards." That's because it was thought that dinosaurs were, in fact, very lizard-like—slow, sprawling, and cold-blooded. As a result, they were called "saurs," which is Greek for "lizards."

This term still makes perfect sense if you think of reptiles in general as basically lizard-like. What's more, dinosaurs are descended from lizards—or, at any rate, from reptiles that descended from other reptiles from which lizards also descended. So we might as well call them "lizards" if we want.

But then again, it makes about as much sense to call people two-footed, talking rodents. From a reptile's point of view this may seem about right, but from our point of perspective, this is a hasty generalization. Rodents are just one group of mammals, just as lizards are a special group of reptiles.

> **Dig This**
> The first reptiles were discovered from 300 million-year-old fossils that date to the Carboniferous Period. These fossils, known as romerids, were little skeletons found inside petrified tree stumps, where the creatures had evidently been hunting for grubs and insects. Although the first true lizards did not evolve until much later, the romerids resemble modern lizards in lifestyle, size, and appearance.

To be more accurate, then, true lizards set off on their own evolutionary path before dinosaurs came along. Lizards date to the Upper Permian Period, predating dinosaurs by about 25 million years. Several major lizard families—including the gekkos and chameleons, the iguanas, and the skinks—took shape by the Cretaceous Period and are still around today.

Loose Lips

Lizards continue to be a successful and varied group, with thousands of different species all over the world. They have remained successful in part by staying small: Because of their small size, lizards can move quickly despite their typical lizard posture—sprawling with their legs flung out to the side.

Perhaps the real key to lizard success—and the trait that sets them apart from the early reptiles they resemble—is their flexible jaw design. Lizard jaws are extremely flexible, allowing the creatures to snap at prey very quickly and to swallow it without chewing.

> **Dig This**
> As lizard skulls and jaws became much lighter, some unneeded bones eventually floated around loose in the reptiles' heads. These developed into ear bones that resonate with sound waves, enabling lizards to notice even the slightest noises.

Snakes Alive

Jaw flexibility is taken to an even greater extent in a group of reptiles that branched off from lizards during the Cretaceous Period: the snakes. Many snakes have such flexible jaws that they can swallow prey even bigger than their heads! Snakes may have descended from burrowing lizards, which have shown a tendency to develop long, snaky bodies and short, inconsequential limbs.

Dig This
Another jaw adaptation that some snakes—the vipers—have developed are retractile fangs. These remain folded up into the upper jaw when not in use but flick forward like switchblades when it's feeding time.

Fossils of primitive snakes have bones that are vestiges of the hips of their lizard ancestors. Modern snakes, though, have lost even these traces of lizard legs. Although snakes have been around since Cretaceous times, most modern snakes didn't evolve until the Miocene Period—about 25 million years ago. These snakes evolved so late probably because they have adapted to a life of eating small mammals that have also evolved only recently.

All Wet

While dinosaurs were dominating the land during the Mesozoic Period, undersea life was flourishing, too—so much so that there really isn't enough room in this book to mention all of it. In addition to shellfish and other invertebrates, all kinds of bony fish, lobe-finned fish, and so-called cartilaginous fish (including sharks) inhabited the sea.

In addition to these dyed-in-the-wool sea creatures, other sea creatures descended from land creatures—reptiles that moved back to water. These evolutionary back-sliders had fins and flippers derived from legs and feet that once adapted for running around on land. Of course, some of these aquatic retreads were more fish-like than others. Among the fishiest Mesozoic water reptiles were the ichthyosaurs (fish lizards).

Boning Up
Origins of the ichthyosaurs are uncertain. Their emergence in the Early Triassic Period is late enough for them to be thecodonts—a theory possibility supported by the fact that many had socket teeth. On the other hand, these creatures are so specialized for undersea life that many believe they evolved from much more primitive reptiles that hadn't adapted to living on land as well as the thecodonts.

Flukes of Nature

Ichthyosaurs were quite common throughout the Mesozoic Period, but like so many other creatures of that time, they died out by the end of the Cretaceous Period. In fact, the ichthyosaurs didn't even make it that far, but fell into extinction a little more than halfway through the Cretaceous Period. They may have been squeezed out of existence by sharks or other marine reptiles.

An ichthyo might be thought of as something of a cross between modern sharks and dolphins. The creatures had bottle-shaped noses like a dolphin; some had lots of shark-like teeth, while others were toothless; they each had four fins derived from legs, plus a dorsal fin on their backs; and many had flukes on their tails.

The largest known ichthyos were 30 feet long. They lived mostly on fish, although fossils show that they also ate pterodactyls from time to time. Many ichthyo fossils are extremely well-preserved—some even show them in the process of giving birth. The young, born alive, emerge tail first.

Flippery When Wet

Less obviously adapted for undersea life were the nothosaurs (false lizards) and the plesiosaurs (ribbon lizards). Many of these closely resemble long-necked land reptiles; that's especially true of the nothosaurs, whose fins look very much like feet. The nothos' near descendants, the plesios, had flippers.

Who needs a chandelier when you've got a plesiosaur hanging from the ceiling? This plesio, an Elasmosaurus, *lends a touch of elegance to a party at the Academy of Natural Sciences in Philadelphia.*

(Ewell Sale Stewart Library, the Academy of Natural Sciences of Philadelphia)

Plesios cruised through the depths not with a front-to-back breast stroke, but by flapping their flippers up and down, much as a bird flaps its wings. Nothosaurs are known only from the Triassic Period, but plesiosaurs lived throughout the Mesozoic Period to the end of the Cretaceous Period.

Plesiosaurs are evidently extinct—unless you happen to believe in the famous Loch Ness Monster, which, with its long neck, looks like a plesiosaur. Plesio necks may have been useful for catching fish, and the animals may have been quite strong and fast so they could snatch darting fish they could not otherwise have caught up to. Although their flapping flippers would not have allowed them to dart through the water, their long, quick necks may have taken up some of the slack of their slow-mo swimming.

> **Fossil Fallacy**
>
> One of the most famous goofs in the history of paleontology concerned the reconstruction of a fossil skeleton of the plesio known as *Elasmosaurus* (plated lizard). This goof touched off a bitter feud between two rival paleontologists, Edward Cope and O.C. Marsh. After Cope described the fossil, Marsh pointed out that he had placed the head at the end of the tail! This fostered ill will between the two that was never resolved.

In addition to the long-necked plesios, some short-necked sorts existed. These resembled whales and could grow to huge sizes—one skull, identified as *Kronosaurus* (time lizard), is 8 feet long. In contrast, long-necked plesios have relatively short skulls.

Lizards Below

One scary but short-lived sort of marine reptile was the mosasaur (lizards from Meuse), which is known only from the Cretaceous Period. (The mosasaur *Tylosaurus* is depicted in one of the color plates.) These reptiles were equipped with large heads and big, powerful, toothy jaws. They propelled themselves around with their tails, eating all manner of things—possibly including plesiosaurs. Some mosasaurs measured more than 30 feet in length, and all had especially flexible, double-jointed jaws. Mosasaurs qualify as lizards precisely because of these flexible jaws, and they're one of the few true lizards ever to take to the sea. In fact, they bear an uncanny resemblance to the mythical sea serpent, even though they became extinct long before sailors began telling their stories.

> **Dig This**
> The first mosasaur skull was discovered in Belgium early in the 19th century. It became a source of controversy when possession of the skull was claimed by French republican forces.

The Shellfish Kind

Still another Mesozoic water reptile was the placodont (flat teeth). These creatures were similar to sea turtles in many respects: They had squarish, beaked heads, and some had armor plating on their backs that resembled a turtle's shell. Unlike turtles, however, some placos had long tails they used to propel themselves through the water; others, like turtles, had only short tails.

Placos were not speedy swimmers. They evidently spent most of their time scuttling across the floors of silent seas with their ragged claws, scraping around for shellfish. Their flat teeth seem well-designed for breaking clamshells.

Herd of Turtles

Much as some of the placodonts resemble turtles, they do not appear to be closely related. The first turtles arrived during the Upper Triassic Period both by land and by sea—and they're still zooming along today. Early turtles had teeth, unlike their modern counterparts, and were not able to tuck their heads and limbs entirely into their shells. Placodonts grew to be as large as 12 feet long.

The Least You Need to Know

➤ The thecodonts gave rise to the dinosaurs, the pterosaurs, and the crocodiles.

➤ Crocodiles haven't changed much in more than 200 million years.

➤ Lizards and snakes have extremely flexible jaws.

➤ Many reptiles adapted successfully to undersea life in the Mesozoic Period but have since died out.

Chapter 17

Warm Fuzzies

> ### In This Chapter
>
> ➤ The origin of mammals
>
> ➤ Pelycosaurs
>
> ➤ Therapsids
>
> ➤ Early mammals

Some of the nicest creatures we know are mammals—warm, covered with fuzz, good parents to their children. They've worked out a pretty good life for themselves, but it hasn't always been so easy. In fact, mammals have gone through a lot to get where they are today.

Some of the toughest times for mammals were right when they started out, during the days of the dinosaurs. It was rough for a while, but the mammals learned from experience. They learned to be themselves and not let bigger critters push them around. And they learned all this without sacrificing their family values.

The mammals' development is really remarkable when you consider what they were like before they became mammals—big, cold, low-down tough types who took whatever they wanted by force. After 50 million years of lording over everyone else, though, they learned their lesson the hard way—with a taste of their own medicine. Only after that did mammals really come into their own.

A Long Line

Paleontologists used to believe that mammals evolved from reptiles (and we've all met people who lead us to believe this is the case!). Today, however, it's clear that mammals and reptiles evolved separately from an older group of amniotes—the first creatures capable of laying eggs on land.

Back in Carboniferous times, the amniote evolved into two different types: the sauropsids, which gave rise to the reptiles, and the synapsids, which eventually gave rise to the mammals. Before the synapsids became mammals, however, they became a group of land animals known as *pelycosaurs* (bowl lizards, named for the shape of their hips). The pelycosaurs were the first big land animals ever—they grew to be up to 20 feet long.

Fossil Fallacy

The term "synapsid," meaning *fused arch*, is misleading. This term refers to a window formed in the skull of these creatures that was once thought to have evolved when the two windows in the skulls of diapsid (*two-arched*) reptiles merged together. Scientists have since concluded, however, that the synapsids evolved before the diapsids, so their windows could never have "fused."

Strutting Their Stuff

Museum Exhibit

Boning Up
The amniotes were the first land animals to lay eggs with shells. (This is in contrast to amphibians, who laid shell-less eggs in the water.) The amniotes take their name from the amnion, which is a special membrane inside the egg that encloses the embryo in its own sack of fluid. These two new features—the shell and the amnion—enabled the amniotes to lay their eggs on dry land.

The pelycosaurs were a diverse and successful group of the Late Carboniferous and Early Permian eras. As big as they were, the pelycosaurs still walked with their legs sprawled out to the side, like modern-day newts and salamanders. Nevertheless, they were the latest thing in land animals, not only because of their size but also because of their teeth and jaws. Although they didn't exactly chew, the teeth did more than simply catch food—they actually cut the food up a little, too.

It Takes All Kinds

Some pelycosaurs were meat-eaters, some ate insects, and some ate plants. In fact, the first plant-eating land animal ever to evolve was a pelycosaur called *Edaphosaurus* (earth lizard). The *Edaphosaurus'* eating habits added a new wrinkle in the game of survival, enabling these animals to survive longer than any other kind of pelycosaur.

Pelycos moved into environments that the reptiles hadn't filled while keeping a toe-hold in the swamp, where they had their roots. Because some ate plants and insects, these varieties moved into the forests, where they had the whole place to themselves. The only predators forest-dwelling pelycos had to worry about were other meat-eating pelycos.

The best-known pelyco meat-eater is *Dimetrodon* (two-sized tooth). True to its name, this pelyco had an ordinary set of sharp, curved teeth as well as two fangs placed strategically toward the end of its snout. Like *Edaphosaurus*, *Dimetrodon* was a sail-backed reptile.

Pelycosaurs came in different sizes. Plant-eaters such as *Edaphosaurus* were the largest, but meat-eaters such as *Dimetrodon* got pretty big too—up to 11 feet long. Among the smallest were the insect eaters, and from these pelycos evolved a whole new group of synapsids.

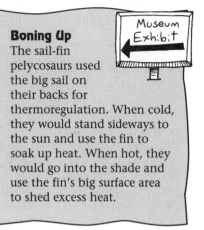

Boning Up
The sail-fin pelycosaurs used the big sail on their backs for thermoregulation. When cold, they would stand sideways to the sun and use the fin to soak up heat. When hot, they would go into the shade and use the fin's big surface area to shed excess heat.

Museum Exhibit

The Dimetrodon *is not a dinosaur; it's a pelycosaur that lived years before the dinos came along.*

(Department of Library Services, American Museum of Natural History; Neg. no.:315862; Photo.:Julius Kirschner)

Permian Wave

This new synapsid group is known as the therapsids (beast arches). These creatures developed a number of characteristics that enabled them to compete successfully against the pelycosaurs—in fact, they helped drive the pelycos to extinction. By the end of the Permian Period, the pelycos had been almost completely replaced by therapsids—plant-eaters as well as meat-eaters.

Close to You

Therapsids were the final evolutionary step before the arrival of true mammals. These reptiles may have developed a number of mammalian characteristics, including hair, although this is impossible to tell for sure from the fossil record.

Like the pelycosaurs—only more so—the therapsids branched into different species and followed different lifestyles to eventually dominate the land. Therapsid varieties included several different kinds of vegetarians, meat-eaters, and insect eaters of different sizes. Some even became specialized for night life: Small seed and insect eaters avoided the big predators by sleeping through the day.

> **Dig This**
> The first herbivores found world-wide were therapsids known as **dicynodonts**. These herbivores came in all sizes, some as big as rhinos and others as small as rabbits. Many of the smaller dicynodonts dug burrows in the ground like modern-day woodchucks and prairie dogs. In a spectacular fossil find in South Africa, several complete skeletons of dicynodonts were discovered still in the spiral-shaped burrows they had dug more than 250 million years ago.

Best of Breed

Take a look at this list of some of the therapsid groups.

➤ **Dinocephalians** (terrible heads)   10-foot-long, 1-ton herbivores of the Permian Era. They developed bony eyebrows and possibly horns, evidently used in head-butting contests among themselves.

➤ **Dicynodonts** (two dog teeth)   Herbivores that dominated the Triassic Period thanks to improved jaws equipped with a pair of powerful tusks.

➤ **Gorgonopsians** (gorgon face; a Gorgon was a Greek mythical creature that turned whoever looked at it to stone)   Big, saber-toothed meat-eaters specialized to prey on large herbivores such as the rhino-sized dicynodonts. Gorgonopsians were top predators for much of the Permian Period. They died out abruptly at the end of the era and left no descendants.

➤ **Cynodonts** (dog teeth)   The most advanced meat-eating therapsid. They took over during the Permian Period before losing out—temporarily—to the thecodonts and, later, to the dinosaurs. Among their descendants are the modern mammals.

Going Places

A number of characteristics made the therapsids more successful than the pelycosaurs, enabling them to dominate the first half of the Triassic Period. For one, therapsids walked with a more upright and streamlined gait, which meant they were able to move around more efficiently than the slower, waddling pelycosaurs.

When pelycosaurs walked, their whole bodies shifted from side to side because their legs stuck out so much. The therapsids moved straight ahead, wasting less energy in the process. Because they could move more quickly than the pelycos, the therapsids may have been able to keep themselves warmer, too. Generating more of their own body heat may have enabled them to move farther away from warm, tropical regions into colder territories they could have all to themselves.

Fast Food

Another significant new development that first appeared in therapsids is a palate separating the sinuses from the mouth—this made it possible to eat and breathe at the same time. Pelycosaurs had less need for this because they had a lower metabolism and thus didn't need to breathe as much. Pelycosaurs could easily breathe between mouthfuls.

> **Dig This**
> Some therapsids, notably the dicynodonts, apparently kept cool in hot weather much as hippos do today—by wallowing in mud. This is evident from the fact that some dicynos have been fossilized in a standing position, which suggests they died while standing deep in mud.

Therapsids, however, ran at a higher speed, so they needed more air as well as more food. Their mouths eventually evolved to let them get both at the same time. This trait is especially significant because it later enabled suckling, or breast-feeding, which evolved not long afterwards in mammals, if not in the therapsids themselves.

What's more, the cynodont therapsids became specialized chewers with precisely designed sets of teeth of different sizes. Like mammals of today, cynodont therapsids had teeth for stabbing, teeth for cutting, and teeth for grinding—all attached to the same pair of jaws. With teeth that worked as efficient food-processing equipment, they could digest their food much more rapidly.

A Fuzzy Distinction

The therapsids may well have developed still other traits that increased their advantage over the pelycosaurs. Some of these traits, such as hair and the suckling of young, may have been features that we associate with mammals, but it is impossible to tell precisely when these traits evolved because they didn't become fossilized.

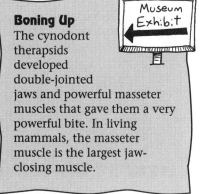

> **Boning Up**
> The cynodont therapsids developed double-jointed jaws and powerful masseter muscles that gave them a very powerful bite. In living mammals, the masseter muscle is the largest jaw-closing muscle.

Because we can't tell just when these definitive mammalian feature evolved, scientists recognize a technical distinction between mammals and therapsids that hinges on the way their jaw joints connect. Apart from this distinguishing feature, the more advanced therapsids may have been very similar to the first mammals.

Out After Dark

Although no fossil record exists of the precise origin of many features we associate with mammals, some mammalian traits are evident in therapsid fossils. Among these traits are whiskers; some therapsid snouts have marks that suggest the presence of big hair follicles.

These fossil snouts belonged to some of the smaller seed- and insect-eating therapsids. These creatures may have developed whiskers as an adaptation to a nocturnal lifestyle. Whiskers are useful at night because they can tell you when something's right in front of you when it's too dark to see. It's also possible that therapsids developed coats of hair or fur that helped them conserve body heat.

Twice Bitten

The therapsids developed and passed along to the mammals the practice of growing two—and only two—sets of teeth. By keeping the same set of teeth longer—a set of "milk" teeth in immature animals, and a replacement, adult set—the more advanced therapsids avoided gaps in their specialized set of choppers.

In contrast, pelycosaurs and their distant cousins, the reptiles, had teeth that could be replaced throughout their entire lifetimes. This meant that they were often likely to have missing teeth as the new ones began to grow in. Because these creatures used their teeth for stabbing rather than slicing, missing teeth were not a big deal. However, for the therapsids—whose teeth formed a specialized slicing mechanism—missing teeth could gum up the works. Placing a limit on tooth replacement helped minimize this problem.

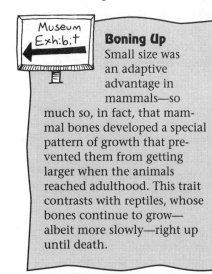

Boning Up
Small size was an adaptive advantage in mammals—so much so, in fact, that mammal bones developed a special pattern of growth that prevented them from getting larger when the animals reached adulthood. This trait contrasts with reptiles, whose bones continue to grow— albeit more slowly—right up until death.

Win Some, Lose Some

Some of the more sophisticated characteristics developed by the therapsids helped them take over from the pelycosaurs as dominating land animals. Other traits, however, developed later in response to the fact they, in turn, were being dominated—first by the thecodonts and then by the dinosaurs.

The therapsid heyday drew to a close near the end of the Triassic Period. By this time, the bigger therapsids died off in the face of predation and competition from their archosaur rivals. Only the smaller, agile, nocturnal therapsids held on, and these animals evolved into small, agile, nocturnal mammals.

Hearing of New Things

We mentioned that the official difference between the first mammals and the last of the therapsids has to do with their jaw joints. Admittedly, this doesn't seem like an especially exciting development. From a broader perspective, however, jaw development in mammals is one of those miraculous evolutionary events, similar to the development of breathing air or flying.

New Vibrations

As mammal jaws developed, they came to rely increasingly on a single bone in the lower jaw. Because mammals were specialized chewers, they needed strong, efficient jaws instead of the reptiles' complex, multiboned jaws designed more for swallowing big, struggling mouthfuls than for chewing.

The extra reptilian bones didn't disappear entirely from mammal jaws, however—they got put to use in a completely new way that helped mammals to survive in their nocturnal environment. These bones became the hammer and anvil bones of the middle ear, capable of picking up sounds too faint for most reptiles to hear.

In fact, the evolutionary process that resulted in mammalian ear bones is mirrored in the development of mammal embryos. This mirroring is especially clear when comparing mammal embryo growth to that of reptiles. Mammal embryos and reptile embryos appear to have very similar jaw bones. In reptiles, these bones develop into jaw bones, but in mammals, they develop into the hammer and anvil bones of the ear.

Sensing the Possibilities

Sharp hearing came in handy for the nocturnal mammals, who were unable to rely on their vision to tell them what was out there. Along with their resonating ear bones, these mammals also developed fleshy ears for focusing sounds.

In addition to keen hearing, mammals also developed a keen sense of smell that helped them determine what they were up against in the dark. Developing these senses was not simply a matter of growing better ears and noses; it also involved developing more sophisticated brains for processing the sensory information. As a result, the early mammals had large brains compared to their small sizes.

> **Dig This**
> Early Triassic reptiles who lacked a sophisticated hearing mechanism may well have "listened" by setting their jaws on the ground to pick up vibrations. This would have been easy for them to do because they ordinarily held their heads close to the ground anyway—and most of the things walking around were really, really big.

A Little Goes a Long Way

Life for the early mammals as small, timid, nocturnal creatures prompted them to develop a number of other miraculous features, including live birth and suckling of the young. These characteristics helped mammals to remain small, a trait that enabled them to survive the age of the mighty dinosaurs.

By staying small, early mammals stayed out of the way of predators. During the Triassic Period, mammals grew to be no more than 4 inches long. Their babies, of course, were even smaller. Because they were so little at birth, it took these mammals some time to develop to the point of being able to care for themselves. For one thing, unlike reptile babies, infant mammals were born without teeth, so they were totally unable to feed themselves. This meant that at least one parent—in the mammals' case, the mother—had to take care of the babies.

Boning Up
Birds, of course, do not nurse their hatchlings the way mammals nurse their babies. They do, however, have a specially evolved part of their bodies, called an incubation patch, on which the feathers are especially downy and well-suited for keeping the eggs—and later the hatchlings—warm.

Definosaurus
The **placenta** is a mammalian female organ that connects the mother's bloodstream to her babies', supplying them with all their physical needs. The **marsupium** is an analogous organ belonging to a different kind of mammal. It's a pouch in which a newborn, undeveloped baby can stay and feed until it becomes mature enough to stand on its own two feet.

This care involved protecting as well as feeding the little ones. The first mammals were egg-layers, and the mother probably stayed with the eggs (and later with the hatchlings) almost all the time, keeping them warm and feeding them. Of course, it's hard to get food for your babies and keep them warm at the same time. It was a good thing for the baby mammals, then, that suckling evolved.

Mother's Milk

Scientists think suckling evolved gradually as babies started licking the fur of their mothers, which may have been bathed with sweat and other secretions that provided nourishment in the form of fats, salt, and other nutriments.

In fact, this form of fur-feeding is actually practiced today by an ancient group of mammals known as *monotremes*. This living group of egg-laying mammals includes the spiny anteater and the duckbilled platypus. Monotreme mothers don't have teats. Instead, their milk glands are connected to simple open pores in their bellies. Monotreme hatchlings lap the fur on their mother's stomach to receive the milk she secretes for them.

It seems likely that the suckling of milk developed from the sort of fur-lapping practiced by monotremes. Suckling provides a significant adaptive advantage to species with helpless young, because milk is extremely nourishing and is right there on tap where the little ones can reach it.

To the Manner Born

Live birth ranks as another major mammalian improvement. Live birth means Mom has to spend less time sitting on the nest waiting for the eggs to hatch. Instead, the embryos develop inside the uterus. In fact, mammals have evolved two different techniques for bearing live young.

The common technique today involves an organ called the *placenta*, which is developed specifically for the purpose of nourishing the embryo. The placenta actually connects the babies' vital processes to those of the mother, providing food and oxygen through a dense mass of vessels and tubes. The other technique involves a kind of second womb—a pouch known as a *marsupium*.

Apart from monotremes, who still lay eggs, mammals are divided into two kinds: placental mammals (like you, me, and your pet gerbil) and marsupials (including possums, kangaroos, koalas, and Tasmanian devils). Instead of a placenta, marsupial mothers have a pouch where the baby—which is, at first, even less developed than a newborn placental mammal—can nurse and grow.

Boning Up

Although placental mammals and marsupials evolved side by side, placentals won out over their pouchy competitors, nearly driving them to extinction in most of the world. Fortunately for the marsupials, they remained alive in large numbers on an island continent—Australia—where no placental rivals existed.

Getting Ribbed Off

One additional achievement of the mammals that allowed them to stay small and agile is the disappearance of a number of ribs just above the hips. You may be able to tell for yourself that your ribs don't run all the way down to your hips—they stop about three-quarters of the way from your armpits. In the early mammals, fewer ribs made birth easier and also made it easier to hop around.

What's more, mammals' exceptional agility allowed some of them to emerge from the cover of darkness into a new environment where they could be safe from the dinosaurs—the trees. In fact, it was from these tree-climbing mammals that human beings eventually descended.

Inheriting the Earth

Not until after the non-bird dinosaurs died out did mammals come out of hiding and take over the planet. Why the dinosaurs died remains a mystery, but it seems likely that they weren't killed off by the fuzzy, 4-inch mammals who occupied the planet at the time. Having survived the dinosaurs, however, the mammals were ready to populate a whole new world.

The Least You Need to Know

➤ Mammals descended from a group of amniotes called synapsids.

➤ The first large land animals were mammalian ancestors, the pelycosaurs.

➤ The therapsids, from whom the mammals evolved, dominated the Late Permian and Early Triassic periods before losing out to the archosaurs.

➤ Many mammalian characteristics developed as adaptations to small size and a nocturnal lifestyle.

➤ Mammals include the monotremes (who still lay eggs), the marsupials (whose young develop in pouches), and the placental mammals (like us).

Part 5
Famous Finds

The history of the search for dinosaur fossils spans about 200 years and includes episodes that took place all over the world. At first, only a few 19th-century naturalists had any idea that dinosaurs existed. As more fossils were found, however, more people became interested. Private collectors and museums launched expeditions all over the world. People started to pay attention as more fossils came to light and scientists continued to develop ideas about what dinosaurs were and how they lived. Throughout this process, money, politics, and professional rivalries played as big a part as in any other scientific pursuit.

Chapter 18

Lost and Found

Of course people haven't always known about dinosaurs. Their discovery involved the pooled resources of many countries and many scientific disciplines. In fact, the scientific background necessary for recovering and interpreting the fossil record has developed only fairly recently—since the late 18th century.

Now that this science is available, the ancient rock formations seem like big lost-and-found boxes for us to rifle through and look for all kinds of cool stuff we never realized we had. At first, though, it was hard for people to understand what they were looking at when they were confronted with dinosaur fossils. What's more, the new discoveries made some people uncomfortable because they meant that some long-held ideas about the nature of life had to be revised—ideas, for example, about the role of living things on earth.

At the beginnings of dinosaur science, the revision process and the new discoveries were closely tied together. New finds demanded significant new ideas to account for them. The new ideas weren't always right of course, but most of them make pretty good sense when you consider how unheard-of dinosaurs were.

Old Bones, New Views

For all we know, people may have been digging up dinosaur fossils since before they invented the wheel. The problem was, it wasn't until well into the 19th century that people began to figure out what these fossils actually were—remains of a large, extinct group of creatures that dominated the planet long before human beings lived. To achieve this recognition of dinosaur fossils, the science of paleontology had to establish itself.

They Might Be Giants

Before the early years of the 19th century, a few scattered references to strange bones left by mysterious and perhaps magical creatures were found in old books. In 1676, for example, a book by Robert Plot describes what he identifies as the scrotum of a giant human being. This curious item has since been lost, but judging from the description of the find, its location, and the drawing included in Plot's book, it seems to have been part of the thigh bone of a *Megalosaurus*.

Boning Up

Fossils generally do not stay preserved as well when they are exposed to the air as they do underground. To prevent fossils from crumbling, scientists often coat them with shellac or some other fixative.

It is likely that many other dinosaur bones have been lost or simply eroded away because people didn't realize what they were. The famous explorer William Clark (as in "Lewis and Clark") described some partially crumbled bones he identified in 1806 as belonging to a giant fish. No one knows what became of these bones, but they were discovered in what is now the famous Hell Creek formation, a site rich in dinosaur fossils—they may well have been dinosaur bones. Who knows how many others have stumbled on dinosaur bones, picked them up, shown them to their friends as curiosities, and then simply lost them, having no idea what they actually were.

Vive la Difference!

Before the modern concept of the dinosaur could emerge out of the fossil record, scientists had to learn to see life on earth in a complete, systematized way. Back in Chapter 4, we mentioned the work of the Swedish naturalist Carl Linnaeus, who developed a system for classifying living things. With the Linnaean system in place, scientists became more methodical in identifying creatures.

In fact, many started collecting fossils not just out of curiosity, but to learn more about life in general by comparing fossil specimens to one another and to living creatures. Thanks to careful scientific study and comparison, it became gradually clear that creatures existed long ago unlike any creatures still alive today. One of the first scientists to reach this conclusion was the French anatomist and paleontologist Baron Georges Cuvier.

They Don't Make 'Em Like They Used To

Cuvier conducted a study of elephant bones, comparing fossil specimens to skeletons of modern species. He noticed that different skeletons had bones that corresponded to one another but had different particular shapes that indicated they belonged to different species. As a result of this study, Cuvier found that some groups of elephant were no longer around. Two kinds of ancient elephant, the mastodon and the mammoth, were clearly different from living elephants.

Because of his fame as a fossil anatomist, Cuvier was called upon to offer his opinion on a huge set of jaws and teeth recovered in the Netherlands, evidently belonging to an ancient marine animal. Some believed this jaw belonged to whale. Others noticed, however, that the fossil had characteristics in common with modern lizards. This was baffling, as no known species of lizard lives in the ocean.

Cuvier supported the view that the jaws belonged to an ocean lizard (later named *Mosasaurus*) and suggested that the kind had died out. At the time, this was controversial because the concept of extinction was unknown to most people, and it was unacceptable to many others for religious reasons. They believed God would not create creatures only to allow them to die out.

> **Dig This**
> The first mosasaur jaws were discovered in a Late-Cretaceous chalk quarry in Maastricht, Holland. This site is famous for its fossils, including many ancient sea shells. The quarry is carved into the heart of a mountain and consists of huge manmade caverns with roofs supported by vaulted stone archways. In honor of this important site, a section of geologic time has been named the Maastrichtian stage.

Perfect World

This way of thinking was not simply a traditional religious view; it reflected ideas from 17th- and 18th-century enlightenment philosophy about the perfection of the universe. Many of Cuvier's contemporaries saw the universe as a complicated but perfectly designed machine, in which all the parts—including living things—were necessary to keep the whole running smoothly.

The notion of extinction made the universe seem messy and imperfect. As a result, many refused to accept Cuvier's ideas and insisted that the creatures he said were no longer alive continued to exist in unknown regions of the world. Ultimately, however, extinction became impossible to refute in the face of increasing fossil evidence.

Fossil Firsts

A great deal of the evidence for extinction, of course, comes in the form of dinosaur fossils. The first dinosaur fossils to be discovered and written up in a scientific paper included a jaw, a pelvis, part of a shoulder, and some vertebrae. These bones were described by the English cleric and geologist Dean Buckland, who said they belonged to a "giant reptile" he called *Megalosaurus* (giant lizard).

Mantell Pieces

The very next year, in 1825, another fossil was described by the English physician Gideon Mantell. Earlier, in 1822, Mantell had written a book on fossils found in South Downs, England. During that same year, Mantell's wife, Mary, discovered some fossilized teeth in a pile of rocks. Mary Mantell shared her husband's interest in fossils and drew a number of illustrations for the book.

Dental Work

Mantell believed these fossils were the teeth of a big, ancient reptile, and he sought confirmation on his view from his countryman Buckland and from the eminent Frenchman, Cuvier. Buckland disagreed with Mantell's view of the teeth's age, suggesting that they might have come from more recent sediments that got mixed in with the older layers of rock that formed the site. Cuvier's assessment was even more disappointing—he suggested the teeth belonged to a rhinoceros!

Mantell, however, was not convinced. Shortly thereafter, he met an anatomist named Samuel Stutchbury, who said the teeth resembled large versions of those on a modern iguana. This observation reinforced Mantell's view that the teeth belonged to a large lizard. In 1825 he published the second scientific description ever written of a dinosaur fossil, which he called *Iguanodon* (iguana tooth).

Getting Organized

Not until many years later were *Iguanodon* and *Megalosaurus*, along with a recently discovered specimen named *Hylaeosaurus*, named "dinosaurs." This name resulted from the studies of the English anatomist Sir Richard Owen, who said these three creatures belonged to a single group of giant reptiles.

Owen was the leading anatomist in England, and his view, presented in 1841 at a meeting of the British Association for the Advancement of Science, met with praise and excitement. By now a considerable number of scientists, including Owen and Buckland, had come to accept the idea of extinction, despite deep religious convictions.

When Bad Things Happen to Good Dinosaurs

In fact, Buckland and Owen were religious themselves. They looked at extinction as an act of God, resulting from the kind of catastrophe described in the book of Genesis in which God sends a flood to kill everything on earth except for Noah, his family, and his boatload of animals. Owen believed there may have been a number of catastrophes similar to the biblical flood—this view is known as *catastrophism*. According to this view, after each catastrophe, God repopulated the planet with a whole new set of living things.

Catastrophism made sense of the fossil record by using ideas found in the Bible to explain the existence of fossilized creatures no longer alive. Such fossils could be considered "ante-diluvian" (before the flood) or even "pre-adamic" (before Adam, the first man created by God). These fossils could be interpreted as God's way of warning human beings not to be evil—or risk suffering the same fate!

The Latest Rage from Another Age

Owen was highly regarded during this time in his career. He was known as "the English Cuvier" and was personally acquainted with Queen Victoria, who was greatly interested in Owen's work. Owen visited the palace from time to time to speak with her about paleontology. In addition to knighting him, the Queen gave Owen an estate to which he moved with his family, living there the rest of his life.

Yesteryear's Models

Thanks largely to Owen's work, fascination with dinosaurs caught on in subsequent years. Owen was offered the job of overseeing the construction of life-size models of the three first-known dinosaurs, to be set up in Sydenham, an estate in the suburbs of London.

Definosaurus — Glossary

The view that extinction takes place when God periodically annihilates living things by means of a flood or other disaster is known as **catastrophism**. This view reconciled the idea of extinction with biblical thinking during the mid-19th century.

Boning Up — Museum Exhibit

One of the opening sentences of Charles Dickens' novel *Bleak House* alludes to the connection between a catastrophic flood and the dinosaurs: "As much mud in the streets as if the waters had but newly retired from the face of the Earth, and it would not be wonderful to meet a Megalosaurus, forty feet long or so, waddling like an elephantine lizard up Holborn Hill."

These models were added to an exhibit known as the Crystal Palace, which was originally installed in Hyde Park in London at the very first world's fair. This display was big news at the time, and tourists can still see the famous exhibit, even though it no longer enjoys the cutting-edge status it had in Owen's day.

Dig This

Hawkins was offered the opportunity to construct more of his dinosaur models in Central Park in New York City. Hawkins eagerly accepted and traveled to America. Midway through the planning stages, however, funds were cut off due to the growing influence of the Tammany Hall political machine, run by New York's infamous Boss Tweed.

Owen developed his conceptions of *Megalosaurus*, *Hyleaosaurus*, and *Iguanodon* with the sculptor Coleman Hawkins, who constructed models according to Owen's specifications. These models were based on scant information about what these creatures were really like and, as we now know, reflect a somewhat inaccurate conception of dinosaurs. The *Iguanodon* model is especially speculative, based on little more than a few teeth.

Owen imagined his dinosaurs basically as lizards with the shape and size of a large hippopotamus. The models are crouched on four massive legs and look like they are waiting for a chicken-sized fly to come along so they can snap it up in their jaws. We now know that only *Hylaeosaurus*, of the three dinosaurs represented, was actually four-footed.

In the Belly of the Beast

Although the squat, four-footed posture of the *Iguanodon* model hasn't stood up to subsequent anatomical findings about the animal, the model was especially useful for an 1853 New Year's Eve dinner held in honor of the exhibit. For this dinner, a platform was built around the *Iguanodon* model, its back was taken off, and seats were put in so that 21 honored guests could be served dinner inside it. Owen sat at the head of the table, just behind the head of the *Iguanodon*.

Owen's position as head man in dinosaurs, however, did not last much longer. A new way of thinking was in the wind that transformed the way people thought not only about dinosaurs but about life in general. This was Darwin's theory of natural selection, a theory that Owen strongly opposed.

Bridging the Gap

Although many joined Owen in opposing Darwin's theory, the philosophy had important supporters, too. Among the most important of these was T.H. Huxley, a British paleontologist who was the first to use dinosaur fossils as evidence for evolution. Huxley believed that dinosaurs represented an intermediate step in the evolution of birds from reptiles. He was especially interested in the bird-like characteristics of dinosaurs, including the three-toed feet of *Iguanodon*.

Eating in style inside Hawkins' reproduction of Owen's Iguanodon.

(Ewell Sale Stewart Library, The Academy of Natural Sciences of Philadelphia)

Born in the U.S.A.

A number of important new finds provided Huxley with evidence that dinosaurs served as an evolutionary link between birds and reptiles. Among these finds was the first of many dinosaur skeletons to be discovered in North America. This was described in 1858 by the American anatomist Joseph Leidy, who named the specimen *Hadrosaurus*.

The hadro bones were discovered by an amateur collector from Philadelphia named William Foulke. Foulke heard that a neighbor had once found a number of large vertebrae on his farm. Unfortunately, this was 20 years before, and these bones had since been distributed among visitors.

> **Dig This**
> An *Iguanodon* fossil discovered in Maidstone, England, identified the first iggy jaw yet found. In honor of this discovery, the city altered its coat of arms to include a heraldic *Iguanodon* rather than the more conventional griffin or lion.

Undaunted, Foulke got permission to dig around on the farm for more fossils. After a lot of searching and digging, Foulke's crew of hired helpers uncovered a partial skeleton.

Leidy later identified the find as a dinosaur closely related to *Iguanodon*. This was important not only as the first major North American dinosaur fossil and as the discovery of a new dinosaur genus, but it also led to a drastic revision of what dinosaurs were assumed to be like.

The first dinosaur found in America was this Hadrosaurus. *We now know that this fossil was assembled with the wrong head.*

(Ewell Sale Stewart Library, The Academy of Natural Sciences of Philadelphia)

SKELETON OF THE GREAT FOSSIL LIZARD OF NEW JERSEY.

Standing Up for Evolution

One of the most surprising and significant features of the new *Hadrosaurus* was the fact that its forelimbs were quite a bit shorter than its hind limbs. To Leidy, this creature looked very little like the dinosaurs as Owen imagined them. Instead, it obviously moved around upright, on its hind feet.

Dig This
Leidy led a distinguished career as a professor, trustee, and finally president of Philadelphia's Academy of Natural Sciences. Today a big bronze statue of Leidy stands in front of the academy.

Huxley was especially interested in this fact. He even suggested that Owen's models were inaccurate because they depicted the dinosaurs on all fours. Perhaps *Iguanodon*, like *Hadrosaurus*, was a bipedal creature. The possibility excited Huxley because it meant that dinosaurs were even less like modern lizards than previously believed—and more like birds.

Huxley's belief that many dinosaurs were bipedal was born out by two important finds. The first was a series of fossil trackways, thought at first to belong to birds but later identified as Triassic dinosaur footprints, found in the Connecticut valley.

Making Tracks

These tracks, popularly referred to as prints left by "Noah's raven," were collected and studied by geologist Edward Hitchcock. Hitchcock believed the tracks were left by wading birds, despite their enormous size. He imagined these birds were like enormous ostriches, up to 20 feet tall. Huxley agreed that the smaller prints were left by ancient birds but suggested the larger ones were made by bipedal dinosaurs. In fact, it seems clear today that all of Hitchcock's tracks were left by dinosaurs, as they predate the evolution of birds.

Working in the Coal Mine

Irrefutable evidence that *Iguanodon* was bipedal arrived with another important find made in a coal mine in Bernissart, Belgium, in 1878. During the Cretaceous Period, the mine had evidently been a ravine, into which at least 31 *Iguanodons* fell to their deaths before being quickly buried and eventually fossilized. These 31 iggies were dug up, reassembled, and put on display in the Brussels Royal Museum of Natural History, where they can still be seen.

On their way from the mine to the museum, however, these fossils became the subject of a thorough, lifelong study by the French paleontologist Louis Dollo. Dollo had the opportunity to study dinosaurs in a way no one could before, by comparing the fossils of a number of individuals of the same species. In fact, he became a Belgian citizen so that it would be easier for him to spend all his time with the *Iguanodons*.

Dollo took advantage of his opportunity by expanding the field of paleontology to include the lifestyle of the extinct animals. He focused not only on the bones and their structure but also on their functions. He even studied the area where the fossils were found in an attempt to recreate the environment of the original iggies.

Dollo confirmed that iggies were bipedal—and what's more, his findings supported Huxley's view of iggies as having features in common both with birds and with crocodiles. He also revised one more conception of the iggies stemming from the early work of Richard Owen. Associated with the fossils Owen worked with was a big spike. Owen placed this at the tip of the snout, where it looked like a horn, but Dollo showed that each iggy had two spikes—not on their snouts, but on their thumbs.

Boning Up

Huxley's claim that dinosaurs represent an evolutionary step between reptiles and birds was the result of his first attempt to find evidence for evolution in the fossil record. His second try, even more convincing, was based on a more complete sequence of fossils. He showed that modern horses, with their single "toe," or hoof, descended from a dog-sized, five-toed creature originally named *Eohippus* (dawn horse) and now called *Hyracotherium*.

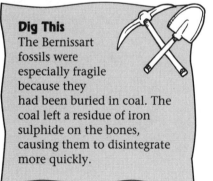

Dig This

The Bernissart fossils were especially fragile because they had been buried in coal. The coal left a residue of iron sulphide on the bones, causing them to disintegrate more quickly.

Right from the Start

With these and a number of other important early finds, the field of dinosaur study had taken shape and was off to a good start. In some ways, the start was better than people realized, because a number of speculative ideas about dinosaurs put forward at the time have turned out to be correct.

Among these are ideas that were rejected shortly afterward but that have since become widely accepted. For example, Owen's claim that dinosaurs constitute a single group of related creatures was rejected for a while when scientists came to the conclusion that the bird butts and the lizard butts (Saurischians and Ornithischians) were not closely related. These days, however, it seems that Owen was right in the first place.

Another early idea that was rejected and later accepted was Huxley's view of dinosaurs as the ancestors of birds. In fact, given that this idea is by now almost as old as Darwin's theory of natural selection, it seems a little surprising that it has made such a splash in recent years. You'll read more about this controversy in Chapter 24.

The Least You Need to Know

➤ Baron Georges Cuvier was the first to demonstrate the existence of extinct creatures.

➤ The first dinosaur fossils were discovered in England in the 1820s by Dean Buckland and by Gideon and Mary Mantell.

➤ Sir Richard Owen first identified dinosaurs as a group in 1841.

➤ T.H. Huxley was a strong advocate of Darwin's theory of natural selection who saw dinosaurs as an evolutionary step between reptiles and birds.

➤ Edward Hitchcock discovered and catalogued a number of dinosaur trackways in the Connecticut valley—but thought they were made by giant birds.

Fossil Frontiers

One of the great sagas of the American West is the discovery and recovery, from the 1860s to the early 20th century, of a wealth of dinosaur fossils. During this time, fossil prospectors uncovered veritable bone bonanzas, including some of the largest finds ever, many of which consisted of complete and nearly complete skeletons. When people took it into their heads to actually go looking for fossils, it was astonishing how many were out there.

In true Wild West fashion, big careers and lots of prestige were made and lost, lots of money was spent, and lots of people braved freezing snow and desert heat in search of big, heavy bones. As big and heavy as they were, these bones were worth their weight in gold, both for the public interest they could generate and for their scientific value.

The legacy of this chapter in the history of dinosaur discovery fills the halls of major museums around the world. After all, the incentive for collecting fossils is not simply that scientists want to study them, but that ordinary people want to see them, standing straight and tall like living creatures once again.

Fossil Feud

Dinosaur discovery in America during the late 1800s was dominated by a pair of strong-willed scientists named Othniel Charles Marsh and Edward Drinker Cope. Through their prodigious efforts, well over a hundred new species of dinosaurs were discovered, along with hundreds of tons of fossils for the scientists and museums back east. The names Marsh and Cope have become almost inseparable: They shared many of the same ambitions, explored many of the same fossil sites, and were often the first to comment on one another's work. As it happened, unfortunately, they were bitter enemies.

Edward Drinker Cope, one of the early stars of dinosaur science.

(Ewell Sale Stewart Library, The Academy of Natural Sciences of Philadelphia)

Good Scientists with Bad Chemistry

Their lifelong rivalry seems to have stemmed from petty motives—professional jealousy and personal dislike for one another. Each was a character in his own way. Cope was impetuous and high-strung; Marsh was crusty and proud. Their bad personal chemistry led to a number of unpleasant incidents throughout their parallel careers. On the positive side, it also spurred them both to achieve great things in their efforts to outdo one another.

Both men were of independent means. Marsh's uncle was the wealthy banker and entrepreneur George Peabody. Peabody paid for Marsh's education at Yale, and later, at Marsh's suggestion, endowed Yale's Peabody Museum of Natural History, along with a professorship for Marsh. Marsh's professorship involved a comfortable living and no teaching duties, so he was free to devote himself to his obsession with dinosaur fossils. He also had the money to hire helpers, which enabled him to amass an unprecedented collection.

Child Prodigy

While Marsh was good at managing people, Cope had a way of drawing attention to himself. He was an eager student of living things and, at 18, published his first scientific paper on the classification of salamanders. He went on to become a professor at Haverford College at 24 but soon left because he wanted to look for dinosaur bones.

Dig This
While Cope was a child prodigy, Marsh was something of a late bloomer. He delayed going to school for many years because he had no money to go. By the time he went, he was so much older than his classmates that they nicknamed him "Daddy."

On leaving Haverford, Cope bought a house in Haddonfield, New Jersey, where the first *Hadrosaurus* skeleton had been found. He began traveling to stone quarries in the area, introducing himself and asking to be notified in case any fossils were found. His plan worked. In 1866, when some quarrymen came upon some old bones, Cope was called in right away.

Cope identified the fossils as a new kind of meat-eating dinosaur, which he called *Laelaps aquilingis* (Laelaps is the name of a dog from Greek mythology that was turned into stone). Cope suggested that *Laelaps* leapt after its prey like a kangaroo with claws on its feet. The find brought Cope considerable notoriety.

Shortly afterward, Cope was sent a 40-foot reptile fossil found in Kansas. He spent years restoring and describing this find and eventually called it *Elasmosaurus* (ribbon lizard) because of its long, snaky neck and tail.

Cope's restored elasmo, which we now know is a kind of plesiosaur, went on display at the Academy of Natural Science Museum in Philadelphia. In addition, he published a description and a drawing of the skeleton, indicating that it was one of the most peculiar creatures that ever lived.

Cope's drawing (done on the back of a letter) of his first big discovery, which he called Laelaps.

(Ewell Sale Stewart Library, The Academy of Natural Sciences of Philadelphia)

Bones of Contention

In 1870, Marsh visited the museum, where Cope personally showed him the mounted elasmo and explained its unusual features. The neck, in particular, was extremely flexible, unlike any other creature's. Marsh then pointed out that what Cope was calling the neck was actually the tail. Cope had put the skeleton together with the vertebrae facing the wrong direction and with the head attached to the end of the tail!

Dig This
Cope was so embarrassed by his *Elasmosaurus* mistake that he attempted to buy up all the published copies of his description of the fossil.

The incident sparked bad feelings between the two that were never resolved. From that point on, each did whatever he could to make the other look bad. Many years later, for example, Marsh pointed out that the name *Laelaps*, which Cope had given more than 10 years ago to his first new dinosaur, had already been taken. Marsh proceeded to give it a new name, *Dryptosaurus*. Cope responded by objecting to a name Marsh had given to one of his prize finds, a big sauropod he called *Titanosaurus*.

Top Dog Gets the Bones

The rivalry became more intense because both men were widely recognized as experts. In 1877, a man named Arthur Lakes discovered some huge dinosaur bones near Morrison, Colorado, just southwest of Denver, and he sent some of them to Marsh. When Marsh didn't respond, Lakes sent some more bones to Cope.

Cope was excited by the find and immediately set to work on a paper describing the fossils. At this point, Marsh belatedly wrote to Lakes, sending money and telling him to keep the fossils a secret. With money in his pocket from Marsh, Lakes wrote to Cope saying Marsh had bought the fossils and requesting Cope to send them to their owner.

Meanwhile, Marsh sent a helper to the Morrison site and arranged to have it excavated. The site was rich in fossils, and it looked like Marsh's luck was good. Shortly afterward, however, another collector exploring the Morrison formation further south sent some fossils to Cope.

Cope immediately hired a crew and sent them to Colorado, where they worked nearly side-by-side with Marsh's men amid an atmosphere of tense suspicion. A particularly special find for Cope was a nearly complete skeleton of an enormous sauropod he named *Camarasaurus* (chambered lizard). In fact, finds made by both groups shed light on the big brontosaur-style dinos, fueling international speculation about whether they lived under water or fed from the treetops like giraffes.

> **Dig This**
> Both Cope and Marsh's crews improvised techniques for excavating and preserving fossils. Cope's men made protective coverings called "jackets" for fossils out of burlap bags dipped in paste made of overboiled rice. When the rice paste hardened, the fossils could be shipped back east more safely.

Dinosaur Derby

The fossils from further south, where Cope's group worked, turned out to be larger and easier to get, so Cope had the upper hand for a time. It wasn't long, however, before the tide turned in Marsh's direction once more. That same year, Marsh received word of huge fossil fields in Wyoming at a place called Como Bluff (about 100 miles northwest of Laramie, today).

This word came from a couple of railroad men who noticed the fossils while workin' on the railroad and decided they would have a better time in the dinosaur-digging business. These men had obviously heard that fossils were hot items that wealthy paleontologists back east were squabbling over, so they took on phony names for secrecy and got in touch with Marsh.

Marsh sent one of his assistants to look the site over. Then he hired the railroad workers, along with some helpers of his own, to excavate. Como Bluff soon turned out to be even richer than the Morrison formation. In fact, Marsh's men worked the area for 12 years, sending back hundreds of fossils—including duckbills, which became something of a specialty for Marsh, who published a number of papers on them. In addition, Como Bluff yielded an exotic new dinosaur, which Marsh named *Stegosaurus*.

> **Dig This**
> Marsh became internationally famous for his fossil discoveries at Como Bluff. The attention, however, wasn't always flattering. He was represented in a cartoon published in England as a ringmaster at a circus, dressed in a stars-and-stripes tuxedo with dinosaur skeletons performing around him. Clearly the cartoonist was making fun of Marsh for walking a fine line between science and showmanship.

Live By the Shovel, Die By the Shovel

While Marsh's men worked at Como Bluff, Cope came west himself to search for fossils in Montana. He ultimately lost out to Marsh in the race for dinosaur bones, though. Unfortunately, Cope made some bad investments in mines and lost almost all his money, so he could no longer finance full-scale fossil expeditions.

Cope and Marsh are often remembered more for their feuding than for their discoveries. Despite their sometimes petty treatment of one another, however, they were both distinguished scientists. Two years before his death, Cope was elected president of the American Association for the Advancement of Science. Marsh became president of the National Academy of Sciences.

Building with Bones

The wild and woolly days of Cope and Marsh gave way to a calmer approach to fossil hunting. For one thing, subsequent excavation parties tended to be less antagonistic to one another. For another, it was no longer the rule for expeditions to be funded by individual private paleontologists. Instead, professional fossil hunters were usually backed by museums, which were often backed, in turn, by tycoons such as J.P. Morgan and Andrew Carnegie.

Exhibit A

Perhaps the world leader in dinosaur exhibits among museums today is the American Museum of Natural History in New York City. The museum's dinosaur reputation was built largely through the efforts of Henry Osborn, the founder of the museum's Department of Vertebrate Paleontology, and later the museum's president.

Osborn became interested in paleontology as an undergraduate at Princeton after attending a course in geology and hearing about the Marsh's exploits out West. A friend suggested they organize an expedition of their own.

Years later, while working for the American Museum, Osborn recognized how valuable a good collection of dinosaur fossils would be for the museum's prestige. He therefore arranged in 1897 for a group to go back to Como Bluff, Wyoming, from which Marsh's crew had departed less than 10 years earlier.

Dinosaur Express

In fact, the Marsh expedition hadn't exhausted the Como supply of valuable fossils. Dinosaur bones were still so abundant that some turned up as building materials in a cabin belonging to a sheep herder. In its honor, the site became known as Bone Cabin quarry.

This trip was funded with the help of the famous J.P. Morgan. The millionaire's money came in handy not only for paying the workers who dug up and packed the bones, but also for transporting the fossils back east by train. On average, the expedition sent back more than 10 tons of fossils every year for six years. Included in these shipments were spectacular skeletons that spurred other museums to launch expeditions of their own.

Outstanding in the Field

One worker involved with the Como Bluff diggings was a fossil collector named Barnum Brown. Brown went on to explore and develop other sites and, backed by the American Museum, became one of the most successful fossil hunters in history. In fact, many of the dinosaur fossils he collected remain on display in the museum.

> **Dig This**
> Brown worked for New York's American Museum of Natural History for 60 years, until his death in 1957. About 50 years of this time was spent in the field collecting dinosaur fossils.

Twin T's

One of Brown's early successful expeditions after working at Como Bluff was the Hell Creek site, a Cretaceous formation in eastern Montana. Here he uncovered huge skeletons, including some duckbills and two magnificent T-rexes. He dug up one T-rex for the American Museum and another for the Carnegie Museum in Pittsburgh.

From Hell Creek, Brown moved on to Alberta, Canada, to explore formations along the Red Deer River. From here, he and his crew shipped out dinosaur fossils by the boatload, returning to the site seasonally for several years in a row. In fact, bordering the river were two Cretaceous formations of different ages. The presence in one region of two formations of nearly (but not quite) the same age provided a rare opportunity to trace evolutionary development.

Dinosaur Deficit

Brown was so successful in Canada that a number of Canadians grew alarmed. Although he had permission from the Canadian government to collect fossils, no one realized how

Dig This
Among the museums for which the Sternbergs dug fossils was the British Museum in London. These fossils were shipped across the Atlantic in 1916, during the first World War. Unfortunately, the ship carrying the fossils was sunk by a German U-boat's torpedo.

many he would actually make off with. Fortunately, the Canadians responded not by restricting Brown's activity but by launching fossil expeditions of their own.

For these, Canadian researchers hired a family of fossil hunters—a father and three sons—the Sternbergs. The father, Charles, had collected fossils for Edward Cope. The Sternbergs uncovered a number of valuable fossils in Canada both for Canadian museums and for museums in the United States. Among these is a famous duckbill fossil that includes one of the finest dinosaur skin impressions ever found.

Top of the Heap

One of Brown's late successes was his work at a site in Wyoming called Howe Quarry. Here, bones and skeletons somehow became jumbled together in a big heap. As a result, digging them up and sorting them out was a delicate operation. A map made by the excavation crew indicates that the quarry contained the most dense tangle of dinosaur bones ever found within an area of 20 square yards.

Unlike the famous Cleveland Lloyd Quarry in Utah (mentioned in Chapter 8), Howe Quarry was evidently not a predator trap because it contained mostly plant-eating sauropod dinosaur bones. Instead, these fossilized plant-eaters may have been faced with a serious water shortage and came crowding into a muddy pool for a last drink before getting stuck.

Monumental Projects

One of many important museums to catch dinosaur fever was the Carnegie Museum in Pittsburgh. Scientists associated with the museum got wind of possible dinosaur bonebeds in Utah and sent a fossil collector named Earl Douglass to investigate. The museum would not be satisfied with a few odd bones: It was interested in some serious digging for large quantities of fossils.

Spadework

To find this sort of promising Mesozoic strata required an extensive knowledge of geology. It also required a lot of traipsing around in the desert. This is just what Douglass did once he identified a likely Jurassic formation. Eventually, he found just what he was looking for: a number of huge vertebrae that were still *articulated*—connected much as they were when the beast was still alive.

The fact that these bones were still articulated provided good evidence that there were more skeletons throughout the area. Already exposed were eight tail bones of a big *Apatosaurus*. As it turned out, the site was rich in sauropod skeletons. Among the biggest trophies the Carnegie Museum expedition unearthed was a new species of the sauropod *Diplodocus*, which the director of the museum wisely named *Diplodocus carnegiei* in honor of the steel tycoon who bankrolled the expedition.

Fossil Philanthropy

Carnegie was so pleased with the find that he supplied funds to have each bone from the complete skeleton cast in plaster and replicated many times. This was no easy job, because the original skeleton included more than 300 bones. When the casts were finished, they were distributed as gifts to natural history museums throughout the world, including museums in London, Paris, Frankfurt, Vienna, Mexico City, and La Plata, Argentina. The director of the Carnegie Museum, W.J. Holland, made a world tour of these other museums to personally present the plaster skeletons and to supervise their installation.

Rolling Over in the Grave

The Carnegie Quarry, located in the Uinta Basin in Utah near the Green River, proved to be the richest site in dinosaur fossils ever discovered. Douglass soon realized that excavating the site was going to take at least the rest of his life, so he moved away from Pittsburgh with his family and built a homestead near the quarry. Here, in addition to digging fossils, he raised cows, chickens, and vegetables.

Digging dinosaur bones at the Utah site was an interesting challenge. The layer of rock containing the fossils had been turned on its side, so a big vertical trench had to be dug. Rail cars like those used in mines were installed to cart excess rock out of the trench. Eventually, this trench got to be about 80 feet deep and 600 feet long, with sedimentary stone walls on either side.

Definosaurus

Articulated bones are connected to one another in their original configuration. When an articulated fossil skeleton of a dinosaur is discovered, it means the bones have remained undisturbed for millions of years since the death of the dinosaur.

Dig This

Additional casts of *Diplodocus carnegiei* were later made in fiberglass. This glass dinosaur still stands along the highway near the quarry.

Boning Up

Douglass suggested that so many dinosaur skeletons ended up so close to one another at the Carnegie quarry because they drifted downstream before becoming lodged in a sandbar and finally being buried in river sediment. Evidence for this includes the fact that one side of the skeletons is better preserved than the other, indicating that they were buried sooner by a gradual accumulation of silt.

Park It Here

Although Douglass and his crew didn't have any rival fossil hunters to contend with, a different sort of problem arose when, while they were still excavating, the government opened up the land to homesteaders. This meant that anyone who wanted to develop the land could claim it and throw the fossils off.

Although this never happened, it was a legitimate worry, so Douglass filed a mining claim hoping to secure the right of the museum to dig fossils. The claim was rejected, however, because the court ruled that dinosaur bones did not qualify as minerals.

It would have been a shame to shut down the greatest dinosaur excavation site because a homesteader wanted to start a sheep farm, so the Carnegie Museum joined forces with the director of the Smithsonian Institute in Washington and took the problem to President Woodrow Wilson. The president made an executive decision on behalf of the dinosaurs. In 1915, he allocated 80 acres in and around the quarry to be set aside as a national park known as Dinosaur National Monument. Since then, park lands have expanded to include even more of the surrounding territory.

The Monument quarry has since been developed into a museum in its own right. In fact, in 1923, before all the fossils had been removed from the site, the Carnegie Museum decided it had done enough excavating. At that point, the job was taken over by a division of the Smithsonian Institute, the United States National Museum.

Running into a Wall

At this point, Douglass proposed an idea he'd had for many years. He suggested that the Monument quarry be turned into an exhibition where dinosaur fossils could be displayed while still embedded in the rock in which they were found. The vertical wall of layered Jurassic rock could be used as the actual wall of a museum building. The National Park service liked the idea.

Dig This
The rock wall of the museum at Dinosaur National Monument is especially well-suited to display purposes because it slants backward about 15 degrees. As a result, fossils in the wall can be seen more easily.

Unfortunately, money for the project was in short supply. Andrew Carnegie had died, and the government found itself in the midst of the Great Depression before it could get around to putting a big museum in the middle of the Utah desert. In the meantime, unemployed people were given government jobs doing a limited amount of fossil excavation at the site.

Not until 1958 was a building completed to house the excavation site/museum. Since becoming a museum, in fact, excavation of the quarry has continued, yielding still more valuable finds. This may be the only museum that enlarges its rooms by digging exhibits out of its walls!

The Least You Need to Know

➤ Edward Cope and Othniel Marsh were rivals in the race to find and describe dinosaur fossils.

➤ Henry Osborn organized an important expedition to Como Bluff for New York's American Museum of Natural History.

➤ Barnum Brown was one of the most prolific fossil collectors of all time.

➤ Earl Douglass developed the site in Utah that later became Dinosaur National Monument.

Dinosaurs International

Just like everyone else, dinosaurs come from all over the world. Some have distinct characteristics as a result of where they're from; others traveled around, picking up worldly ways in the process. Scientists around the world have challenged themselves to figure out how far dinosaurs moved and to what extent the evolution of stay-at-home dinosaurs was shaped by their local environments.

One reason that's a big challenge is that during the Mesozoic Period, the continents didn't stay put much more than the dinosaurs did. Land masses themselves have globe-trotting tendencies, so it becomes especially hard to pin down the comings and goings of the creatures who lived on them many millennia ago.

The job of tracking dinosaurs in faraway places is hard for another reason, too—it can sometimes lead to bureaucratic and political entanglements resulting from the way human history has divvied up the planet into separate countries. These human boundaries sometimes stand in the way of tracing dinosaur populations.

Fossil Politics

As the first dinosaurs were discovered in Europe, European countries were maintaining colonies in foreign territories. Colonialism served a variety of purposes, including the military, economic, religious, and scientific interests of the folks back home. Dinosaurs had at least a small role to play in this colonial situation. Not long after the first dinosaur fossils were discovered in Europe, more dinosaurs were discovered by European scientists abroad.

Picking the Bones

Researchers have developed a number of explanations for the late 19th- and early 20th-century practice of collecting dinosaur fossils in far-away lands. Many non-European countries—especially countries in Asia and Africa—had better fossils than those in Europe, and these fossils could sometimes be excavated with the help of inexpensive native labor.

Fossils enhanced the prestige of the European countries that dug them up, and the bones wound up in their museums not only as scientific exhibits but as trophies representing their influence abroad. This helped reduce unpleasant thoughts about colonial activity in the minds of Europeans: You can forget that your country is exploiting other countries for military and economic purposes if your country is also making scientific discoveries and collecting artifacts for its museums.

Live and Let Live

Definosaurus
Fauna means animal life. The term is often contrasted with **flora**, which means plant life. Scientists also talk about specific faunas, the kinds of animals found at a particular time and place.

It would be unfair, however, to represent all fossil collecting abroad as merely a show of power. Many European scientists wanted to collect and study fossils for purely scientific reasons. For one, populations of living animals, or *faunas*, can vary according to both location and geologic age. Studying the way faunas differ can tell us things about animal life as a whole.

Even when faunas outside Europe and North America do not differ significantly, this information is still quite valuable. Similarities and differences among the faunas of different regions provide evidence for migration and geographic isolation of certain species.

Taking the Good with the Bad

Sometimes, especially during the early days of dinosaur discovery, good and bad motives for fossil hunting in foreign countries could be hard to distinguish. Scientists abroad could learn more about paleontology while being paid by governments and museums back home to collect impressive fossils.

More recently, however, scientific study abroad—including the collection and study of dinosaur fossils—often involves constructive exchanges between countries and promotes international cooperation. Hopefully, this will continue to occur in the future.

Ground-Floor Finds

Dinosaur fossils were found in Africa almost as soon as dinosaurs were recognized as a distinct group. The bones of the prosauropod dinosaur *Massospondylus* (big back-boned creature) were discovered in South Africa and sent back to England, where Richard Owen described the animal in 1854.

Countries in southern Africa turned out to have dinosaurs not found anywhere else. In addition, these countries are rich in fossils belonging to synapsids and therapsids. These fossils attracted scientists interested in studying the origin of mammals. In fact, some of the first Mesozoic fossils found in Africa were found by scientists who went there to look for them.

Bone Bandwagon

The most spectacular African fossil find, however, was not made by scientists but by an engineer who worked for a German mining company. This engineer was exploring possible sites for mining operations in what was then colonial German East Africa (and what has since become Tanzania). Instead of finding minerals, he came upon some very large, very old bones.

As it happened, a German paleontologist named Eberhard Fraas was in the area. When he was called in to examine the site, he thought he had died and gone to dinosaur-hunting heaven! Dinosaur bones were sticking up out of the ground everywhere! Fraas gathered up some samples and went back to Germany to spread the word.

The director of Berlin's Humboldt Museum was especially interested. He persuaded the city of Berlin, the Imperial government, two academies, and about 100

Dig This

It's become something of a cliché in historical costume dramas—the proper Victorian in the equatorial wilderness insists on wearing his or her formal attire regardless of the circumstances. In fact, Robert Broom, a 19th-century British doctor and paleontologist in Africa, regularly went out fossil collecting in the sweltering savanna in a black dress coat and tie.

private citizens to help pay for a massive excavation of the site, known as Tendaguru. The Germans back home came through with funds for a big dig, and the project got underway.

Skeleton Crew

Hundreds of natives were hired to do the digging, with additional workers hired on in subsequent years. By the fourth year, 500 Africans were employed to dig dinosaur bones out of the Tendaguru bonebeds. These laborers built a semi-permanent field camp for themselves, where many of them lived with their families, although food and water shortages became a problem as the operation continued.

> **Dig This**
> Fossils were hauled out of Tendaguru on foot by African porters who carried them on litters to the seaport. Each trip took four days. In the first three years, workers carried out some 200 tons of fossils.

In four years, from 1908 to 1912, the workers of Tendaguru dug, packed up, and shipped out some 4,300 Jurassic fossils. Included in these bones were some prizes for scientists and for the Humboldt Museum: a new species of stegosaur named *Kentrosaurus*; two new genera of sauropod; a magnificent display-quality skeleton of a 40-foot-high *Brachiosaurus*; and a pterosaur called *Rhamphorhynchus*.

Before the fossil wealth at Tendaguru could be fully excavated, World War I broke out and digging operations ceased. After the war, German East Africa became British East Africa. Eventually, in 1924, the British picked up where the Germans left off, and the site continued to yield fossils for years afterwards.

Hot Spot

Tendaguru is one of the most bountiful dinosaur bone sites ever found, a fact stemming from some unique circumstances. Evidently, during the Jurassic Period, Tendaguru was a big sandbar in the middle of an estuary where lots of bone-preserving sediment flowed in and was dumped—sometimes from up-river, sometimes from the ocean. Sediment at the site is made up of alternating river and marine deposits.

Certainly the environs around this Jurassic estuary were popular for dinosaurs. Perhaps the river was a good swimming spot or watering hole. At any rate, a number of dinosaurs must have died from year to year, and their bodies floated downstream before foundering on the sandbar, where they were soon covered with sand and silt.

Chinasaurs

Many fossil collectors also have been drawn to the Far East, looking for fossil evidence that animals and early humans migrated between Northeast Asia and North America. In fact, the first full-scale fossil-hunting expedition to China set off not in search of dinosaur fossils, but of early human remains.

Seek and Ye Shall Find

The China expedition was led by an American paleontologist named Roy Chapman Andrews, who was backed by the American Museum of Natural History. The plan was to search the Gobi Desert for fossil remains of human beings, but though Chapman and his crew were unsuccessful in locating human fossils, they did find a number of significant dinosaur fossils.

The Gobi Desert was an unlikely place in which to search for fossils. The only fossil found there prior to the Chapman expedition was a single rhinoceros tooth—and this was thought to have belonged to an animal that lived somewhere else entirely. It may have been carried there and dropped by traders!

Boning Up
A number of scientists earlier in this century entertained a theory that humans evolved not in Africa, as most fossil evidence indicates, but in Asia, where they left to migrate to other parts of the world. Paleontologist Steven Jay Gould says this theory is, in effect, racist, as it is based not on evidence but on the desire to promote Northern people as ancestors of all humanity.

Hot Wheels

Nevertheless, Chapman believed he could locate fossils where other fossil hunters had failed. One reason is that he had automobiles—previous expeditions relied solely on camels, which moved much more slowly. With the ability to cover more ground, Chapman felt his crew had a better chance of finding fossils.

In fact, they found a number of important fossils that made the expedition famous. The most notable find was a new genus of dinosaur called *Protoceratops*, a small-beaked dinosaur that appears to form an evolutionary link between the parrot-billed *Psittacosaurus* and the big-horned dinosaur, *Triceratops*. To make this discovery even more significant, this new dinosaur was found in association with a nest of fossilized eggs, believed at the time—1923—to be the first dinosaur eggs ever found.

Fossil Fallacy

In truth, Andrews' eggs were not the first dinosaur eggs ever found. Fossil eggs found previously in Southern France proved later to be dinosaur eggs. What's more, Andrews' eggs were not laid by *Protoceratops*, as he thought, but by *Oviraptor*—Andrews had found the bones of this dinosaur near the nest, but he thought the creature had been stealing the eggs!

A Little Nest Egg

Evidence that dinosaurs laid eggs was particularly exciting—and also lucrative. After Chapman sold one of the eggs on behalf of the American Museum to Colgate University for $5,000, the Chinese government soon became irritated that the museum was making so much money from fossils found in China. What's more, political upheavals in China made continued permission to search the Gobi for fossils impossible to get.

The expedition worked the Gobi Desert site seasonally for many years from 1922 to 1929—and would have kept coming back, but the Chinese government refused permission. Andrews called the site the Flaming Cliffs because he saw the sun glinting like flames off the dinosaur bones embedded in the rock face.

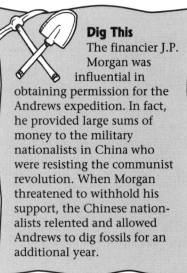

Dig This
The financier J.P. Morgan was influential in obtaining permission for the Andrews expedition. In fact, he provided large sums of money to the military nationalists in China who were resisting the communist revolution. When Morgan threatened to withhold his support, the Chinese nationalists relented and allowed Andrews to dig fossils for an additional year.

Behind the Dinosaur Curtain

After the communists came to power in China, the Gobi Desert was closed to democratic fossil collectors. In their place, Soviet, and later Polish, paleontologists worked the site at Flaming Cliffs. Though the Soviets, in conjunction with the Chinese, met with limited success, a number of Polish expeditions turned up some spectacular fossils.

Four expeditions between 1963 and 1971, led by the female paleontologist Zofia Kielan-Jaworowska, uncovered some prizes for museums in Poland as well as Mongolia. One of these appears to be a fossilized battle between a *Protoceratops* and a *Velociraptor*. These animals must have been buried in sand in the middle of a fight. Another famous fossil recovered by the Polish crew was a pair of huge shoulders, forelimbs, and foot-long claws—each one was more than 8 feet long. The unusual find is known as *Deinocheirus* (terrible claw).

Although the Poles had permission from the local Mongolian government to continue digging for fossils, the Soviet Union refused them the privilege. Leaders in Moscow were evidently jealous of the success the Poles were having, so they nixed the project to launch one of their own. Soviet scientists then proceeded to explore and excavate Flaming Cliffs, where they found a number of brand-new dinosaur species.

Dinosaur Diplomacy

Since the collapse of the Soviet Union, paleontologists from a number of countries have sought permission to collect fossils in the Gobi Desert but have been refused by the Chinese. Finally, in the mid-1980s, the Canadian government made the Chinese an offer they couldn't refuse.

This arrangement, known as the Dinosaur Project, has enabled Canadians to travel to China to search for fossils with Chinese paleontologists, who in turn traveled to Canada to work with the Canadians. They agreed that each country could keep the fossils found within its borders but would loan them out to other countries for display.

The Dinosaur Project collected a number of valuable fossils, both in Canada and in Mongolia. In Canada, the group found a *Troodon* braincase that stimulated research suggesting that this was the smartest of all dinosaurs. In Mongolia, they found a new species of sauropod called *Mamenchisaurus*. This dinosaur is estimated to have been 100 feet long, with the longest neck of any known living thing.

Dig This
The Chinese were reluctant to supply the Canadian paleontologists working in Mongolia with geological maps of the area because the maps identified classified missile-testing sites.

Another especially striking discovery was a cluster of five baby dinosaurs all huddled on top of one another. These belong to a genus of ankylosaur known as *Pinacosaurus*. The babies had yet to develop the tail clubs and bony armor characteristic of the adults.

Brothers Under the Skin

These and many other fossils found in Mongolia are similar to the kinds of fossils found in North America. In spite of the fact that some new species have been found in Mongolia, the similarities between Mongolian and North American dinosaurs suggest that dinosaurs were able to migrate between Asia and America during the Cretaceous Period. Differences between Mongolian and North American species may reflect differences in habitat between the two areas rather than diverging evolutionary trends caused by separation.

Headin' South

Australia has, so far, been much less rich in dinosaur fossils than the other continents. Nevertheless, fossil hunting in Australia has turned up some interesting finds. One is a new species of hypsylophodont named *Leaellynasaura*, for the daughter of the husband-and-wife team of paleontologists who discovered it. For its size, this turkey-sized plant-eater has one of the largest brains of any dinosaur.

Dig This
In the process of mineralization through which fossils are preserved, some dinosaur bone fragments found in Australia have turned into hydrated silicon dioxide—in other words, precious gems known as opals!

Pulling Teeth

Most dinosaur fossils uncovered in Australia have come from some seaside cliffs called Dinosaur Cove. This site has been difficult to excavate because it requires some tricky tunneling through hard sedimentary rock. This work would probably not have been carried out were it not for strong public interest in Australian dinosaurs.

In fact, fossils at Dinosaur Cove—including fragments, scattered bones, and teeth—were excavated and prepared with the help of volunteer workers, who donated food and equipment in addition to labor. The crew went on to find a number of skeletons of dinosaurs that had not yet reached adulthood. These fossils have led to speculation that the site was once a kind of dinosaur nursery.

Still in the Dark

Dig This
In their zeal for collecting fossils in Argentina, American paleontologists Alfred Romer and Jim Jenson ran into difficulties with the local police. Some of their fossils were impounded; others they made off with before the police could stop them!

The crew at Dinosaur Cove found species of dinosaur not found anywhere else in the world. While these dinosaurs may have migrated to the spot during a time when Australia was connected to Antarctica, they may also have been especially well-adapted to life near the South Pole. Although this region was warmer during the Cretaceous Period than it is today, dinosaur evolution at the poles may have been affected by long periods of darkness during winter, when there was no sunlight.

Old as the Hills

Each continent seems to have distinct conditions influencing not only dinosaur habitat and evolution, but also the geological conditions affecting the preservation of fossils and the possibilities for excavating them. This is certainly true of South America, where conditions are especially well-suited for hunting the oldest dinosaur fossils.

Dig This
One paleontologist who has collected *Lagosuchus* and *Herrerasaurus* fossils in recent years is Paul Sereno from the University of Chicago. Sereno's career epitomizes the international character of fossil collecting. He has collected fossils in virtually all parts of the world, including China and Mongolia, the erstwhile Soviet Union, Australia, Africa, South America, and the United States.

In Argentina, especially, huge formations from the Triassic Period—220 million to 230 million years old and earlier—are exposed. Here researchers found the remains of the most viable candidate for oldest-known dinosaur—the peculiar and primitive four-toed meat-eater named *Herrerasaurus*. Also found in Argentina was the archosaur near-ancestor of the dinosaurs, the small, agile meat-eater *Lagosuchus*.

Back to the Bare Bones

Increasingly, dinosaur hunting has become a cooperative international effort. Countries share fossils, scientists, technology, and sometimes money and equipment. At the same time, the days of enormous bone bonanzas and huge, expensive expeditions, seem to be over for now. Most fossil hunting today is done by a handful of scientists affiliated with universities who collect fossils as research.

The Least You Need to Know

➤ International dinosaur hunts have involved both conflict and cooperation.

➤ One of the largest bonebeds ever excavated was Tendaguru, in what is now Tanzania.

➤ The Flaming Cliffs in the Gobi Desert have been rich in fossils, including *Protoceratops*.

➤ Australia's Dinosaur Cove has yielded a disproportionate number of juvenile dinosaurs.

➤ Some of the oldest-known dinosaur fossils have been found in Argentina.

On the Cutting Edge

In This Chapter

➤ New species, new ideas, and new technology

➤ John Ostrom's *Deinonychus*

➤ Jim Jenson's *Supersaurus* and *Ultrasaurus*

➤ David Gillette's *Seismosaurus*

➤ Sonar, radar, computer imaging, and DNA

➤ Jack Horner's *Maiasaura*

➤ Giganotosaurus and Carcharodontosaurus

Thanks to the large-scale fossil-collecting efforts of days gone by, natural history museums all over the world are well supplied with display-quality dinosaur skeletons, including plaster casts and original fossils. In fact, some museums today have fossils coming in from the field faster than they can be prepared for study and exhibition.

This doesn't mean that the days of the front-page fossil finds are over. A number of significant fossil discoveries have been made over the past 40 years. These include skeletons of unprecedented size, as well as important new species that have changed our conception of what dinosaurs are.

Meanwhile, scientists have been developing new techniques both for collecting and analyzing fossils. Some of the more sophisticated techniques attract attention for their own sake, apart from what they tell us about dinosaurs. It remains to be seen how successful high-tech approaches to dinosaur science really can be, but they are showing signs of revolutionizing a field with a long history of big surprises.

Back to the Drawing Board

One of the most significant finds of the last half-century was a new dinosaur named *Deinonychus* (terrible claw). This predacious dinosaur belongs to the dromaeosaurs, the group known for its big sickle-shaped, retractile toe-claw. *Deinonychus*, closely related to *Velociraptor*, has sparked some serious rethinking of dinosaur behavior and evolution.

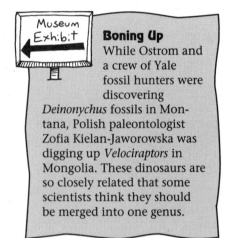

Boning Up
While Ostrom and a crew of Yale fossil hunters were discovering *Deinonychus* fossils in Montana, Polish paleontologist Zofia Kielan-Jaworowska was digging up *Velociraptors* in Mongolia. These dinosaurs are so closely related that some scientists think they should be merged into one genus.

Hot to Trot

Found in 1964 in southern Montana, *Deinonychus* helped change the prevailing view of dinosaurs in general—that dinosaurs were cold-blooded and sluggish. Its discoverer, Yale paleontologist John Ostrom, found that his new dinosaur was built for rapid movement and could maintain high speed for much longer than modern cold-blooded lizards.

The size of a human being or smaller, *Deinonychus* has unusually long, slender legs. This suggests how active and agile dinosaurs could be. As highly active predators, they are likely to have been warm-blooded.

Winging Their Way

In addition, *Deinonychus* has specially adapted finger bones and wrist joints, resembling corresponding bones in the claw-like wings of early birds. Ostrom's study of his new dinosaur provided convincing evidence that birds descended from a dinosaur-like *Deinonychus*.

Ostrom's theory that birds are dinosaur descendants has found support among a number of paleontologists who have confirmed Ostrom's findings with the help of a new system for analyzing evolutionary change. This approach, known as *cladistics*, is increasingly popular for figuring out how different living things are related. (We talked about cladistics previously in Chapter 4.)

Cladistics is a breakthrough in paleontology in that it provides a more specific way of identifying evolutionary links, enabling scientists to point to particular features of the fossils they study as evidence for the relationships they see. Cladistic studies of birds and dinosaurs, for example, have enabled paleontologists to develop a long list of specific anatomical features that dinosaurs have in common with birds. See Chapter 24 for more on dinosaur-bird similarities.

Biggest Brontos

Not long after Ostrom published his provocative description of his agile, bird-like predator, even more earth-shaking fossils were found in western Colorado. These were enormous plant-eating sauropod dinosaurs—serious contenders for the title of largest land animals ever.

Shoulder to Shoulder

In 1972, a fossil collector known as "Dinosaur" Jim Jenson set off with a crew to explore a site called Dry Mesa in search of big, meat-eating dinosaurs. Instead of big meat-eaters, though, his group found an even bigger plant-eater—or at least an 8-foot-long shoulder blade and some neck vertebrae. Depending on the kind of dinosaur to which these bones belong, they could have come from a record-breaking animal of up to 140 feet long.

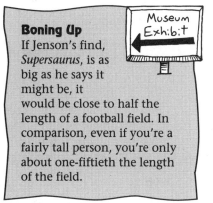

Boning Up
If Jenson's find, *Supersaurus*, is as big as he says it might be, it would be close to half the length of a football field. In comparison, even if you're a fairly tall person, you're only about one-fiftieth the length of the field.

Years later, in 1979, Jenson went back to the same site and found an even bigger shoulder bone—this one 9 feet long—quite close to where the first big blade was found. Jenson said that the longer shoulder blade actually came from a shorter, heavier dinosaur. He named this heavier find *Ultrasaurus*. The previous find, the extra-long dinosaur, he named *Supersaurus*.

Big Doubts

Unfortunately, Jenson was not consistent or thorough enough in his descriptions of these fossils to satisfy some dinosaur paleontologists. These critics say it isn't clear whether the big bronto-like finds are a new species of *Diplodocus*, a new species of *Brachiosaurus*, or no new species at all. Figuring out the groups to which *Ultrasaurus* and *Supersaurus* belong is crucial in estimating their size, and it's hard to do this conclusively based on Jenson's work.

To make matters more confusing (but also more exciting), another enormous dino bone was discovered at the same site almost 10 years later, in 1988, within 30 paces of the earlier finds. This was a huge pelvis, 6 feet long and weighing 1,500 pounds. Scientists disagree about which dinosaur the huge hip belongs to—and they're not entirely sure it doesn't belong to a completely different dinosaur!

Size Mo' Seismo

Meanwhile, in New Mexico, another enormous fossil was discovered by some backpackers: huge tail bones sticking out of a stone mesa in which Indian petroglyphs—symbols in stone—had been carved. The dinosaur these bones belong to is still another contender for biggest of the big, estimated to be from 110 to 140 feet in length. This is the sauropod dinosaur named *Seismosaurus* (earthquake lizard).

Dig This
Some 230 gastroliths, or stomach stones used for digesting vegetation, were found in the vicinity of the *Seismosaurus* fossil.

A number of tail vertebrae, a few backbones, and the pelvis of this animal have been recovered by David Gillette, a paleontologist at Utah State University. It seems likely that more of the skeleton remains buried in the solid rock of the mesa. Unfortunately, funds for excavating dinosaurs in New Mexico have been in short supply, and carving the rest of *Seismosaurus* out of its stone wall looks like an expensive project. To make the work easier—and perhaps cheaper—scientists have tried to implement several high-tech labor-saving ideas.

Tricks of the Trade

To make the digging as easy as possible, it would help to know exactly where the bones are buried in the rock face. In hopes of getting this information, planners at the *Seismosaurus* site have brought in a technique for creating sonic images of underground objects. This technique has been used to find buried weapons and buried containers full of toxic waste; it was actually demonstrated as a technique for finding dinosaurs a few years later in the hit dinosaur movie of 1993, *Jurassic Park*.

Here's how it works: A shotgun is fired straight into the ground, sending sound waves through the rock and whatever the rock has buried inside it. These sound waves travel at different speeds depending on the density of the material they are penetrating at the time. These speeds can be traced and fed into a computer that produces an image of the underground terrain.

Dig This
David Gillette, the paleontologist in charge of excavating *Seismosaurus*, estimates the cost of finishing the project at one million dollars.

In the movie, this technique worked perfectly, producing a clear picture of a dinosaur skeleton buried several feet in the ground. Unfortunately, the real-life sonic scanning in New Mexico failed to produce definitive results. Evidently, the rock inside the mesa where the rest of the seismo's bones reside is made up of all kinds of different material. This uneven mix of stone produces a very garbled picture of whatever might be buried in it.

Those involved with the project didn't give up on high-tech solutions for their stony problem. They tried radar scanning but met with similar results. The stone inside the mesa wasn't uniformly grained enough to provide a clear background for dinosaur fossils, and the matter did the same funny things to radar waves that it had done earlier to sound waves.

Radioactive Research

Scientists considered still more cutting-edge technology. Many dinosaur fossils contain traceable quantities of uranium, so a gamma-ray spectrometer, used for tracing radiation leaks, might have pin-pointed any seismo fossils in the mesa. Unfortunately, this technique works only at short range, and the bones in question are too deep to show up on a radiation detector.

Finally, to check for fossils that may have already eroded out of the mesa but were missed by preliminary excavations, the seismo crew went out at night with ultraviolet lightbulbs. If you've ever worn a black shirt to a disco that has an ultraviolet ("black") light, you probably noticed the light made the little pieces of lint on your shirt shine with an unearthly glow. The same effect can be produced on dinosaur fossils scattered on the ground in the dark. In this case, however, no new fossils were found.

Blast from the Past

Ironically, while these high-tech methods have met with limited success, an old-fashioned method has succeeded in recovering some of the *Seismosaurus* bones from the mesa—blasting with dynamite. Of course, dynamiting for dinosaurs is a risky job because it involves potential danger to the fossil itself—and to the workers trying to recover it. Nevertheless, thanks to the blast, enough of the skeleton was recovered to support the likelihood that seismo is, in fact, the biggest dinosaur.

Back to Nature

One of the most illuminating dinosaur discoveries ever happened within the last 20 years. This find not only added another new species to the list of known dinosaurs, but it revealed astonishing evidence about this species' behavior. This find was the duckbill dinosaur known as *Maiasaura*, named after Maia, the Roman nature goddess.

> **Dig This**
> The Roman nature goddess, Maia, gave her name not only to the duckbill dinosaur, *Maiasaurus*, but also to the merry month of May.

Dinos in the Hood

Some new species of dinosaur have been identified on rather fragmentary evidence—a few teeth and a piece of jawbone, for example. This is not true of *Maiasaura*, which was discovered not as a few bones from a single skeleton, but as a whole fossilized neighborhood that included individuals of all ages—from new-laid eggs to adults.

This *Maiasaura* community was discovered by paleontologist Jack Horner, a duckbill specialist who deliberately explored formations that were up in the hills during Cretaceous times; Horner believed that highlands would have been likely nesting grounds for duckbill dinosaurs. Of course, he was right and, in Montana in 1978, found the first dinosaur eggs and nests known in North America.

Pulling Out Plums

The eggs included embryos in various stages of development. In addition, Horner found newborn hatchlings and young dinosaurs of various ages, in addition to adult duckbills. Taken together, these finds provided a perfect opportunity to study the social significance of duckbill nesting habits, and Horner was just the paleontologist to conduct the study. As a result of his work on these fossils, he was able to argue convincingly that baby *Maiasaura* were cared for by the grown-ups.

Evidence for Horner's theory includes trampled eggshells (which suggest adults were near the eggs after they had hatched) and regurgitated vegetation (which suggests the adults actually helped feed the little ones). It seems that the babies needed all the help they could get, because their bones were not fully developed at birth. The young probably weren't able to move around much, unlike most other dinosaurs born with sturdier bones.

Eggs-Ray Vision

Since Horner found the maiasaur nesting community, eggs and dinosaur development have become a hot topic among paleontologists. This new interest has emerged just in time to take advantage of a new use for CAT-scan technology. With the help of this sophisticated medical equipment, dinosaur scientists can produce 3-D images of the insides of dinosaur eggs without having to break the shells.

Song of the Dinosaur

Still other innovative techniques for studying fossils are being explored, suggesting whole new avenues for paleontological research. One far-out new approach has recently been carried out on the duckbill dinosaur, *Parasaurolophus*. This dinosaur has a huge crest extending from its snout well back over the top of its head.

The crest is an extension of the duckbill's nasal passages and evidently served as a kind of resonating chamber for its calls and cries. In an effort to learn what these duckbill dinosaur calls may have sounded like, 3-D replicas of a crest were simulated with the help of a computer process known as "stereolithography." With data on the shape and size of the crest stored in the computer, scientists can run simulated tests to see how that shape affects sounds that are channeled through it.

Dino DNA

Another avenue of scientific investigation into dinosaurs has generated a lot of pretty far-out speculation: the study of dinosaur proteins, amino acids, and even dino DNA. *Jurassic Park* author Michael Crichton used the idea of cloning dinosaurs from fossilized DNA as a premise for his best-selling novel (which later, of course, was turned into a hit movie). In *Jurassic Park*, as you may know, the dino DNA is found in blood that has been sucked out by mosquitos that have been preserved in amber.

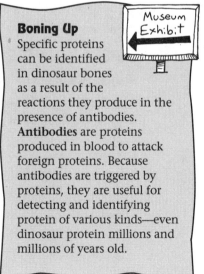

Fossil Fallacy

In reality, no dinosaur DNA has been found inside fossilized mosquitos. Most insects that have been preserved in amber date to a later epoch, the Cenozoic age.

Though complete DNA molecules aren't readily available, fragments of DNA molecules consisting of amino acids and proteins have been recovered from dinosaur bones in Alaska. These bones were fossilized under especially cold conditions, so traces of soft tissue have been preserved.

While it seems unlikely at this point that dinosaurs can be cloned from the fragmentary genetic material paleontologists have been able to recover, it does seem possible that dinosaur fossils may someday be identified by tiny residual amounts of organic material that has been incorporated by the minerals during fossilization. In addition, tracing proteins from dinosaur to dinosaur may even provide a way of establishing evolutionary relationships.

Boning Up

Specific proteins can be identified in dinosaur bones as a result of the reactions they produce in the presence of antibodies. **Antibodies** are proteins produced in blood to attack foreign proteins. Because antibodies are triggered by proteins, they are useful for detecting and identifying protein of various kinds—even dinosaur protein millions and millions of years old.

Giant Killers

A couple of additional finds have been making headlines in scientific journals very recently: enormous predacious dinosaurs that rival T-rex as the biggest meat-eaters of all time.

What's Growing On

One of these is *Giganotosaurus*. A complete skeleton of this killer, found in Argentina, was reassembled and put on display in Philadelphia in 1997. *Giganotosaurus* is 45 feet long and $14^1/_2$ feet high. In contrast, T-rex has been estimated to be up to 50 feet long and 20 feet high. Even so, *Giganotosuarus* seems to have outweighed T-rex. Its estimated weight is 8 tons, a full 2 tons larger than T-rex is thought to have weighed. What's more, *Giganotosaurus* has the largest skull ever found, 6 feet long. Its brain, however, was smaller than T-rex's.

Getting Around

The other huge predator recently discovered is *Carcharodontosaurus* (great white shark-toothed lizard). This dinosaur, a kind of megalosaur, was found by paleontologist Paul Sereno, one of the most widely traveled fossil hunters in recent years. Although the species (a kind of allosaur) was first identified back in the '20s, none this size has ever been found before.

Boning Up
In addition to being one of the most well-traveled dinosaur hunters, Sereno is one of the first dinosaur scientists to apply the method known as cladistics to the study of dinosaur evolution.

Carcharodontosaurus may be the longest-known meat-eating dinosaur, stretching out to a length of 50 feet. What's more, like the deadly shark for which it's named, it has huge teeth.

Sereno found *Carcharodontosaurus* in Morocco, where he was been investigating the relationship between dinosaur distribution and continental drift. He claims that his big find supplies evidence that the supercontinent Pangaea held together longer than was previously thought, allowing dinosaurs to travel north and south during the Late Cretaceous Period.

The Least You Need to Know

➤ Ostrom's discovery and description of *Deinonychus* supplied crucial new evidence that dinosaurs were warm-blooded and closely related to birds.

➤ Jenson's *Supersaurus* and *Ultrasaurus*, and Gillette's *Seismosaurus*, are candidates for the world's largest dinosaurs.

➤ Horner's discovery of *Maiasaura* nesting colonies provided clear evidence of parental care among dinosaurs.

➤ Recently discovered candidates for world's largest predator are *Giganotosaurus* and a new skeleton of *Carcharodontosaurus*.

➤ Recent techniques for excavating and analyzing fossils include radar and sonar, CAT scanning, gamma-ray spectrometry, amino acid and DNA analysis, and cladistics.

Part 6
Earthshaking Theories

Debates about dinosaurs are inescapable. The creatures are too important and too mysterious for people to resist generating—and arguing about—theories to explain what they were like. The history of dinosaur studies is full of some fascinating theories that have either become accepted as fact or have fallen by the wayside. Some still tantalize people, waiting to be decided one way or the other.

Of course, this is basically how science always works. People observe facts, construct theories, test the evidence, revise or discard the theories, and so on. With dinosaurs, however, the evidence tends to be especially scanty and the theories, as a result, are especially speculative. As a result, they also tend to be especially interesting.

Chapter 22

Recalled Models

In This Chapter

➤ Erroneous conceptions about dinosaurs

➤ Owen's *Iguanodon*

➤ Marsh's *Apatosaurus*

➤ Hay's *Diplodocus*

➤ Lambe's *Gorgosaurus*

➤ Wilfarth's *Hadrosaurus*

➤ Abel's *Hypsilophodon*

In 1988, British dinosaur enthusiast Dougal Dixon came out with a book of dinosaurs that never really existed, *The New Dinosaurs*, based on a combination of evolutionary principles and his own fertile imagination. The idea of the book was to depict imaginary animals that might have evolved from dinosaurs—animals that are both fantastic and believable. Examples of the creatures described in his book are the sailbacked "dingum," the armored "turtosaur," and a descendent of *Pachycephalosaurus* called the "numbskull."

Dixon's book crosses the fine line that separates the study of dinosaur evolution from imaginative speculation. As unusual as his book is, however, he is by no means the first to describe dinosaurs that never actually existed. In fact, paleontologists have come up with quite a few fantastic creatures in their attempts to understand the dinosaurs that did exist. Some of these animals represent ingenious theories based on sketchy, insufficient information that just didn't hold water in the long run.

Dinosaurs, then, aren't the only things that have evolved and adapted. Ideas about what they're like have evolved, too, as new information comes to light and new studies are conducted. This chapter covers some theoretical dead ends—interesting ideas about dinosaurs that proved to be mistaken.

Mind Games

Some erroneous notions about dinosaurs have stemmed from the excitable imaginations of the people who have studied them. Peculiar traits that are hard to account for can give rise to some daring ideas. Other errors, however, result from what we might call a lack of imagination—from mistaken assumptions that dinosaurs are like creatures that are more familiar. Both these tendencies are evident through the history of dinosaur science.

Where Does It End?

We already mentioned a few dinosaur designs that turned out to miss the mark. One famous mistake was not technically a dinosaur—Edward Cope's *Elasmosaurus*. This creature was a plesiosaur whose bones Cope assembled and described as one of the most unusual creatures ever found. One reason the creature seemed so peculiar was that Cope had put the skull on the wrong end—at the end of the tail!

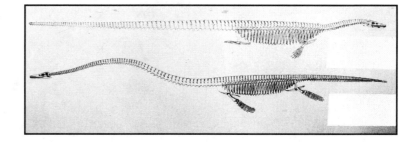

Heads or tails? The upper drawing with the long tail was one of the most embarrassing mistakes in the history of paleontology. The lower, long-necked drawing is correct.

(Ewell Sale Stewart Library, The Academy of Natural Sciences of Philadelphia)

Knowing Squat

Another early and famous dinosaur to be wrongly redesigned was Sir Richard Owen's *Iguanodon*. With the modern-day lizard in mind, Owen pictured his iggy on all fours like a big, ponderous rhinoceros. Hulking, slow-moving, and with a purely decorative horn on the end of its snout, Owen's iggy reflected the partial knowledge of dinosaurs available at the time and the partial skeleton Owen had to study.

More complete skeletons and a fuller knowledge of dinosaurs in general have since produced a picture of *Iguanodon* as bipedal, capable of running swiftly, and having a large claw on each of its thumbs rather than a horn on its nose. In fact, once the idea that dinosaurs were bipedal caught hold, paleontologists assumed that they all walked around on two legs. Even one of the big four-footed "brontosaurus"-like sauropods was briefly thought of as a two-footer, before scientists took a good look at its massive, pillar-like front legs.

> **Boning Up**
> Together with *Megalosaurus*, *Iguanodon* was one of the first dinosaur fossils to be discovered and described. Like the iggy, Owen pictured the megalo as being a hefty four-footed swamp creature.

Museum Exhibit

Coming to a Head

Heads, as well as legs, have been a problem in the history of sauropod anatomy. One famous example occurred in the 1880s when the paleontologist and dinosaur hunter Othniel C. Marsh was putting together a sauropod skeleton for Yale's Peabody Museum. This skeleton was a magnificent *Apatosaurus*, but it had a serious defect—its skull was missing.

> **Fossil Fallacy**
> In addition to its missing head, Marsh's *Apatosaurus* suffered from an identity crisis. Marsh named the fossil *Brontosaurus*, a name that became widely recognized before it was found that the same animal had already been given the name *Apatosaurus*. Thus one of the best-known dinosaur names, "bronto," turns out to be a misnomer.

Marsh made his best guess about the sort of skull the big browser must have had, and his thinking was influenced by the fossil material available at the time, which included a sauropod skull that had been recovered not far from the rest of skeleton. This skull belonged to a sauropod named *Camarasaurus*, a creature that Marsh believed to be very similar to *Apatosaurus*. He attached this skull to the long, snaky neck of the fossil put on display in the Peabody Museum.

Two Minds, One Head

In subsequent years, however, some disagreement arose as to whether this skull was the right one; the debate was fueled by the fact that Marsh's skeleton was taken as a representative fossil for *Apatosaurus*. Some scientists, most notably W.J. Holland of the Carnegie Museum, believed that apato had the wrong head. Others, including Henry Osborn of the American Museum, felt that Marsh got it right the first time.

Holland argued that *Apatosaurus* resembled *Diplodocus* more closely than *Camarasaurus*. He pointed out similarities between the skeletons of apato and diplodo, and he also pointed out that another apato skeleton was found in Utah with a partial skull that closely resembled a diplodo head.

Losing Your Head

To underscore his feelings on the matter, Holland removed the *Camarasaurus* head from the skeleton on display at the Carnegie Museum. When Holland died, however, the headless dinosaur was fitted with a skull like the one Marsh selected for his sauropod. In fact, museums all over had apatos with the sort of skull Marsh had originally picked out for them.

Dig This
The *Apatosaurus* skeleton in the American Museum of Natural History had a *Camarasaurus* head for 90 years before it was replaced by the skull of a *Diplodocus*.

Fairly recently, however, in 1978, the head business was re-examined by paleontologists Jack McIntosh and David Berman. After retracing the steps leading through the debate, they concluded that Holland was right. Their argument has convinced dinosaur experts to this day. As a result, apatos all over the world had their *Camarasaurus* heads popped off and were given new diplodo skulls.

Water World

Speaking of sauropods, we already mentioned in Chapter 10 that these were originally thought to be aquatic creatures due to their long, snaky necks and relatively delicate teeth and jaws. Supposedly, they were too heavy to carry their own weight comfortably on land. What's more, their dainty mouths supposedly showed that they could eat only soft water plants, which they sucked in while standing on the bottom of lakes and lagoons, using their long necks to sweep the surface.

Careful studies of the sauropods' leg bones have since shown that the creatures were perfectly capable of supporting their massive bodies. What's more, they didn't need powerful teeth and jaws because they hardly chewed their food; they relied instead on gastric mill stones inside their bodies to grind up their leafy mouthfuls. As a result, the aquatic bronto has been replaced by an earthshaking land rover that used its long neck for cropping vegetation high in the treetops.

Standing Tall

The idea that sauropods were aquatic was slowto die, however, partially because the idea of such huge creatures stomping around on land was hard for many people to swallow. The question of the lifestyle and stature of the sauropods achieved international attention early in this century as a result of casts that were produced and distributed of *Diplodocus carnegiei*, the sauropod collected by the Carnegie Museum in Pittsburgh with the help of funds by the museum founder, the famous steel tycoon Andrew Carnegie.

These casts were given to museums around the world, along with advice by Carnegie Museum Director W.J. Holland on how to mount them. Holland's idea of the skeleton as straight-legged and upright was criticized by the American Oliver Hay and the German Gustave Tournier, who said that the big *Diplodocus* could not have stood upright. Instead, they claimed, it crawled with its legs sticking out to the side, like a crocodile or a modern-day lizard.

Dig This
Social commentators of Carnegie's day came up with an analogy between the fact that the *Diplodocus* named in his honor was a huge creature controlled by a very small brain and the fact that Carnegie's steel empire was a huge enterprise controlled by only him!

Friends in the Swamp

Hay and Tournier supported their claim by arguing that sprawling posture would have made it easier for the diplodo to rest on its belly when it wasn't crawling or slithering around. What's more, they said that the diplodo could not have stood upright without having its feet sink and get stuck in the mud.

Obviously, Hay and Tournier assumed that the big sauropod lived in a swampy environment. Hay even published a drawing that depicted a couple of diplodos sprawled out on the banks of a lagoon, resting contentedly on their tummies with their legs sticking out to the sides. In the background, the head and back of a third sauropod is sticking out of the water, as it swims toward the others.

Design Flaws

Holland fought back with some arguments and drawings of his own. He said that Hay and Tournier's conception of the diplodo was based on a faulty understanding of the creature's anatomy. To emphasize his point, he drew a skeleton of a sprawling *Diplodocus* in which the bones were skewed and the joints dislocated, suggesting that for a diplodo to have sprawled, it would have had to undergo some impossible contortions.

Holland also drew a sprawling diplodo skeleton that was not contorted. It did, however, have a ribcage that extended several feet below the level at which the feet were standing. For the sprawling diplodo to walk around, it would have had to straddle a trough big enough for its huge body to fit into!

Boning Up
Since Holland's day, the idea that dinosaurs in general walk with an upright posture has been identified as a factor leading to their evolutionary success over other land animals. London paleontologist Alan Charig proposed the idea that an upright stance allowed dinosaurs to move more efficiently and to compete successfully against slower creatures.

Museum Exhibit

Holland's view that *Diplodocus* had an upright posture has stood the test of time. This is fortunate for all the museums around the world that have a cast of *Diplodocus carnegiei* on display, assembled with Holland's instructions.

Lazy Lizard

Boning Up

Gorgosaurus is named for Greek mythological creatures known as Gorgons (such as Medusa, who was beheaded by the hero Perseus), who could turn whoever looked at them to stone. Studies of *Gorgosaurus* from the 1970s show that it's quite similar to the Canadian predator identified as *Albertosaurus*. When two names refer to the same animal, the first-given name takes priority. Gorgo is now properly known as alberto.

Erroneous views of sauropod posture stemmed in part from the idea that these creatures were sluggish swamp-dwellers. A similar misconception influenced an early description of the Canadian predator *Gorgosaurus*, made by Lawrence Lambe in 1913. Even though Lambe rightly observed that this 29-foot-long therapod was bipedal, he believed it spent most of its time in a prostrate position with its head, neck, and belly resting on the ground.

Lambe saw *Gorgosaurus* as a cold-blooded reptile that would not have had the energy to carry itself around on its feet throughout much of the day. What's more, even though its long, sharp teeth and claws indicate clearly that it was a meat-eater, Lambe believed the *Gorgosaurus* was incapable of hunting. Instead, it lived by scavenging dead carcasses of other dinosaurs.

Lambe's *Gorgosaurus* was the kind of animal you could poke with a stick and it wouldn't even roll over. Since then, however, paleontologists have come to see this carnosaur as a fierce, fast, and agile predator that could bite your head off before you could jump.

Ducks in the Pond

A number of mistaken ideas about dinosaurs stem from the notion that they were cold-blooded, swamp-dwelling creatures. Because dinosaurs were often seen as "primitive" creatures, early dinosaur scientists had a tendency to place them in or near the water. It was probably inevitable, then, that the hadrosaurs—the duckbilled dinosaurs—have been seen as aquatic creatures, given their superficial resemblance to modern ducks.

In keeping with this idea, some paleontologists have come up with some creative explanations for how duckbill crests may have been suited to life underwater. We mentioned that these crests—situated on top of the snout and head—were extensions of duckbill nasal passages. In the earlier part of this century, paleontologists suggested these crests were adaptations for breathing underwater.

Skin-Diving Dinosaurs

Martin Wilfarth of Germany suggested in 1938 that hadrosaur crests were only the base where a long, fleshy trunk was attached. This trunk, said Wilfarth, could have been used as a snorkel under water, allowing the duckbill to breathe without coming up for air. This trunk might also have been used for plucking underwater vegetation, much as an elephant uses its trunk for feeding on land.

A major problem with this view is that hadrosaur nostrils are located at the tip of the snout. An animal with a trunk would be more likely to have nostrils closer to the top of its skull, like an elephant or a tapir does. Another problem is that a trunk used for feeding suggests a completely different lifestyle from that implied by the hadro's duckbill. In short, a beak and a trunk are two completely different and incompatible adaptations.

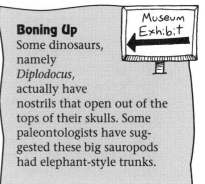

Boning Up
Some dinosaurs, namely *Diplodocus*, actually have nostrils that open out of the tops of their skulls. Some paleontologists have suggested these big sauropods had elephant-style trunks.

Room to Breathe

Another popular, but temporary, suggestion was that duckbill crests were used as storage chambers for an auxiliary air supply while the animal was underwater. This idea seems unworkable, not only because there would have been no way to transfer the extra air to the lungs without also letting in water, but because the crests can contain only a very small, essentially useless amount of air anyway. Currently, duckbill crests are seen as adaptations for display and for amplifying and resonating cries and calls. This view is in keeping with the current consensus that duckbills were land animals that lived by grazing.

Up the Creek Without a Paddle

Another dinosaur that has been mistakenly identified as a water creature is the small meat-eater *Compsognathus corallestris*. This view is based on a compie fossil found in France that seems to bear the impression of flippers around the bones of the forelimbs. The fossil has led to speculation that the compie paddled around in lakes and lagoons, using its tail and flippers for propulsion.

This theory of compie lifestyle fails to hold water, however, because other fossils of the same species lack flippers. What's more, close examination of the flippery fossil suggests that the fin-like markings around the forelimbs aren't really flippers—they're simply aberrations in the stone.

Boning Up
Most paleontologists today agree that theropods, including *Compsognathus*, were probably good swimmers. Even so, they appear to have been even better land predators. Largely for this reason, it seems that compies spent most of their time on land.

Out of Its Tree

Something as small as a single bone out of joint can make a big difference in our understanding of a particular kind of dinosaur. This is true in the case of the small plant-eating *Hypsilophodon*. A primitive dino with four long toes on each foot, hypsie was described as a tree-climber by James Hulke, the first to study it in 1882.

Hulke's view gathered steam 30 years later when the Austrian paleontologist Othenio Abel examined the hypsie's tootsies and concluded that the big first toe stuck out backwards behind the foot to grab onto branches while perching. Abel and others believed *Hypsilophodon* lived a lifestyle similar to that of an Australian tree kangaroo. They saw the feet as poorly designed for running. By climbing trees, however, it was thought to be able to avoid predators.

Abel even believed that the hypsie fossil proved that all dinosaurs descended from reptiles that climbed trees. This view was rejected early on, but the idea that the hypsies were tree-climbers persisted well into this century. In fact, it wasn't until 1974 that Peter Galton of the University of Bridgeport refuted the tree-climbing theory and brought the hypsies back down to earth for good.

The Least You Need to Know

➤ Many mistaken ideas about dinosaurs stem from the notion that they were cold-blooded, lizard-like swamp creatures.

➤ Owen's *Iguanodon* had a nose horn rather than a claw on each thumb.

➤ Marsh's *Apatosaurus* had the head of a *Camarasaurus*.

➤ Hay's *Diplodocus* did not stand upright, but had a sprawling posture like a lizard's.

➤ Lambe's *Gorgosaurus* spent most of the day stretched out on the ground to conserve energy.

➤ Wilfarth's *Hadrosaurus* breathed underwater through a snorkel-like trunk.

➤ Abel's *Hypsilophodon* perched in the branches of trees.

Body Heat

Dinosaurs have become "hot" in recent years thanks in part to a combination of increased media attention and exciting new scientific theories of what they were like. Symbolic of this popularity is a controversial claim that they were "hot" back in their own day, too—that they were not simply cold-blooded lizards but warm-blooded like birds and mammals of today.

This body-heat theory is controversial both because it is exciting (it suggests dinosaurs were dynamic characters) and because it is hard to prove. Fossil evidence reveals a number of suggestive clues, but not enough to let us decide for certain—even though scientists have sifted through various areas of dinosaur science.

Debates about body heat have helped to produce a highly appealing picture of dinosaurs that has fueled the interest of the general public in dinosaurs. Many scientists are concerned, however, that this new picture is not based entirely on reliable scientific conclusions. In fact, many who disagree with the view of dinosaurs as warm-blooded are more opposed to the reasoning behind the idea than to the idea itself.

Heating Things Up

The question of how dinosaurs maintained their body temperature has become important largely as a result of the work of contemporary paleontologist Bob Bakker. Bakker argues that dinosaurs were warm-blooded in his 1986 book *Dinosaur Heresies*. In doing so, he shows that warm-bloodedness has important implications for how we understand not only dinosaur metabolism but also dinosaur lifestyles, habitats, evolutionary success, ecosystems, and origins.

In the Beginning

The fossil record indicates clearly that dinosaurs evolved from archosaur ancestors, emerged during the Middle Triassic Period and proceeded to dominate the planet for the next 140 million years. Losing out to the dinosaurs during these years were the early mammals and their ancestors, the mammal-like therapsids. Less clear, however, is why things happened this way.

Lazy Days for Dinosaurs

Paleontologists have come up with a number of explanations. One theory holds that the climate during much of the Mesozoic Period was especially hot and dry, favoring the evolution of animals that could conserve moisture in their bodies. Unfortunately for this theory, we don't know whether the climate during dinosaur days was really hot and dry. It was definitely warmer than it was today, but it may have been exceptionally wet and rainy. What's more, there may have been pronounced seasonal differences.

Boning Up

Many of the rocks that make up Late Triassic formations have a distinct reddish color. Some hold that this redness indicates a hot, dry climate at the time these rocks were formed. Others believe the rocks were formed in a seasonal climate in which dry and wet seasons alternated.

Another possibility as to why the dinosaurs came to power is that some global misfortune may have befallen the creatures competing with dinosaurs for evolutionary space. With the field clear of rivals, the dinosaurs could easily have radiated into available Mesozoic habitats. This theory doesn't explain what killed off the dinosaurs' competition, however, or why the dinosaurs weren't killed off as well.

An additional problem with both these theories—hot climate and no competition—is that neither gives dinosaurs much credit for their success. In both of these views, the point is not that dinosaurs were particularly well-adapted to succeed but that the competition was held back. Neither of these theories, then, challenges the long-held notion that dinosaurs were slow, sluggish, ponderous, and cold-blooded—in other words, just big lizards.

Fossil Fallacy

So-called "cold-blooded" creatures do not actually have cold blood. In fact, their bodies may be as hot or hotter than that of so-called "warm-blooded" creatures. Some lizards, for example can tolerate a body temperature well above 100 degrees Fahrenheit for an extended period of time.

Jumping to New Conclusions

By the time Bakker came along, a lot of new ideas about dinosaurs implicitly opposed the "just big lizards" take on dinosaurs. One was Alan Charig's claim, made in 1972, that the characteristically straight posture of the dinosaurs probably gave them a big advantage over other reptiles.

In addition, by 1969, John Ostrom had discovered and described *Deinonychus*, a predacious dinosaur that attacked its victims by leaping at them with its clawed hind feet. This approach to hunting obviously required considerable athletic ability. Dinosaurs, then, could be agile and speedy.

Among scientists, the "big lizard" idea was slowly and quietly falling apart. No one tried to change the way people in general thought about dinosaurs until Bakker came along. Bakker pointed out that most people failed to give dinosaurs much credit for their evolutionary success and set about mustering evidence for how well-adapted dinosaurs were—not only for particular environments, but for competition with other creatures.

Definosaurus

"Warm-blooded" animals are **endothermic**. This doesn't necessarily mean they have higher temperatures than "cold-blooded" or **ectothermic** animals. Instead, endotherms are self-heating and keep themselves warm by their metabolic processes. Ectotherms rely on the heat of the sun for warmth, and they tend to eat less and move less than endotherms.

Fire in the Belly

Bakker focused this evidence by using it to support his theory that dinosaurs are hot-blooded, or *endothermic*, as opposed to cold-blooded, or *ectothermic*. For Bakker, dinosaur body heat is an indication of how well-equipped they were for survival. The view that dinosaurs were slow, lizard-like, and cold-blooded prevented people from appreciating this.

Hot Talk

Bakker argued that dinosaurs took over the Mesozoic world because they benefited from their advantages as endothermic animals—active creatures with efficient metabolisms. Of course, this is difficult to prove, because dinosaur hearts, lungs, and blood—the parts that could tell us for certain how dinosaurs stayed warm—are not preserved as fossils. Nevertheless, important evidence resides in the physical characteristics of dinosaurs that we *can* study—characteristics that can be compared to those exhibited by living creatures.

Hot Gators

Bakker was not the first to be curious about how dinosaurs maintained their body temperatures. During the 1940s, paleontologist Edwin Colbert conducted studies on alligators to see how long it took to raise their body temperatures when exposed to direct sunlight. He used gators of various sizes to test the effect size had on body heat.

The alligators were placed in full sun and had their temperatures taken every two minutes or so—with rectal thermometers! Unfortunately, two alligators died from overexposure to the sun during the course of this experiment. Colbert found that the larger the gator, the slower it heats up and loses heat. The temperature of smaller animals responds much more rapidly to external heat, suggesting that the larger dinosaurs could maintain a high body temperature as ectotherms. In fact, this idea has persisted in complicating Bakker's body-heat theory.

> **Dig This**
> In addition to testing the effects of size, Colbert tried to test the effect of upright posture on body heat by constructing frames that would support his alligators in an upright position while being heated in the sun.

Since Colbert's studies, Bakker and other scientists have collected a variety of information in an attempt to show whether dinosaurs were self-heating. Much of this information suggests important differences between dinosaurs and reptiles of today, as well as similarities between dinosaurs and modern endotherms, both mammals and birds.

Heads Held High

One feature that links dinosaurs with the warm-blooded creatures of today is their upright posture. Dinosaurs, both bipedal and quadrupedal, stood straight up with their legs underneath them. Today, almost all endotherms carry themselves in the same way, while virtually no ectotherms do.

> **Boning Up**
> Most, but not all, mammals have an upright posture. Exceptions are aquatic and semi-aquatic mammals—dolphins, whales, seals, sea lions, and walruses. All reptiles today seem to have a sprawling posture, with the possible exception of the chameleon, which is capable of standing straight up on its legs.

In keeping with their upright postures, many dinosaurs carried their heads high in the air, well above their hearts. This means they may have had relatively high blood pressure in comparison with today's reptiles. Among today's animals, high blood pressure is consistent with endothermy.

To take an extreme dinosaur example, the Chinese sauropod *Mamenchisaurus* had a neck that was 33 feet long. For its heart to pump blood all the way up to its brain, it had to generate extremely high blood pressure—high enough to risk bursting the little vessels in the lungs unless the heart was divided, sending blood to the head and to the lungs at different pressures. This sort of divided heart is also characteristic of endotherms.

Even so, it is possible that long-necked sauropods had other ways of dealing with their blood-pressure problem. For example, they may have had special valves and muscles in their necks for shoving the blood upward, much like giraffes have.

The point is, even though having your head high above your heart is a tendency exhibited by endotherms of today, there is no necessary correlation between that and body heat. In fact, the same may be said of upright posture; the fact that today's endotherms are generally upright doesn't prove that upright dinos were endothermic.

Big Heat

In the case of the big sauropods, as well as for other large dinosaurs, endothermy may not have been necessary simply because of their size. Extremely large creatures have an easier time preserving a constant body temperature because larger bodies gain and lose heat more slowly than smaller ones.

Perhaps you've noticed that a gallon of water takes longer to boil than a cup does. By the same token, once it's hot, the gallon takes longer to cool down. This same theory seems to make it easier for some large creatures to survive as cold-blooded animals. Preserving a constant body temperature through size is known as *gigantothermy*.

Large size in many dinosaurs may have made endothermy impossible: We don't know how a huge, self-heating dinosaur could shut off its furnace before roasting itself in its own big body. Large endotherms such as elephants frequently cool down with a dip in lakes and rivers—perhaps big dinos did, too. Some dinosaurs may even have used different heating strategies as youngsters than they used as adults.

Simply put, there's a lot we don't know about dinosaur physiology. The whole body-heat debate underscores how different dinosaurs were from animals today. Nevertheless, comparing dinosaurs with living creatures remains one of the best ways to develop and test the body-heat theory.

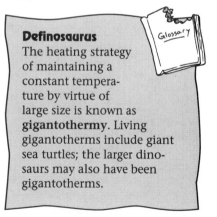

Definosaurus
The heating strategy of maintaining a constant temperature by virtue of large size is known as **gigantothermy**. Living gigantotherms include giant sea turtles; the larger dinosaurs may also have been gigantotherms.

Taking a Look Around

While it's useful to compare dinosaurs with living creatures, it's also important to study them in the context of their Mesozoic environments. This means looking at how they lived and how they fit into their ecosystem. Factors such as feeding habits, social behavior, and climate also enter into the debate on body heat.

Pretty Swift

A significant dinosaur feature associated with endothermy is an active lifestyle. Many dinosaurs were fast runners and even leapers. It takes a high metabolism to maintain high levels of activity over a period of time—the ability to burn a lot of food to produce energy. This suggests endothermy in some, but not all, dinosaurs.

Boning Up
Theropods and ornithopods had brains that were as large or larger than your typical modern lizard, relative to body size. Frilled dinosaurs, stegosaurs, and ankylosaurs had smaller brains. As for the sauropods, you'd have to bring a magnifying glass when you shinnied up their long necks!

Boning Up
Dinosaurs' diverse habitats also indicate that they were endothermic. Some dinosaur species ventured as far as the Arctic, where, some argue, it would have been too cold for ectothermic animals to survive. Others reject this, saying that the earth was considerably warmer during dinosaur days, so dinosaurs may have migrated to the poles during the warmer seasons and back to milder latitudes during the cold seasons.

Another possible sign of endothermy in some dinosaurs is their large brains relative to their size, comparable to the brains of many mammals and birds. Dinosaurs' high IQs made possible the kinds of activities that endotherms practice, including social behaviors such as caring for their young and sexual display. Again, however, not all dinosaurs had large brains—many, in fact, had extremely diminutive noggins.

A correlation may exist between dinosaur brain size and level of activity. The dinosaurs that seem to have had the largest brains—the smaller and medium-sized theropods and the ornithopods—also seem to be the most capable of sustained activity, judging from the shape of their skeletons and from the evidence of fossil trackways. It may be that these dinosaurs were, in fact, endothermic, while slower, small-brained dinosaurs were not. Again, however, this line of reasoning is inconclusive.

Lonely Hunters

In addition to physical characteristics, paleontologists have considered environmental evidence for endothermy in dinosaurs. One of Bakker's most notable claims is that dinosaur ecosystems consisted of a small ratio of dinosaur predators to their prey. This relatively small number of dinosaur predators, says Bakker, is consistent with endothermy.

Because endotherms eat more than ectotherms, it takes a lot of meat to feed one warm-blooded hunter. The available supply of plant-eaters can support only a limited number of hot-blooded predators. If dinosaurs were ectothermic, says Bakker, we would expect to see a much higher ratio of predators to plant-eaters. The fact that the fossil record shows a large number of plant-eaters for every predator is thus evidence for endothermy.

This evidence, too, is somewhat indirect; other factors may have limited the number of predacious dinosaurs per vegetarians. What's more, the fossil record may reflect an incomplete picture of dinosaur ecosystems. Perhaps fewer predators became fossilized, for some unknown reason.

Hot Bones

Still another episode in the dinosaur body-heat debate began with some bone analysis by French scientist Armand de Ricqles. Using a special saw, Ricqles cut thin cross-sections of dinosaur bones and examined them under the microscope, where he could see structures indicating their growth patterns. Ricqles found that dinosaurs sometimes grew rapidly in spurts.

A few years later, Bakker got hold of Ricqles' work and used it as evidence for his body-heat theory. Bakker claimed that fast periods of growth are typical of endotherms, whereas ectotherms grow more slowly. This, said Bakker, can be seen in the more even patterns in the bones of modern reptiles.

Since Bakker made this claim, more studies have shown that cold-blooded creatures also exhibit growth-spurt patterns in their bones. Apart from this, Ricqles himself has questioned Bakker's use of his study as evidence of dinosaur endothermy. Growth speed does not necessarily go along with self-generated body heat.

Mixed Review

The question of warm-bloodedness in dinosaurs has not been decided to every-one's satisfaction, and some think it never will be. Many believe, however, that some dinosaurs—the smaller, more active theropods and ornithopods—may have been hot-bloods, while the rest were most likely ectothermic.

In any case, the debate has served a useful purpose in drawing the attention of scientists as well as the public to dinosaurs as a unique group of creatures with unusual characteristics. As a result, the traditional view of dinosaurs as "just big lizards" has been pretty thoroughly debunked.

The Least You Need to Know

➤ The ability to heat themselves internally may or may not have given the dinosaurs an adaptive advantage over their rivals.

➤ Comparing dinosaurs to animals living today yields inconclusive evidence as to whether they were warm-blooded.

➤ Evidence about dinosaur lifestyle and environment is suggestive but inconclusive as to dinosaur body heat.

➤ The larger dinosaurs probably relied on gigantothermy to maintain their body temperature.

➤ Smaller theropods and ornithopods may well have been warm-blooded.

Dinosaurs of a Feather?

Almost as soon as the first dinosaur fossils were identified, scientists have noticed similarities between dinosaurs and birds, and a continuous flap has ensued about whether dinosaurs are bird ancestors. For years, arguments on both sides have been built on feather-weight evidence, due to a lack of available fossils.

You might think Mesozoic bird-watching would be easy. After all, unlike birds of today, their fossilized forebears hold still. The fact is, though, early bird fossils are hard to come by. Their bones were very light and apt to crumble. Even rarer than fossilized bird bones are fossilized feathers. As a result, dinosaur detectives have found it difficult to pick the likely bird suspects out of the lineup.

It now seems entirely likely, however, that birds are, in fact, descended from dinosaurs. The new conclusion is based on new evidence and new methods for analyzing it, as well as a closer, revised look at fossils that have been around for more than a century. This view has detractors but is quickly gaining acceptance as more and stronger evidence comes to light.

Airy Notions

As early as 1868, the English paleontologist T.H. Huxley began arguing that an evolutionary relationship existed between reptiles and birds. His claim was especially surprising at the time, because existing birds and reptiles differ so clearly from one another. The differences between them make sense in evolutionary terms, said Huxley, if we consider the possibility that there may have been creatures resembling both reptiles and birds that no longer exist. These extinct creatures would be the descendants of ancient reptiles and the ancestors of modern birds.

Missing Links

Huxley advanced his ideas about bird origins largely in defense of Darwinian evolution, which was an extremely controversial notion at the time. Some who opposed Darwin's theory of evolution through natural selection saw birds and reptiles as too different to be linked by evolution. Huxley refuted these naysayers by claiming that the link once existed but had since become extinct.

Fortunately for Darwin's theory, Huxley had dramatic evidence to support his claim—a bird-like reptile, or a reptilian bird, known as *Archaeopteryx*, whose fossil remains had been recently discovered in Germany. This creature was clearly reptilian because it had teeth, a long tail, and front claws; but it was also clearly bird-like because it had feathers. The fossil provided made-to-order confirmation of the idea that species evolved.

The famous Archaeopteryx *from limestone deposits in Germany in 1861. After all this time, it remains the most likely candidate for the title of oldest bird.*

(Department of Library Services, American Museum of Natural History; Neg. no.:34711; Copied by AMNH Photo Studio)

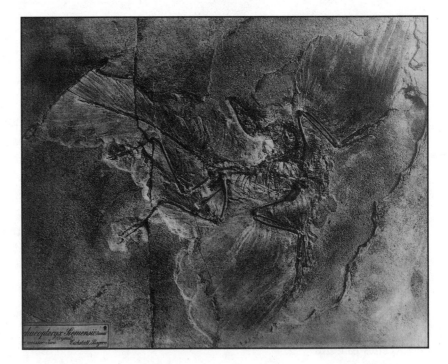

Dinos for Darwin

Huxley believed this creature was closely related to the dinosaurs. What's more, he suggested that just as *Archaeopteryx* helped bridge the evolutionary gap between reptiles and birds, dinosaurs helped bridged the gap between reptiles and the archie. In support of this point, he noticed a number of similarities between dinosaurs and modern birds, including three-toed feet and bipedal walking.

Huxley argued convincingly that birds and dinosaurs are closely related. Open to debate ever since is whether the dinosaurs were ancestors of birds, or whether dinosaurs and birds had a common ancestor. This debate has flared up a number of times since Huxley's day, most recently within the past few years. As a result of the latest dinosaur-bird controversy, most paleontologists think the theropod maniraptor dinosaurs were, in fact, birds about to happen. This is a switch from the opposing view that has dominated dinosaur science since the 1920s.

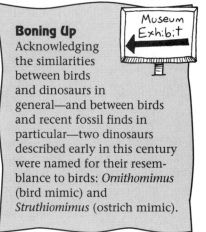

Boning Up

Acknowledging the similarities between birds and dinosaurs in general—and between birds and recent fossil finds in particular—two dinosaurs described early in this century were named for their resemblance to birds: *Ornithomimus* (bird mimic) and *Struthiomimus* (ostrich mimic).

A Chance Meeting

During this time, birds weregenerally thought to be descended from reptiles that preceded the dinosaurs, thanks in large part to the work of Danish anatomist Gerhard Heilmann. In 1916, Heilmann wrote an influential book called *The Origin of Birds*, which was translated into English in 1926. Heilmann's book argued against dinosaurs as bird ancestors, despite the many similarities between birds and theropod dinosaurs.

Heilmann acknowledged that small theropods and birds share many features, but he claimed these features stemmed from convergent evolution. In other words, these features evolved in both early birds and dinosaurs not because they are closely related, but because both kinds of animals lived a similar lifestyle. (Convergent evolution explains similarities between many unrelated creatures including dolphins and fish, and birds and bats. For more information, see Chapter 4.)

The Well-Tempered Clavicle

Heilmann concluded dinosaurs were not the grandparents of modern birds largely on the strength of one crucial bit of evidence. Dinosaurs, he said, do not have a clavicle, or collar bone. Birds, in contrast, have distinctive clavicles, otherwise known as wishbones. Bird wishbones are important adaptations, helping to stabilize their shoulders and making it possible for them to fly.

Heilmann believed that for birds (which have clavicles) to be descended from dinosaurs (which do not have them) bird clavicles would have to re-evolve from nothing. This was considered impossible, thanks in part to the work of the French paleontologist Louis Dollo. Dollo claimed that no structure that has disappeared during the course of evolution can reappear later. This idea became known as "Dollo's law." Unfortunately for Dollo and Heilmann, Dollo's law has since been proven wrong.

Fossil Fallacy

Louis Dollo, the French-Belgian paleontologist famous for his work on the Bernissart *Iguanodons* is also famous for Dollo's law, the dictum that a structure that has disappeared cannot re-evolve in descendent species. This "law" turns out to be false, however; it seems that characteristics that disappear are sometimes preserved in a latent state in a creature's DNA. This latent information may be "remembered" and reappear. This sort of re-emergence of lost characteristics is evident in some horses of today that are born with several toes in addition to their main, single toe, known as a hoof. Horses with multitoed hooves are reminiscent of their ancient ancestors.

Heilmann was mistaken not only in thinking that lost traits cannot re-evolve; he was also wrong in his belief that theropod dinosaurs had no clavicles. Dinosaurs that most resemble birds did, in fact, have collar bones, although these are rather small and were hard to see in the fossils known to Heilmann at the time. Since Heilmann published his book, scientists have discovered more fossils of small theropods that have distinct clavicles.

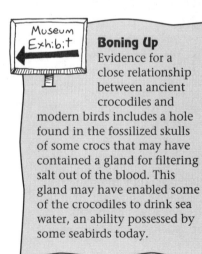

Boning Up

Evidence for a close relationship between ancient crocodiles and modern birds includes a hole found in the fossilized skulls of some crocs that may have contained a gland for filtering salt out of the blood. This gland may have enabled some of the crocodiles to drink sea water, an ability possessed by some seabirds today.

Despite this fact, no one noticed Heilmann's oversight until almost 50 years later. In fact, Heilmann's work was so persuasive that few scientists cared to argue with his conclusions until new evidence emerged in the 1960s—Ostrom's discovery and description of the theropod maniraptor, *Deinonychus*.

Down-to-Earth Evidence

Before Ostrom's raptor came along, most scientists believed that birds were descended from a group of thecodont reptiles. The most likely candidate was even given the name *Ornithosuchus*, which means "bird-crocodile." The skull of this reptile is distinctly bird-like, as are the skulls of many crocodilian reptiles, both ancient and modern. Some scientists believed that *Ornithosuchus* had descendants that were adapted for climbing trees. These tree-climbing crocodiles were thought to be the immediate ancestors of birds.

The question of bird ancestry continued to rest on sketchy evidence. The fossil record was simply not complete enough to show conclusively where birds came from. A major breakthrough came, however, when Ostrom discovered *Deinonychus*.

Preparing for Lift-off

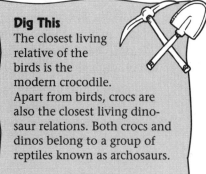

Dig This
The closest living relative of the birds is the modern crocodile. Apart from birds, crocs are also the closest living dinosaur relations. Both crocs and dinos belong to a group of reptiles known as archosaurs.

Ostrom worked not only on his newly discovered *Deinonychus* but also on the famous feathered *Archaeopteryx*. He noted many similarities in the skeletons of maniraptors and those of *Archaeopteryx* and other birds. These similarities have been confirmed by other scientists using the newly developed technique of evolutionary analysis called cladistics (see Chapter 4).

This list details some of the features shared by maniraptor dinosaurs and birds.

➤ **Flexible shoulders and wrists**   In raptors, this flexibility helped in snatching and holding on to small prey. In birds, this led to the downward and backward motion of the wings used in flight.

➤ **Long forelimbs**   These helped raptors hunt and became adapted for flight in birds.

➤ **Hollow bones**   Air pockets in bones promoted agility in raptors and are a big help to birds in getting off the ground.

➤ **Three-fingered hands and three-toed feet**   Bird wings are adapted from the three fingers of raptor forelimbs. Perching bird feet derived from the famous bird-like feet of theropod dinosaurs.

➤ **Deeply angled collar bone**   In raptors, this promoted balance and stability while running; in birds, this became the wishbone, necessary for flight.

➤ **Shape of the pelvis**   *Archaeopteryx* and maniraptors had pelvises of a very similar shape. These pelvises evolved into the characteristic bird pelvis only later.

Swivel Hips

The hip business linking birds and dinosaurs can be confusing. Maniraptors are members of the Saurischian (lizard-hipped) order of dinosaurs, as opposed to the Ornithischian (bird-hipped) dinosaurs. Ornithischian pelvises, then, resemble bird pelvises more closely than do Saurischian hips. In fact, scientists have attempted, unsuccessfully, to find bird ancestors among the Ornithischians. Traditionally, *Archaeopteryx* was thought to have had the characteristic bird-shaped pelvis, too, but this turns out not to be the case. At some point before becoming fossilized, the pelvis on the holotype specimen of *Archaeopteryx* became broken and bent into a shape resembling the shape of the pelvis on modern birds, making the archie appear to have a more modern pelvis than it actually possessed. It now seems that archie pelvis closely resembles the Saurischian hips found on maniraptors. Only later did the shape of this pelvis change as modern birds evolved.

These features supply the main evidence that birds are, in fact, closely descended from maniraptor dinosaurs, or from dinosaurs who were ancestors of both the birds and the maniraptors. An additional trait that birds may share with maniraptor dinosaurs is warm-bloodedness. As Chapter 23 discusses, warm-bloodedness in dinosaurs has not been proven; but if any dinosaurs were self-heating, it is likely to have been the small, active, intelligent maniraptors.

Counting on Their Fingers

A majority of paleontologists today are persuaded that maniraptors are closely related to birds. It isn't surprising, though, that some scientists remain skeptical and have pointed out problems with the idea. One problem has to do with just which fingers form the forepaw in raptors and the wings in birds.

> **Dig This**
> Whatever creature gave rise to the first birds, there is no doubt that birds first emerged during the Mesozoic Era and immediately began to diversify. Most of the first bird species, however, died out before the end of the Cretaceous Period.

Both raptors and birds have three "fingers," or digits, on their forelimbs. These forelimbs evolved from a more primitive five-digit forefoot. Studies of bird embryos suggest that the bird wing is made up of the second, third, and fourth digit. In contrast, the maniraptor foreclaw is generally thought to consist of the first, second, and third digit. Bird wings, then, may have evolved separately from raptor foreclaws.

Defenders of the case for raptors as bird ancestors point out that we cannot make studies of raptor embryos like we can on modern birds. As a result, no evidence exists that the digits of bird wings and raptor claws are different. To the contrary, they look very much the same in raptors and *Archaeopteryx*, especially in the way they are attached to the wrist.

All in the Timing

A second problem stems from the fact that known maniraptor fossils have not been old enough to be ancestors of the first birds, which predate them. Whereas *Archaeopteryx* dates to the Late Jurassic Period (140 million years old), *Deinonychus* and *Velociraptor* are Early Cretaceous creatures (only 107 million years old). Quite recently, however, in 1996 and 1997, two finds in China have brought to light new raptor species as old or older than *Archaeopteryx*.

These new Chinese fossils are named *Sinosauropteryx* (Chinese lizard wing) and *Protarchaeopteryx* (first *Archaeopteryx*). *Sinosauropteryx* initially caused a great deal of excitement among dinoscientists because it appeared to be covered with feathers. It seemed that proof had finally been found that feathers evolved first in dinosaurs that did not fly, and that birds later modified these feathers for flight. Closer examination of the supposed ridge of feathers along the back of *Sinosauropteryx* revealed, however, that the structures are simpler than true feathers—sort of like half-formed feathers instead.

The second Chinese find is even more exciting, because *Protarchaeopteryx does* have true feathers running the length of its tail, with additional feathers attached to its forelimbs—and *Protarchaeopteryx* is clearly a dinosaur that did not fly. (These feathers were probably used for insulation. For more on the evolution of flight and feathers, see Chapter 15.) Both *Sinosauropteryx* and *Protarchaeopteryx* are much older than *Deinonychus* and *Velociraptor*, and much closer in geologic time to *Archaeopteryx*, although their exact age has not yet been precisely determined.

Fossil Fallacy

Perhaps because of their intermediate status as both birds and dinosaurs, more than one *Archaeopteryx* fossil has been misidentified. One was thought for many years to be a specimen of the small theropod dinosaur *Compsognathus*. Another was identified as a pterosaur.

Who's on First?

Because the maniraptors and *Archaeopteryx* are so similar, the strongest case for dinosaurs as ancestors of the birds depends on the status of *Archaeopteryx* as one of the first birds. This status has been challenged by a find made in 1988 of fossil remains dating from the Late Triassic Period. This creature was found in Texas by paleontologist Sankar Chatterjee, who called his discovery *Protoavis* (first bird).

On making his discovery, Chatterjee claimed it was the oldest bird fossil yet discovered. If so, that means *Archaeopteryx* may be an evolutionary dead end. *Archaeopteryx* is clearly a primitive bird, but it may have coexisted with more advanced birds descended from *Protoavis*. What's more, *Protoavis* is much too old to have a maniraptor as an ancestor. If *Protoavis* is a bird, it puts bird origins back about 80 million years.

A Mixed Bag

Before Chatterjee had a chance to publish his results, people got wind of his find and eagerly awaited his account of the fossil. They wanted to know if this was, in fact, the oldest known bird. When Chatterjee published his description and made the fossil available to others, however, some paleontologists disagreed with his interpretation and said he was too quick to conclude that he had discovered a bird. They said not only that its bird status is unclear, but that it may even consist of two or more different kinds of animal.

Others agreed with Chatterjee, but Chatterjee and his supporters are in the minority. Since the discovery and description of *Protoavis*, cladistic analysis of the kind used to confirm the relationship between the raptors and *Archaeopteryx* has become widely accepted. The recent discoveries of *Sinosauropteryx* and *Protarchaeopteryx* in China also lend support to the view that raptors gave rise to the first birds.

Aves for Dinos

If this interpretation of the fossil record is correct, it is exciting for bird-lovers and dinophiles alike—it means we know where birds come from, and it means dinosaurs are still around. It also emphasizes how different non-bird dinosaurs were from reptiles of today. If the group known as dinosaurs includes not only Ornithiscians, Saurischians, and aves (birds), it certainly seems large and diverse enough to warrant designation as a class, along with mammals and reptiles, rather than a mere order.

The Least You Need to Know

➤ T.H. Huxley made a case for the relationship between birds and dinosaurs in the 1860s, but for most of this century, scientists believed that dinosaurs could not have given rise to birds.

➤ The case for dinosaurs as bird ancestors is based on similarities between maniraptors and *Archaeopteryx,* the earliest known bird. Although it has wings and feathers, *Archaeopteryx* also has teeth, a long tail, and claws on its wings like a dinosaur.

➤ *Sinosauropteryx* is a dinosaur that has much of its body covered with simple feather-like structures, or proto-feathers.

➤ The recently discovered Chinese dinosaur *Protarchaeopteryx* has true feathers attached to its tail and forelimbs. Although it has true feathers, *Protarchaeopteryx* was a dinosaur that did not fly.

➤ *Protoavis*, a candidate for the oldest bird from the Late Triassic Period, has had its status called into question.

Chapter 25

Real Gone

In This Chapter

➤ Dinosaur extinction

➤ Mass extinctions throughout geologic time

➤ The asteroid impact theory

➤ Objections to the asteroid impact theory

➤ Climate change and related theories

➤ Supernovas, volcanos, and viruses

Non-bird dinosaurs died out by the end of the Cretaceous Period, 65 million years ago—and everyone wants to know why. Invariably, the first question a dinosaur expert gets asked at cocktail parties is, "How did it happen?"

The answer depends on the expert. In fact, there are a number of explanations; all are interesting, and some are spectacularly cataclysmic. Not only are the lives of the dinosaurs at stake, but so is the delicate balance of life on earth during the Mesozoic Period and across still longer stretches of time. It's hard to resist thinking about the global and historical implications of the demise of the dinosaurs. After all, we may be next.

But questions about what killed the dinosaurs extend even beyond the planet to take extraterrestrial phenomena into account. Could an asteroid have triggered the downfall of the dinosaurs? Could this have happened more than once? Could it happen again? In response to these questions, paleo-geologists and astro-physicists have started to compare notes.

These Things Happen

Dinosaurs weren't the only creatures who bit the dust at the end of the Cretaceous Period. In fact, it's been estimated that more than half of the existing species on the planet— both plant and animal—did not survive into the Tertiary Period. Among species to succumb at this time along with the dinosaurs were air creatures (including pterosaurs and many kinds of birds) and sea creatures (including ichthyosaurs plesiosaurs, and mosasaurs).

Fossil Fallacy

Some scientists have suggested that some non-bird dinosaurs survived into the Tertiary Period. This view is based on the fact that some dinosaur fossils were discovered in Tertiary rock formations. The view that these fossils are the remains of Paleocene, rather than Mesozoic, dinosaurs is dubious, however, because they were evidently washed into newer strata by a stream channel that cut across the Cretaceous-Tertiary boundary.

Wipe Out

Because dinos didn't go out alone, whatever killed them must have killed all these other creatures, too. The event is known as the end-Cretaceous *mass extinction*. Mass extinctions have taken place a number of times throughout the history of life on Earth. At such times, a large number of species die off, enabling new and different species to emerge and take their place.

Definosaurus

A **mass extinction** is the dying off of a significant number of species, all within a relatively short interval of geologic time. Mass extinctions have occurred more than a dozen times during the history of life on earth. There have been five times, however, when a mass extinction has been really major—these are known as the "big five."

Curtains

This list details the big five exits from the great stages of natural history:

➤ **The End-Ordovician** About 439 million years ago, before life became well-established on land, many species of marine invertebrates met their fate. Evidence suggests that the damage was done by global cooling that took place at the time.

➤ **The End-Devonian** About 364 million years ago, the first forests had grown up and the first amphibians were emerging onto land. The amphibians were all set to take over but were almost wiped out instead by the second of the "big five."

➤ **The End-Permian**   About 250 million years ago, all the continents got jammed together into the single supercontinent, Pangaea. This caused bad things to happen with the world's climate—deserts expanded across the land, the ocean became stagnant, and volcanoes spewed lava and poisonous gas all over.

➤ **The End-Triassic**   About 208 million years ago, our mammalian ancestors took it in the nose while the early dinosaurs remained relatively unscathed. Thus the dinosaur take-over of Earth was at least partially due to the fourth of the "big five."

➤ **The End-Cretaceous**   About 65 million years ago spelled the end of the dinosaurs, pterosaurs, and marine reptiles.

Space Shot

The end-Cretaceous mass extinction stands out as especially significant, of course, because this was when the non-bird dinosaurs breathed their last. It is significant, though, for an additional reason—special factors may have been at work in snuffing out the dinosaurs that did not influence other mass extinctions.

The most striking evidence that something strange happened to the dinosaurs consists of unusually large amounts of a rare element known as iridium, present in the sediments that make up the boundary between Cretaceous and Tertiary formations. This discovery was made in the early 1977 in what is now Gubbio, Italy, by a team that included physicist Luis Alvarez and his son, geologist Walter Alvarez. Since this initial discovery, other large amounts of iridium have been discovered at the Cretaceous-Tertiary boundary.

Dig This
Evaluating the various mass extinctions strictly in terms of the number of different creatures that died out, the severity of the crisis that killed the dinosaurs pales in comparison with the mass extinction that occurred at the end of the Permian Period, in which close to 70 percent of all known kinds (genera) of living things died off.

Falling Rock

The Alvarezes brought with them the right blend of backgrounds to realize two significant facts about iridium: For one, large amounts of iridium are not usually present in sedimentary rock found on earth. For another, large amounts of iridium are often found in lumps of rock that fall from outer space. They concluded, then, that high iridium levels made their way into Cretaceous-Tertiary stone as fallout from a giant asteroid that smacked into the planet.

Dig This
Early proponents of the asteroid extinction theory include space maven Carl Sagan and paleo-pundit Stephen Jay Gould.

The Alvarez team suggested that a big-enough asteroid could have kicked up enough dust all over the planet to significantly block out sunlight for a period of weeks—or even months. Without enough sunlight, many plants, both on land and in the ocean, could have died off, making things hard, in turn, for the creatures that ate the plants and the meat-eaters that ate the plant-eaters.

Hot Rocks

This list of terms for different kinds of space rocks can help you keep your falling stars from getting crossed.

➤ **Bolide**   Technical term for an extraterrestrial body, such as an asteroid or a comet.

➤ **Asteroid**   Strictly speaking, a member of a group of stones in space that form the asteroid belt orbiting the sun between Mars and Jupiter. These measure from 1 mile to several hundred miles across.

➤ **Comet**   A large bolide with a typical big orbit and a vaporous tail made of carbon dioxide, water, methane, and ammonia. Comets are actually more like icy slush-balls than rocks.

➤ **Meteor**   Technically, a "falling star," or a small asteroid that becomes briefly visible upon entering the earth's atmosphere.

➤ **Meteoroid**   A lump of rock that penetrates the earth's atmosphere, producing the appearance of a meteor.

➤ **Meteorite**   A meteor that makes it all the way to the earth without burning up in the atmosphere.

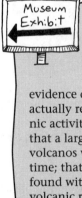

Boning Up
Critics of the asteroid-impact theory say that the iridium used as evidence of an asteroid actually resulted from volcanic activity. They point out that a large number of volcanos were active at the time; that iridium is often found with other elements in volcanic rock but rarely in asteroids; and that the iridium is sometimes dispersed in sediment through thicknesses of several inches in a way that rules out asteroid fallout.

Down to Earth

Many paleontologists think the Alvarezes' asteroid theory is too far out. In response came a barrage of evidence that challenges—or at least complicates—the idea that the dinosaurs were wiped out by a rock from outer space.

Going Slowly

One argument against the asteroid-impact theory is based on evidence that colonies of egg-laying dinosaurs lived close to polar regions year-round. Here, although the temperature was not as cold as it is today, the land would have been in complete darkness during much of the year. This shows that dinosaurs and the plants they ate could live without sunlight for long periods of time.

Other evidence against a dinosaur-killing asteroid includes the precise times when the dinos died off. As the Alvarezes themselves acknowledged, the fall of the dinosaurs does not appear to have been a sudden event. Instead, a number of species died out gradually during the years leading up the end-Cretaceous, when the remaining dinosaurs perished pretty much all at once. This pattern of dinosaur disappearance suggests that other factors were at work apart from—or perhaps in addition to—an asteroid from space.

Getting Cold

In addition, oxygenisotopes in fossilized plankton provide evidence that unusual temperature fluctuations occurred during the end of the Cretaceous Period and the beginning of the Tertiary Period. Changes in temperature may have disrupted the dinosaurs' environment, gumming up the whole ecosystem. These fluctuations are spread out in time and occur both before and after the time when an asteroid may have hit the planet.

Temperature changes, together with indications that many Mesozoic species died out gradually, suggest a much more gradual cause of extinction than the impact of an asteroid. Various theories have been put forward to account for fluctuating temperatures. One such theory holds that climate changes took place as a result of the shifting of tectonic plates as Pangaea, the Mesozoic supercontinent, continued to break up during the Cretaceous Period.

Another explanation has it that volcanic activity was especially high late in the Cretaceous Period. Soot and gasses from volcanos could have trapped heat from the sun close to the earth, producing a greenhouse effect much like that occurring today as a result of automobile exhaust. Meanwhile, hydrochloric acid could have worsened the greenhouse effect by depleting the ozone layer, or could have produced acid rain capable of killing plants.

Paleo Plague

Still another explanation says that dinosaurs died out from disease. This could have happened at the end-Cretaceous because dinosaurs may have become more mobile at this time, enabling diseases to spread. When isolated species suddenly become exposed to one another, they can also be exposed to new germs or viruses against which their bodies haven't developed any defenses.

Boning Up
Fossilized plankton can be dug up from beneath the sea floor only if it is about 200 million years old or younger. Sediment that was laid down prior to this has been pushed down by the moving oceanic plates of the earth's crust into undersea trenches and into the earth's mantle. Here this back-sliding silt melts and later re-emerges as lava in undersea volcanic eruptions.

Boning Up
Shallow seas cut across many Mesozoic land masses that are much drier today. Such seas separated Northern and Southern Europe from one another and from Asia; India and Arabia were also cut off from Asia. What's more, a shallow sea separated North America from South America, and Eastern North America from Western North America.

251

This could have occurred when the warm, wet climate changed to a cooler, dryer one. As a result, the shallow, inland seas that divided many continents dried up. In addition, land bridges between continents were exposed. As dinosaurs traveled across these land bridges and across the dried-up sea beds, species came in contact with each other and became exposed to new diseases.

Weighty Evidence

These ideas do not entirely negate the possibility that an asteroid hit the earth 65 million years ago and killed off the dinosaurs. They suggest, however, that dinosaurs and many other Cretaceous critters may have been in trouble even without an asteroid. Even so, many scientists have remained keenly interested in the possibility of an extinction-causing asteroid, especially as evidence has continued to pile up.

Cretaceous Clues

Evidence for a big rock from space appeared in the form of lumps of glass, called *tektites*, discovered in Haiti in the mid-1970s and later in Mexico. Dating analysis indicates that these were formed just before the last of the dinosaurs died out. Like the layer of iridium discovered earlier, the tektites suggest that an unusual event occurred at the crucial point in dinosaur history.

Tektites require extremely high temperatures to form, so they must have been produced either by volcanos or as a result of an asteroid impact. Some have claimed these particular tektites show no signs of having been forged through volcanic activity since they show no traces of gas or water. They could have been formed, instead, under the impact of an asteroid, which could also have scattered the glass droplets in the process. Years later, unusually high magnetism was detected underground in the Yucatan area of Mexico, again indicating a possible asteroid collision.

Scene of the Crime

Underground samples taken in thearea contained lumps of quartz that had been stressed, or "shocked," by a big impact. This shocked quartz seems to have been formed at about the same time as the tektite glass. Other strange geological clues have been found in the area as well, including sinkholes and sediments that bear the signs of an ancient disturbance.

Dig This

"Chicxulub" is an ancient Aztec word meaning "tail of the devil," a portentously apt name for the site of a cataclysmic asteroid!

Attempts to reconstruct the scene of the impact suggest that an asteroid with a 6-mile diameter fell to earth on top of what is now Mexican seacoast town of Chicxulub. This appears to be one of the biggest rocks ever to collide with the planet—it left a crater of the Gulf of Mexico, while the other half spreads out into the Yucatan Peninsula.

Others Like You?

Many scientists—and ordinary folks, too—are persuaded by the theory that the Chicxulub asteroid rained on the dinosaur's parade. Questions remain, however, because there is so much about dinosaur extinction—and about extinction in general—that the rock from space does not explain. In an attempt to answer some of these questions, scientists have pondered the possibility that the Chicxulub asteroid may not have been a singular occurrence after all.

Studies have suggested that life on earth undergoes periods of crises severe enough to qualify as a mass extinction about every 26 million years. This insight has led to speculation that rocks from outer space may have a tendency to fall to earth about that often. Could unearthly disasters take place like super-slow-motion clockwork?

Under a Cloud

They could, according to some fascinating, if speculative, scenarios. In all these theories, rocks fall to earth from time to time from a supply in space known as the Oort cloud. The Oort cloud is a huge group of floating rocks that sits out there somewhere beyond the orbit of Pluto. Different suggestions have been offered as to why the Oort cloud may rain rocks on earth every 26 million years.

One of these has it that a dark star known as "Nemesis" revolves in a huge, 26-million-year orbit around our sun. When it lines up in the right position and distance from the Oort cloud, this star's gravity yanks a few rocks loose from the cloud and sends them crashing to earth. The fact that no evidence has been found that "Nemesis" exists casts doubt on this theory, however.

Similar to the Nemesis theory is the theory of "Planet X." Planet X is a hypothetical, yet-to-be-discovered member of our solar system that has remained undiscovered because of its enormous, elliptical orbit that takes 26 million years to complete. When Planet X gets to the Oort cloud, it sends asteroids earthward.

A third suggestion is based on the motion of the whole solar system in relation to the rest of the galaxy. As the solar system revolves around the center of the Milky Way, it is affected by the gravitational pull of other heavenly bodies. This is supposed to happen with 26-million-year frequency, causing, once again, the Oort cloud to do its dangerous thing.

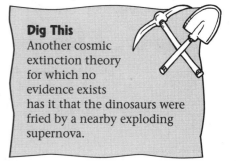

Dig This
Another cosmic extinction theory for which no evidence exists has it that the dinosaurs were fried by a nearby exploding supernova.

All or Nothing

The idea that all mass extinctions, including the "big five," were caused by asteroid impacts remains an interesting but speculative theory. Some evidence exists that the earth may indeed have been hit by a big asteroid during the end-Permian and end-Triassic mass extinctions. Other evidence suggests that a whole series of smaller asteroids may have peppered the earth during the Late Devonian mass extinction.

No evidence exists, however, that the earth was hit by a rock from space during the end-Ordovician mass extinction. Instead, a global drop in temperature at that point in geologic time seems to have done the extinction job all by itself.

Asteroid Smash-teroid!

Some scientists have pointed out that the earth is known to have been hit by asteroids in the past when life seems to have gone on, business-as-usual, without a mass extinction. For example, we know that the earth was hit 36 million years ago by two big rocks from space.

One of these blasted the Popigai crater in Siberia. The second smashed into the eastern coast of the United States, leaving a crater 60 miles wide. Today that crater is filled with water and is known as Chesapeake Bay! Despite these big asteroid impacts, life went on without a hitch.

Gone But Not Forgotten

No definitive answers exist to the question of what killed the non-bird dinosaurs—only a variety of theories with varying amounts of evidence to back them up. From this it seems likely that no single factor triggered the end-Cretaceous mass extinction. Instead, unfavorable circumstances may have accumulated until a last straw—possibly an asteroid—broke the backs of the remaining dinosaurs.

In the wake of this end-Cretaceous ecosystem shakedown, mammals and birds emerged as masters of the dry parts of the planet, while land reptiles continued to hold their own. This twist of evolutionary fate has enabled human beings to emerge and develop their peculiar skills. Thanks to some of these skills, dinosaurs live on in memory, despite the fact that only their fossils remain.

The Least You Need to Know

➤ More than a dozen mass extinctions have taken place since the origin of living things. The worst of these are known as the "big five."

➤ Although the end-Cretaceous mass extinction is the most famous of the "big five" (it killed the dinosaurs), it wasn't nearly as bad as the end-Permian mass extinction; this one wiped out almost all animal life on earth.

➤ Many subscribe to the asteroid impact theory, although some think this is only a partial explanation.

➤ Different kinds of dinosaurs died off gradually throughout the Cretaceous Period before the final catastrophe.

➤ The earth was hit by an asteroid at the end of the Cretaceous Period that blasted a crater in Mexico more than 120 miles wide.

Part 7
Paleo Fever

People like imagining interactions with dinosaurs. Imaginary dinos proliferate in books, movies, TV shows, toys and games, cartoons, T-shirts, and other popular products. Often these imaginary dinosaurs are only distant approximations of the original dinos. However realistic and faithful to current scientific knowledge our imaginary dinosaurs may be, the way they are imagined says as much about us as it does about them. The point of a movie that unleashes a T-rex in a congested American city is not to show what a real T-rex would do in the same situation, but to show what people might do. In other words, we've recreated dinosaurs in popular culture largely for our own benefit to help us think about reality in new ways. Dinosaurs are especially good for this purpose, representing the challenges and rewards of living on Earth.

Novel Ideas

Throughout the 20th century, people have been obsessed with dinosaurs. This is true not only of paleontologists, but of novelists, comic-book writers, and their readers. Throughout this turbulent century, dinosaurs have helped put reality in perspective by providing an imaginary place to escape to—a "lost world" where men are mighty, women are scantily dressed, and dinosaurs must be tamed or destroyed.

Dinosaurs are a prominent feature of a certain kind of fantasy about primitive existence that has had tremendous appeal for millions of readers. According to this "primitive" fantasy, the world is full of dangerous and exotic creatures such as dinosaurs. Whoever conquers them is a hero and gets to be king of the jungle.

Meanwhile, as this fantasy has simmered away on the pages of comics, magazines, and dime-store novels, dinosaurs have been used in a very different kind of fantasy—a "progress" fantasy—by businesses wanting to celebrate the safety and convenience of modern living. Of course, the "primitive" fantasy and the "progress" fantasy are just opposite sides of the same dinosaur coin. In the "primitive" fantasy, the dinosaur must be tamed, whereas in the "progress" fantasy, the dinosaur has been tamed already.

Same Old Story

For almost as long as there have been comic books, dinosaurs have been in them, providing a vital spark to the imaginations of countless pulp-fiction writers throughout the 20th century. The basic formula for most of these stories is simple: an exotic land long ago (or far away), a fearless hero bulging with muscles, a beautiful woman—usually a princess or the daughter of someone rich—and one or more ferocious dinosaurs on the prowl.

Fossil Fallacy

The most basic fossil fallacy is the idea that prehistoric people ever shared the earth with dinosaurs. It never happened, however tempting it may be to think it did.

In some stories, the dinosaurs live in an isolated, forgotten part of the world that is discovered by explorers or scientists. In other tales, the action takes place in an imaginary prehistoric time when (as we know never happened) early humans coexisted with the saurians. In still others, it's anybody's guess where or when the action takes place—the important thing is that a human hero is pitted against dinosaur adversaries.

Digging Up Specimens

Fantasy adventure tales involving saurians really came into their own at the start of the 20th century, but some were written even earlier. Among the first and most notable is Jules Verne's *Journey to the Center of the Earth* (1864), which tells of a scientific expedition down into a volcano. The tale enacts the paleontologist's dream of descending into the earth and finding live Mesozoic creatures rather than fossils!

Despite meeting with incredible adventures, Verne's scientists maintain proper 18th-century conduct throughout, even while being spewed out of the volcano at the end! The tale tries to show the ability of scientists to cope with a bizarre and uncivilized world without getting ruffled. The yarn became a 1959 movie with, yes, Pat Boone.

Early "World"

Another famous fictional scientific expedition to a dinosaur-inhabited realm is Arthur Conan Doyle's *The Lost World* (1912). Doyle is best known as the creator of super-sleuth Sherlock Holmes, but *The Lost World* is a famous work in its own right, setting the precedent for many dinosaur stories to come.

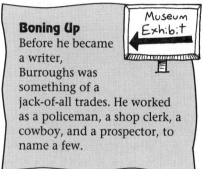

Boning Up
Before he became a writer, Burroughs was something of a jack-of-all trades. He worked as a policeman, a shop clerk, a cowboy, and a prospector, to name a few.

Doyle's tale tells of a team of British explorers in the Amazon led by Professor George Challenger. Sequestered on a high plateau, the team finds the "lost world," where ape-men, pterodactyls, and dinosaurs vie for dominance. The tale was adapted for the silent screen in 1925 and became a talkie starring Claude Rains in 1960. (The 1997 *Lost World* sequel to *Jurassic Park* isn't based on Doyle's tale, but don't be surprised to see a new movie version in the near future.)

Dinosaur Burroughs

Another well-known writer to treat the scientist-discovers-living-dinosaurs theme is Edgar Rice Burroughs (1875–1950). Burroughs is the famous creator of the jungle adventure hero Tarzan. During a career that spanned 44 years, Burroughs wrote more than 70 fantasy-adventure novels depicting imaginary worlds frequently inhabited by dinosaurs and other Mesozoic creatures.

Life Cycles

One of Burroughs' most famous dinosaur adventures is *The Land That Time Forgot* (1918). In this tale, an American soldier fighting in World War I becomes stranded on an island inhabited by various cave people, dinosaurs, and imaginary beings. This story and its two sequels, *The People That Time Forgot* and *Out of Time's Abyss*, make imaginative use of the concept of evolution.

Dig This
At the Earth's Core and *The Land That Time Forgot* both include detailed depictions of an imaginary human culture that coexists with imaginary dinosaurs. Both books were also made into movies: *Land* in 1974 and *Core* in 1976.

It seems that the strange creatures exist in a hierarchical relationship; creatures develop during the course of their lifetimes into more advanced forms, tracing a progressive model of evolution from birth to death. They are reptiles in early childhood and become mammals later in life. During this time, they also migrate further into the imaginary land.

A Hero to the Core

Another of Burroughs' popular fantasy adventures, *At the Earth's Core* (1914), tells of two men who drill their way to the center of the planet in a subterranean vehicle. Here they find a land known as Pellucidar, inhabited by various stone-age people and Mesozoic monsters, including a group of intelligent, telepathic pteranodons called "Mahars." In the process, romantic doings ensue between the explorer-hero David Innes and one of the underground women.

At the Earth's Core was well-received and triggered numerous sequels chronicling the strange goings-on in Pellucidar. Hero David Innes is interested in sharing upper-world technology with his underground friends, including short-wave radio. As his influence in Pellucidar increases, he eventually becomes emperor. All is not well within his realms, however, and he is taken prisoner by pirates.

Tarzan to the Rescue

The heroes of many dinosaur adventure tales are scientists, but more often they come from outside modern society, inhabiting a primitive or natural world where strength, agility, and cunning are more important than book-learning and table manners. One of the first and best-known of such heroes is Burroughs' famous creation, Tarzan. According to tales by Burroughs, Tarzan is the son of an English lord, born in Africa and raised by apes. Burroughs wrote many Tarzan stories, several of which include run-ins with dinosaurs.

One Tarzan adventure is actually one of the many sequels to *At the Earth's Core*. Tarzan visits the underground world of Pellucidar to rescue the emperor, David Innes, from pirates. Tarzan witnesses the exotic dinosaur wildlife of the weird world but becomes trapped himself before making a successful rescue.

Another get-together between Tarzan and Burroughs' imaginary dinosaurs takes place in the tale *Tarzan the Terrible* (1921). In this yarn, Tarzan stumbles across a peculiar prehistoric land called Pal-ul-don while in search of his wife, Jane, who has been kidnapped. Here he learns to ride a species of yellow and blue *Triceratops* called a gryf.

Jungle Fever

Tarzan stories gave rise to numerous films and serialized comics, as well as many spin-offs and spoofs. A host of Tarzan-type muscle men have graced the pages of pulp novels and comics over the years. Frequently, they summon their mighty strength to do battle with dinosaurs and imaginary saurian creatures. Here are just a few of the better-known ones:

➤ **Korak, Son of Tarzan**   He took up in the comics where his dad left off.

➤ **Jongor of Lost Land**   Robert Moore Williams' 1940s hero John Gordon is orphaned in a remote Australian valley that happens to be crawling with dinosaurs.

➤ **Ki-Gor, Jungle Lord**   He starred in comics in the '40s and '50s, doing battle with the saurian "stalkers of the dawn-world" clad in the requisite leopard-skin loincloth.

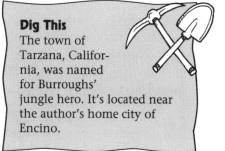

Dig This
The town of Tarzana, California, was named for Burroughs' jungle hero. It's located near the author's home city of Encino.

➤ **Tor**   This dino-fightin' comic-book caveman of the 1950s was created by Joe Kubert.

➤ **Kona, Monarch of Monster Isle**   He kept the Cretaceous killers at bay with his hunting knife.

➤ **Turok, Son of Stone**   The '50s comic starred a Native American in a never-never land of dinosaurs. Turok has recently been revamped as a Nintendo video game called *Turok, Dinosaur Hunter*.

➤ **Conan, the Barbarian**   Robert E. Howard's hero of the sword-and-sorcery set has fought a dinosaur or two.

Others include Jo-Jo, Congo King; Kimbo, Boy of the Jungle; Jungle Jo; Jungle King Torga; and Naza, Stone Age Warrior. In fact, there have been too many jungle- and caveman types to list them all. The comics are also full of jungle- and cave-women in leopard-skin bikinis who fight any dinosaurs that come their way. Among these are Sheena, Queen of the Jungle; Shanna the She-Devil; Rulah, Jungle Goddess; Jann of the Jungle; and Red Sonja.

Jungle Kings

The fantasy of primitive heroism has been a mainstay of pulp novels and comic books for decades. Unencumbered by the trappings of civilization, the jungle king or caveman demonstrates his prowess in life-and-death struggles with nature and, in particular, with predacious dinosaurs. His success not only keeps him alive, but it proves his manhood in physical terms, which can appear absolute in contrast with the elusive and more modest triumphs possible in civilized society.

What's more, the conquering hero typically wins the love of an alluring jungle maiden or a female scientist or explorer. Here again, success takes place independent of the conditions traditionally imposed by civilization. There's no dating in the lost land of the dinosaurs!

Making Progress

While dinosaurs figure into countless fantasy stories as a feature of a primal existence liberated from the restraints of civilization, the creatures have also been used symbolically in other ways. Dinosaurs have long been used as metaphors for failure, especially in the business world. A business that has grown too large and has been around too long to adjust to new demands is often called a "dinosaur," implying, of course, that it won't survive much longer.

Dig This
The "progress" fantasy staged by "The World A Million Years Ago" exhibit was temporarily subverted by a party of nudists who held a wedding at the feet of a mechanical sauropod! This "primitive" fantasy was not welcome and the nudists were arrested.

Fair Game

From a broader perspective, dinosaurs have been used to suggest that progress is inevitable and that humans are succeeding where the dinosaurs have failed. This is the implication behind the many dinosaur exhibits mounted at World's Fairs. The World's Fair celebrates progress and technology, and dinosaur exhibits have held a prominent place in many of them.

In fact, we already mentioned the first World's Fair, held in England in 1851, which centered on the famous Crystal Palace exhibition of dinosaurs designed by Waterhouse Hawkins. This was the first of many instances in which dinosaurs helped suggest the idea of progress through scientific advancement.

The 1933 World's Fair in Chicago, known as the "Century of Progress Exposition," included several dinosaur exhibits—including two with mechanized dinosaurs. It seemed appropriate to use dinosaurs to highlight technological progress because, as prehistoric creatures, they provided a sharp contrast to the high-tech world.

Movers and Shakers

One exhibit, called "The World A Million Years Ago," was built by a company that made mechanized models. The exhibit was advertised as the first "animated museum," and it cost some $200,000 to mount; as reported by a 1933 issue of *Popular Science Monthly*, some models had as many as 16 electric motors inside them.

Another mechanical dinosaur exhibit was sponsored by the Sinclair Oil Corporation, which for years used a sauropod dinosaur as its logo. Motorists could pull in for gas wherever they saw "Dino," the big green dinosaur. The idea behind the dinosaur was to suggest the age of the fossil fuels provided by the company. Advertisements for Sinclair claimed that the best gas and oil comes from the oldest oil wells.

Fossil Fuel

Sinclair's dinosaur exhibit at the World's Fair in Chicago was built with help from Dr. Barnum Brown, a paleontologist with the American Museum of Natural History in New York. The exhibit included six life-size dinosaur statues—*Tyrannosaurus*, *Triceratops*, *Apatosaurus*, *Stegosaurus*, *Corythosaurus*, and *Protoceratops*—together with a nest full of eggs. The dinosaurs were made of steel, rubber, and plaster, and were motorized to move their limbs, heads, and tails.

Sinclair launched other educational dinosaur promotions as well. The company produced its own dinosaur book in the 1930s, again with the help of Barnum Brown, who it gave away free to teachers and librarians. Decades later, Sinclair gave out dinosaur stamps and stamp albums at its service stations.

In 1964 in New York, Sinclair sponsored another World's Fair exhibit called "Dinoland." This exhibit included nine dinosaurs made out of painted fiberglass, as well as some fiberglass sauropod hatchlings.

In addition to the Sinclair exhibit, the New York World's Fair included a dinosaur exhibit sponsored by the Walt Disney Company. This installation was the most high-tech of all: Fairgoers went through the exhibit on a skyway in Ford convertibles, from where they could watch electronically mechanized dinosaurs, including frolicking *Triceratops* hatchlings. The technology that went into the mechanical models was promoted as "space-age technology." The Disney exhibit illustrated like no other that the dinosaurs had been tamed by progress.

It's a Jungle Out There

More recently, the popular "progress" and "primitive" fantasies have been given interesting twists as people increasingly recognize the world of business and technology as a kind of jungle in its own right. These days it's increasingly difficult to escape the world of technology, even in fantasy. Some of the latest dinosaur stories merge technology and fantasy by portraying dinosaurs as technological monstrosities.

Losing Progress

The quintessential example of a high-tech dinosaur thriller is Michael Crichton's best-seller *Jurassic Park*, about a park full of cloned dinosaurs that go on a rampage. At fault for unleashing the deadly dinosaurs is an unholy alliance of big business and advanced scientific technology.

The story reverses the "progress" fantasy by showing technology in the act of unleashing primitive destruction. By the late '80s and early '90s, people were ready to relate to this idea. At this time, many factors contributed to fears of techno-primeval chaos. Well-publicized advances in genetic engineering, the pervasive influence of computers, continuing nuclear fears, and the betrayal of trust by political and business institutions are all reasons technology no longer makes people comfortable, and the *Jurassic Park* dinosaurs symbolize its dangers. The book was made into one of the most successful movies of all time. We'll talk about this picture in more detail in the next chapter.

Armed to the Teeth

The "primitive" fantasy hasbeen technologized not only in books and movies, but also in computer games. We mentioned *Turok, Dinosaur Hunter*, a 1990s computer game based on a 1950s comic series (the comic was also revived in 1996). In this game, players pretend to be Turok and do battle with computer-animated dinosaurs.

Computer technology thus becomes a medium for the "primitive" adventure. In the game, players can choose to fight ordinary fierce predacious dinosaurs, or dinosaurs that are "bionically enhanced" with artillery! The creatures include raptors, *Triceratops*, and *Pteradactylus*.

Players can choose from an arsenal of weapons, including knives, a crossbow, a pulse rifle, a rocket launcher, and even an atomic fusion cannon! As players fight, the game keeps track of their well-being, rating their physical health, weapons supply, and even their "spiritual invincibility." The game shows you can have the latest in high-tech destruction at your fingertips, indulge your primitive fantasies, and still maintain your New Age spirituality!

The Least You Need to Know

➤ Dinosaurs have been staple fare in pulp fiction throughout the 20th century.

➤ Early dinosaur adventure writers include Jules Verne, Arthur Conan Doyle, and Edgar Rice Burroughs.

➤ The "primitive" fantasy in jungle- and cave-hero stories supplies a popular alternative to mundane civilized existence.

➤ The "progress" fantasy at World's Fairs suggests that humans have succeeded where dinosaurs have failed.

➤ The Sinclair Oil Corporation used a dinosaur in its logo and promoted dinosaur education.

From Limestone to Limelight

The history of dinosaur movies develops side by side with the history of movie special effects. Dinosaurs present movie-makers with a special challenge because they're so difficult to represent convincingly—but when filmmakers succeed, it usually means another special-effects breakthrough.

Meanwhile, just as dinosaur movies have developed, so too has dinosaur science, producing its own new pictures of spectacular saurians. There's never been any doubt that dinosaurs must have been a sight to behold, but breakthroughs in dinosaur paleontology indicate dinosaurs were more sleek and streamlined—just plain better-looking—than previously believed.

Developments in dinosaur science and dinosaur-movie special effects culminated in 1993 with the blockbuster movie *Jurassic Park*. By this time, dinosaur science had done justice to the combined power and agility of dinosaurs, and special effects technology—including computer imagery—was ready to do justice to the new scientific view.

Early Effects

While Tarzan and the others have been doing their stuff in the comics, movie-makers have tapped their creative resources in bringing dinosaur spectacles to the screen. We already mentioned several movies involving dinosaur adventures based on novels by Verne, Doyle, and Burroughs in Chapter 26, and there have been plenty of others. In fact, for about as long as motion pictures have existed, special-effects designers have been developing ways to portray dinosaurs on film.

Techniques include cartoon animation, stop-motion photography with models moved by hand, moving mechanical models and puppets, the use of live animals such as lizards, and a technique that has become known as *suitimation*—putting a guy in a rubber dinosaur suit! Many of these gimmicks were pioneering feats in special effects.

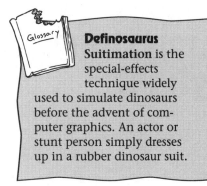

Definosaurus

Suitimation is the special-effects technique widely used to simulate dinosaurs before the advent of computer graphics. An actor or stunt person simply dresses up in a rubber dinosaur suit.

Another First

The first animated cartoon character was a dinosaur named Gertie. A friendly sauropod with a huge appetite, Gertie was created by cartoonist and vaudeville performer Winson McCay in 1912. As part of his vaudeville act, McCay stood on stage next to the screen and would appear to interact with the cartoon, giving it instructions, feeding it, and at the end, seemingly entering the cartoon and riding away on Gertie's back!

Gertie the Dinosaur, the first animated cartoon character ever to appear on a movie screen.

(Photofest)

Frozen in Time

Willis Harold O'Brien was another pioneer in the field of movie dinosaurs. O'Brien was among the first to develop the technique of stop-motion photography—filming models one frame at a time and moving them slightly between each frame so they look like they're moving on their own. This would become a widely used—though painstaking— technique for bringing dinosaurs to life on film.

O'Brien made a number of short dinosaur films using this technique—including *The Birth of a Flivver* (1916), *The Dinosaur and the Missing Link* (1917), and *R.F.D. 10,000 B.C.* (1917)—before using dinosaur animation for his first feature film, the 1925 screening of Arthur Conan Doyle's *The Lost World*. This movie depicts an *Allosaurus* attacking and killing an *Apatosaurus*, an erupting volcano, and a stampeding herd of *Triceratops*.

O'Brien continued to do dinosaur special effects for feature films. His most famous effort is the work he did for the classic 1933 movie *King Kong*. King Kong, as you may already know, is an enormous ape who is captured on a remote tropical island and brought to New York City as a spectacle. Before arriving in the Big Apple, Kong does battle with several Mesozoic creatures, including a T-rex, an *Elasmosaurus*, and a giant *Pteranodon*. O'Brien has been hailed as a master for his special-effects work on *King Kong* and other films.

King Kong makes chicken fingers out of a giant Pteranodon *in the classic film of 1933.*
(Photofest)

269

Snakes Alive

Film pioneer D.W. Griffith's short movie *Brute Force* (1912), about warring cave tribes, earns recognition as well as an early effort to portray dinosaurs in movies. The film uses a live snake and a live alligator, both wearing "costumes" to depict prehistoric saurians. The snake appears with a crest on its head, and the alligator has a horn on its head and two sets of wings attached to its back!

The technique of using live animals to represent Mesozoic creatures was developed further in the Hal Roach film of 1940, *One Million B.C.* (not to be confused with the better-known film *One Million Years B.C.* of 1967, starring Raquel Welch). The 1940 feature, starring Victor Mature as a heroic caveman, treats audiences to the spectacle of man vs. monster by showing enlarged footage of modern lizards and other animals superimposed onto footage of ordinary-sized human actors. Audiences of the '40s thrilled to see Mature and his cohorts menaced by a "giant" iguana, an alligator with a sail attached to its back, and even an armadillo gussied up to look like an *Ankylosaurus*!

Dig This

The live-animal special effects in *One Million B.C.* were recycled numerous times in a host of prehistoric B-movies, including such rarely viewed classics as *Untamed Women* (1952), *King Dinosaur* (1955), and *Teenage Caveman* (1958).

The highly popular 1967 remake *One Million Years B.C.* used model dinosaurs and stop-motion photography to mount dinosaur-caveman battle scenes. These models are reasonably convincing in their own right, though the battle scenes between people and dinosaurs seem a little silly. Though not a clay model, Raquel Welch appears in a fur bikini in the film's now famous publicity poster, which announces the blatant falsehood: "This is the way it was!"

Science and Fiction

Although scores of movies have featured dinosaurs, few make much of an attempt at paleontological accuracy. Dinosaur movies typically show prehistoric people living together with dinosaurs, Triassic and Cretaceous dinosaurs are often portrayed as living at the same time, plant-eaters are sometimes represented as meat-eaters, and dinosaur anatomy is subject to loose interpretation. The point, after all, is not science but make-believe.

Dinosaur Parking

In the blockbuster film *Jurassic Park* (1993) and its sequel, *Lost World* (1997), however, dinosaur science gives the imagination a bigger boost than it does in most films. Recent advances in dinosaur paleontology figure prominently in the plot, and the film isn't set back in prehistoric times or in some undiscovered ecosystem that has escaped the notice of the rest of the world. Instead, dinosaurs are cloned from fossilized DNA. (Although dinosaur scientists are a long way from actually doing this, the movie's high-tech premise is at least based on scientific procedures some paleontologists actually explore in their work.)

Fossil Fallacy

Although *Jurassic Park* emphasizes the role of paleontology in producing our knowledge of dinosaurs, it takes numerous liberties in the way it represents dinosaurs. Even so, director Stephen Spielberg was tempted to go even further and give his raptors the forked, flickering tongues of a snake. He scrapped this idea, however, in favor of greater anatomic accuracy.

Innovations aside, the films explore an idea that is central to many of the older "lost world" stories treated in movies and pulp fiction: Nature is something that science and civilization cannot control. In *Jurassic Park*, however, the world of the dinosaurs does not exist apart from civilization; it is created with scientific technology to serve as a profit-making dinosaur park on a secluded South American island.

Risky Business

The park is master-minded by businessman John Hammond, who is having trouble convincing insurance companies that his park will be safe. To ease their fears, he arranges for noted dinosaur scientist Dr. Grant and his partner, paleobotonist Dr. Satler, to come and endorse the project, along with "chaos theorist" Ian Malcolm. During their weekend visit, the park's computerized security system goes offline and the dinosaurs go on the prowl.

As in the classic film *King Kong*, the attempt to harness a dangerous natural force as a money-making spectacle unleashes its deadly power. In *Jurassic Park*, Ian Malcolm warns against the unholy alliance between scientists who develop dinosaur-cloning technology but who don't consider the practical uses of their discoveries, and business people who don't understand the complexities of the science they put to use. This produces a highly dangerous and uncontrollable situation.

The dangers are unleashed as a computer technician attempts to steal dinosaur embryos to sell them to rival businessmen. In doing so, he shuts down the park's security systems, allowing predacious dinosaurs to roam free in search of human prey. To make matters worse, a tropical storm sets in, making escape from the dinosaurs more difficult.

The dinosaurs and the storm represent the uncontrollable forces of nature that science and business unsuccessfully attempt to harness. The film portrays still

Boning Up

Jurassic Park plays with the fact that the movie, like the park whose story the movie tells, are both designed to be money-making spectacles. In a pivotal scene near the end of the film, the T-rex roars as a "Jurassic Park" banner flutters above him. The movie is publicity for the park is publicity for the movie.

another uncontrollable force of nature that further contributes to the chaotic situation: kids! When the grandchildren of the park's founder are unleashed on the reserved and prickly Dr. Grant, he finds there is no escape. Instead, he must overcome his fear of children and learn to be a responsible protector and role-model.

Evolving Story

Jurassic Park was hugely successful, breaking box-office records as the most popular film yet produced. It ignited a craze for dinosaurs—both as scary movie monsters and as a subject of scientific inquiry. The movie's dinosaurs, created through mechanization and computer imagery, far outstripped previous attempts to bring dinosaurs to the screen in terms of their realism.

The sequel, *Jurassic Park 2: Lost World*, was not as successful, but it continued to develop the theme of the dangerous interaction between civilization and nature. This movie takes place on an island laboratory facility used for breeding dinosaurs for Jurassic Park. Many dinosaurs have survived here and started up a viable ecosystem. A new group of investors wants to bring some of the dinosaurs back to the United States. Meanwhile, a conservationist paleontologist wants to sabotage their plans by releasing the dinosaurs they have captured before they can be transported off the island.

Lost World complicates the idea put forward in *Jurassic Park* that messing with nature is dangerous. While this idea is a theme in the sequel, the second movie also suggests that it can be dangerous to simply leave nature alone. The efforts to release the dinosaurs backfire with deadly results. Setting them free enables them to attack once more.

Dinosaur Camp

This no-win situation, in which interfering with and preserving nature both lead to disaster, also takes place in the campy saur-horror movie, *Carnosaur* (1993). As in *Jurassic Park*, scientists clone dinosaurs. These scientists, however, are twisted and evil. Their carnosaur breaks free and makes a bloody mess out of a group of counter-culture conservationists who have chained themselves to some heavy machinery to protest a building development.

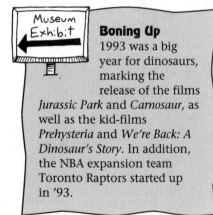

Boning Up
1993 was a big year for dinosaurs, marking the release of the films *Jurassic Park* and *Carnosaur*, as well as the kid-films *Prehysteria* and *We're Back: A Dinosaur's Story*. In addition, the NBA expansion team Toronto Raptors started up in '93.

The terror of reawakened dinosaurs provides a way for movie-makers and storytellers to represent tensions between nature and civilized society. Often, the monsters are somehow of our own creation, and the monster's eventual destruction leads to a humbling realization that human ambitions are often misguided. Versions of this story have been told again and again in the quintessential monster movies starring Godzilla.

New Stomping Grounds

The most extreme cinematic statements about nature running amok in the face of science and civilization are made in the seemingly endless series of Godzilla films. Godzilla is an enormous saurian monster who, in film after film, terrorizes humanity by destroying cities. Sometimes, however, Godzilla is a good monster who defends humanity from other monsters.

Godzilla eats commuter train cars like they were sausage links in the original 'Zilla film, Godzilla, King of the Monsters *(1956).*
(Toho Studios/Photofest)

Checkered Past

Godzilla hails from Japan, where he is known as Gojira. The first Godzilla movie was released in Japan as *Gojira* in 1954 by the motion picture company Toho International. Ever since, Toho has unleashed Godzilla films at an alarming rate. An English version came out two years later, renamed *Godzilla, King of the Monsters*. In this film, scenes featuring Raymond Burr were added.

In this first movie, the monster has been hibernating for centuries before being awakened by atom bomb tests. (Some have suggested that Godzilla is a metaphor for the horrors suffered by Hiroshima and Nagasaki as

Dig This
Godzilla's Japanese name, Gojira, is a combination of the English word *gorilla* and the Japanese word *kujira*, meaning *whale*. Originally, Gojira was the nickname of an employee at Toho International!

a result of nuclear bombing at the end of World War II.) The monster, played by an actor in a rubber suit, goes on a rampage through Tokyo (carefully reconstructed in miniature), destroying everything in its path.

Later Godzilla films are not, strictly speaking, sequels of the original; the Godzilla story is often different from film to film. Different films recount different origins for the monster, give him different "looks," and different personalities. In many films, in fact, Godzilla is a nice monster, protecting humanity from such fearsome invaders as the three-headed Guidrah, the Smog Monster, and Megalon.

Late Shows

Here's a list of some of the better-known Godzilla features. Be forewarned, however, that many Godzilla flicks go by more than one title:

➤ *Godzilla, King of the Monsters* (1956)   This film was the first to treat viewers to a slo-mo destruction of a miniature Tokyo. Godzilla is vanquished in the end by an invention called the oxygen destroyer.

➤ *Gigantis, the Fire Monster* (1959)   Gigantis is a reincarnated Godzilla who does battle with a rubber-suited *Ankylosaurus* named Angurus.

➤ *King Kong vs. Godzilla* (1963)   The meeting was inevitable, but the contest was indecisive.

➤ *Godzilla vs. Mothra* (1964)   This feature pits 'Zilla against a giant moth.

➤ *Guidrah, the Three-Headed Monster* (1965)   Godzilla and Mothra are on the same side this time, defending the earth against the title-role terror.

➤ *Son of Godzilla* (1967)   Godzilla defends his hatchling against mutant insects.

> **Dig This**
> The shortest Godzilla film ever was not made by Toho International but by independent cartoonist Marvin Newland. This is the cult classic *Bambi Meets Godzilla* (1969). All we see of Godzilla is its foot, which squashes Bambi like a pancake!

➤ *Destroy All Monsters* (1968)   Eleven inmates of Monster Island break loose and raise a ruckus.

➤ *Godzilla vs. Megalon* (1976)   Megalon and Gigan take on Godzilla and a robot friend named Jet Jaguar.

➤ *Godzilla vs. MechaGodzilla* (1977)   Godzilla does battle with his mechanical likeness.

➤ *Godzilla, 1985* (1985)   Would you believe they decided to do a remake of the original?

➤ *Godzilla* (1998)   An American 'Zilla film in which the giant menace terrorizes New York City and lays eggs in Madison Square Garden.

The Latest Look

Godzilla's most recent incarnation is the American movie, *Godzilla* (1998), written and directed by Roland Emerich and distributed by Sony Pictures. According to the script, Godzilla is not a reawakened dinosaur as in previous movies, but an iguana that has been mutated by radiation. Despite his iguana heritage, however, Godzilla '98 is agile and bipedal, much like the raptors of the Mesozoic. Thus, the new 'Zilla qualifies as a dinosaur-inspired horror.

The latest Godzilla movie does more with special effects than previous 'Zilla films. Computer-generated imagery makes for a much scarier monster than the suitimation creatures of the past. What's more, the film shows a whole nest of 'Zilla hatchlings in action. Thanks largely to phenominal special effects, it's making monster movie and disaster film fans very happy.

Sauring Sounds

Of course, we express our fascination for dinosaurs in more ways than books and movies. For example, there's dinosaur music. Rock groups include T. Rex of the 1970s and today's Dinosaur Jr. The well-known classical piece "Fossils," from *Carnival of the Animals*, by Camille Saint-Sëans', evokes dinosaurs through the xylophone. The real boom in the dinosaur market, however, is in the realm of kid stuff, as the next chapter indicates.

The Least You Need to Know

➤ Classic dinosaur movies include *Gertie the Dinosaur* (1912), *King Kong* (1933), *One Million B.C.* (1940), and *One Million Years B.C.* (1967).

➤ Dinosaur movies tend to treat the theme of nature vs. civilization.

➤ *Jurassic Park* (1993) is one of the most popular movies ever made.

➤ The Godzilla story changes throughout the many Godzilla movies.

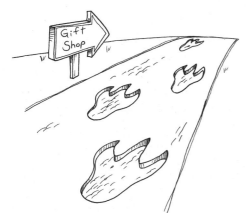

Kid Stuff

The most avid dinosaur fans are kids. Dinosaurs, of course, are inherently cool, and kids can see this as clearly as anyone else. In addition, learning about dinosaurs seems to help kids get a handle on the basic challenges and rewards of existence—dinosaurs lived and died, fought and cooperated, and—just like people—came in all shapes, sizes, and varieties.

What's more, although they once actually existed, they now seem like imaginary creatures. No other subject is both mythic and scientific in quite the same way. As a result, learning about dinosaurs is more exciting than learning about, say, math or geography. Dinosaurs can even be useful for teaching kids about subjects that might otherwise seem boring, difficult, or painful.

Tons of dinosaur books, TV shows, movies, toys, and games are aimed at kids of all ages. Many are educational, but many are intended simply to be entertaining. In either case, they provide kids with intriguing perspectives for thinking about life's problems.

Dino Toons

Of course, lots of dinosaur entertainment can be appreciated by kids as well as adults. For example, many classic cartoons have dealt with dinosaurs. We mentioned Gertie the Dinosaur in the last chapter, the first cartoon character to appear on screen, but since Gertie many more dinosaurs have appeared on the scene.

In one early cartoon, *A Stone Age Romance* (1929), a caveman chases after his future mate amid funny business with dinosaurs and other prehistoric creatures. Still more ridiculous is *Stone Age Stunts* (1930), which includes vaudeville-style song-and-dance numbers performed by dinosaurs.

Dinosaurs have also been featured in the adventures of many classic cartoon characters, including Betty Boop, Felix the Cat, Daffy Duck, Porky Pig, and Mighty Mouse. In fact, in one episode Mighty Mouse overcomes a considerable disadvantage in size as he takes on a sauropod dinosaur!

Hitting Bedrock

A classic cartoon for kids of all ages is Hanna-Barbera's *The Flintstones*. Starting out in the early '60s, the show was the first TV cartoon to premiere as a prime-time series.

The Flintstones show that prehistoric people lived just like they did in the 1960s!
(Hanna-Barbera/Photofest)

In fact, the show was inspired by the popular sitcom, *The Honeymooners,* starring Jackie Gleason, a leading show when *The Flintstones* came out. Like Gleason's character, Ralph Cramden, Fred Flintstone is a loud-mouth who thinks rather too highly of his own intelligence, despite continually appearing foolish.

Modern Living

A recurrent sourceof humor in *The Flintstones* is the fact that, despite the show's prehistoric setting, life in the town of Bedrock is represented as being essentially the same as it was in suburban America during the '60s. People drive around in cars made of wood and animal horn with stone wheels, using their feet to propel them.

> **Dig This**
> The resemblance between *The Flintstones* and *The Honeymooners* was close enough for 'Mooners star Jackie Gleason to consider suing Hanna-Barbera, though he decided not to. He was afraid he'd get a reputation as a crank.

The show's main character, Fred Flintstone, works in a quarry, using a sauropod dinosaur as an earth mover. He belongs to a bowling league and a men's club, called the Loyal Order of Water Buffalo. The family pets, of course, are a sabre-toothed cat and the dog-like dinosaur, Dino.

Household gadgets such as automatic can-openers and vacuum cleaners are provided in the form of animals: A prehistoric bird opens cans with its beak, and a small wooley mammoth sucks up dust with its trunk! The living household appliances occasionally offer droll observations about their work. While the show is something of a spoof on Tarzan and the other "primitive" fantasy heroes we talked about in Chapter 26, it indulges heavily in the "progress" fantasy in which the taming of the dinosaurs symbolizes the success of human beings.

The show was a huge success spawning toys, games, merchandise, comics, and feature-length movies. It was even made into a live action movie in 1994 starring John Goodman as Fred Flintstone. This feature used elaborate models and special effects to simulate the cartoon.

Flakes Off the Stone

The Flintstones was only one of many Hanna-Barbera series based on prehistoric subjects. Needless to say, the others didn't come close to achieving the popularity of *The Flintstones.*

➤ *Dino Boy* 1966 cartoon in which a 20th-century kid gets lost in a valley of dino-saurs. He rides around on his dinosaur, Bronty.

➤ *The Mighty Mightor* 1966 cartoon in which a cave kid with a magic club trans-forms himself into a super-powered hero. He also changes his pet dinosaur into a dragon.

➤ *Valley of the Dinosaurs* Cartoon series of 1974 in which a family finds itself in a lost valley and makes friends with a family of cave people.

➤ *Korg: 7,000 B.C.* Live action series of 1974 about a family of Neanderthals. The show had no dinosaurs.

➤ *Captain Caveman and the Teen Angels* A 1977 cartoon series about a caveman with a magic club who thaws out in the 20th century and turns crime-fighter.

Live-Action Dinos

In 1974, Sid and Marty Krofft Productions came out with a popular live-action Saturday morning dinosaur show, *Land of the Lost*. In this show, a forest ranger named Rick Marshall and his two kids are transported by the greatest earthquake ever known to a strange place inhabited by a variety of weird creatures, including dinosaurs. The family takes up housekeeping in a cave while trying to stay clear of the dangers that inhabit their new neighborhood.

Dig This
A more recent stop-motion dinosaur production is the 1980 short feature *Dinosaurs*, by the famous "claymation" artist Will Vinton.

The dinosaurs are realistic models moved through stop-motion photography. Some become mischievous pets; others are dangerous menaces. There's a "brontosaurus" named Emily, a *Triceratops* named Spike, a *Tyranosaurus* named Grumpy, an *Allosaurus* named Big Alice, a *Coelophysis* named Spot, and a baby *Apatosaurus* named Dopey. There's also their little cave-boy friend, Chaka, and the menacing Sleestaks.

Cold-Blooded Family

Dinosaurs returned to TV in a prime-time sitcom format with *The Dinosaurs*, which ran from 1991–1994. The show centers on the Sinclairs, a puppet family of working-class dinosaurs (who evidently get their name from the Sinclair Oil Company, whose logo featured a dinosaur). The family includes father Earl, a *Megalosaurus*; Mother Fran, an *Allosaurus*; 15-year-old Robbie; 13-year-old Charlene; and a 2-year-old referred to simply as Baby. There's also Grandma Ethyl, who figures into many standard sitcom mother-in-law jokes.

The show deals with the primitive aspects of family life. Family members are typically unable to control their darker feelings and desires. In representing the life of the Sinclairs, the show repeatedly jokes about how beast-like family life can be.

Purple Power

The latest TV dinosaur sensation is aimed at preschoolers and early elementary-school kids: Barney, the purple dinosaur. Don't let the superficial resemblance of this life-size puppet to a meat-eating therapod dinosaur fool you! Barney is every little kid's best friend.

Barney the purple dinosaur is here, and he loves you.
(Dennis Fuller/Photofest)

The show is especially popular for its sing-alongs. Songs are educational and provide emotional encouragement. The show stresses the theme of love among friends and family members. Barney's popularity has given rise to toys, clothing, and other merchandise, including several videos. The feature-length movie *Barney's Great Adventure* came out in 1998.

Younger kids seem to identify strongly with dinosaurs. They sense dinosaurs are special and unusual, just as *they* are, and they see that dinosaurs have been sadly misunderstood by adults. Barney wouldn't get along very well without a lot of kids on his side. By relating to dinosaurs, little kids find a way to deal with their own sense of strangeness in an adult world.

> **Dig This**
> Barney went to South Africa to meet with South African President Nelson Mandela after contributing to the Nelson Mandela Children's Fund.

Kid Flicks

Kids' dinosaur movies have proven immensely popular, especially in recent years. These have tended to portray dinosaurs as misunderstood, lovable misfits. Viewers can relate to the dinosaurs and their friends as they try to get by in world that is too cruel or too busy for its own good. Thus kid movies about dinosaurs show that a world where dinosaurs don't belong is a world that needs changing.

Babes in the Woods

One particular film that achieved tremendous success with young children was 1988's *Land Before Time*, an animated feature-length cartoon directed by Don Bluth. The film tells the story of a baby sauropod dinosaur named Littlefoot, who is orphaned and sets off with his friends in search of a new home.

Littlefoot's companions are also baby dinosaurs. They include Cera, a *Ceratosaurus*; Ducky, a duckbilled dinosaur; Petrie, a *Pteranodon*; and Spike, a *Triceratops*. The youngsters have to stick together for survival as they travel through a fearsome land full of "sharp teeth"—meat-eating dinosaurs. Since the first, four additional *Land Before Time* movies have been made as of 1998: *The Great Valley Adventure* (1994), *The Time of the Great Giving* (1995), *Journey Through the Mists* (1995), and *The Mysterious Island* (1997).

Song and Dance

Another animated dinosaur movie for young children set in modern times is *We're Back: A Dinosaur's Story*, made in 1993. In this yarn, a time-traveling inventor returns to present-day Manhattan with several dinosaurs in tow. He even teaches them to talk (and sing, as the movie is a musical). Meanwhile, an evil scientist wants to get hold of the dinosaurs for himself. The movie features a cast of famous voices, including John Goodman, Charles Fleischer, Rhea Perlman, Martin Short, Julia Child, Jay Leno, Yeardly Smith, and even Walter Cronkite!

A popular comedy for slightly older kids is *Prehysteria!*, still another dinosaur film of 1993. Pigmy dinosaur eggs hatch into pets as bad guys try to steal them from the kid who found them. The kid and the dinosaurs develop a special bond that the rest of the world can't appreciate. A sequel was produced in 1994; a three-quel appeared in 1995.

Grand Finale

A more serious treatment of dinosaurs comes from the famous evolution sequence in the classic Walt Disney Film *Fantasia* of 1940. The segment is accompanied by Igor Stravinsky's famous classical composition, *The Rite of Spring*. As the music is heard, the history of life on earth unfolds, including a memorable look at life during the Mesozoic Period.

Dig This
It has been rumored that Disney Studios is planning a full-length feature devoted entirely to dinosaurs, scheduled for release in 1999.

The film represents numerous animated dinosaurs, including *Triceratops*, *Struthiomimus*, *Apatosaurus*, and several kinds of duckbill. There's also a battle between a T-rex and a *Stegosaurus*. Finally, the dinosaurs fall victim to drought, and they're shown trudging off in search of water. Gradually they fall, die, and decay, leaving their bones to bleach in the sun. It's an evocative portrayal of the demise of the giant creatures.

Prehistoric Pages

Dinosaur books for kids abound. In fact, there are far too many educational books on dinosaurs to list. Libraries and bookstores have entire shelves stuffed full of them. Clearly dinosaurs are a favorite subject for millions of kids—parents often report how far their children outstrip them in their knowledge of Mesozoic creatures!

Not all dinosaur books are educational in a scientific sense. Some are merely entertaining, although they do have lessons to teach about life. In many books, dinosaurs are special friends much as they are in dinosaur movies for kids; other books represent dinosaurs as bad and scary. In books for older kids, dinosaurs appear magical.

Buddies from Way Back

The sauropods are almost always the friendly ones. A famous dinosaur-as-friend book is the classic picture book *Danny and the Dinosaur*, written and drawn by Syd Hoff in 1958. Danny is a kid who rides around town perched high up on the neck of his pet sauropod dinosaur. As you can imagine, this makes Danny pretty special.

Another kind of nutty picture book is *Dinosaur Bob and his Adventures with the Family Lazardo*, written by William Joyce in 1995. Bob is a big sauropod dinosaur who joins the local baseball team—it turns out he's a good player. In the humorous dinosaur book *Mrs. Toggle and the Dinosaur*, by Robin Pulver (1991), Mrs. Toggle is a grade-school teacher who worries about what to do when she hears that a dinosaur will be joining her class.

Facing the Issues

A more confrontational picture book is *Tyrone the Horrible*, (1988) by Hans Wilhelm. This story about a T-rex who needs to learn some lessons in manners shows that dinosaurs are useful in getting kids to think about their own lives.

This idea of representing dinosaurs as inhabitants of a moral universe that kids can understand is the basis of a series of books called *Dino Life Guides*, by Laurie Krasny Brown and Marc Brown. These books depict dinosaurs as being, in essence, people. The guides take on serious subjects, including health, safety, divorce, and even death.

For slightly older kids, there's a series of books based on *Dinotopia* by James Gurney (1992). Dinotopia is a secluded island where dinosaurs are not only still alive, but are capable of interacting with people as part of an imaginary society.

Paleo Pals

Dinosaur toys, too, are available all over the place, ranging from the realistic to the ridiculous. One company, Safari Ltd. of Miami, Florida, makes anatomically accurate plastic models of dozens of dinosaur genera in a range of sizes. Safari also makes wooden skeleton models for assembly at home. Less realistic stuffed animal dinos are easy to find, too.

Another popular kind of dinosaur toy are the "virtual pets," also called "egg watches." An electronic dinosaur "egg" hatches into a small computer dinosaur that you care for and raise to a healthy, full-grown creature. If you don't carry out your responsibilities as a caregiver, however, your dinosaur becomes extinct!

Keep on Digging!

When the kids are tired of playing with their dinosaur toys, reading their dinosaur books, and watching their dinosaur videos, it may be time to take them to see dinosaur fossils at a museum. You can find a museum near you in the list of museums provided in Appendix A, immediately following this chapter.

Other appendices include an annotated list of dinosaurs with pronunciation guides, tables showing how the various kinds of Mesozoic creatures are classified and related in evolutionary terms, a glossary, and a list of books for further reading.

The Least You Need to Know

➤ Dinosaurs are a popular educational subject for kids because they are both scientific and imaginary.

➤ Many classic cartoon characters, including Porky Pig and Mighty Mouse, have had run-ins with dinosaurs.

➤ *The Flintstones* represent prehistoric existence with all the comforts of the modern world.

➤ Kids love Barney, the singing purple dinosaur.

➤ The many *Land Before Time* movies have been immensely popular with little kids.

➤ Dinosaur books for kids range from bizarre to educational.

See 'Em in Museums

This appendix lists the largest dinosaur exhibits in North America.

The National Museum of Natural History
at the Smithsonian Institution
10th Street and Constitution Avenue NW
Washington, D.C. 20560
202-357-2020

The Academy of Natural Sciences
1900 Ben Franklin Parkway
Philadelphia, PA 19103
215-299-1000

The Carnegie Museum of Natural History
4400 Forbes Avenue
Pittsburgh, PA 15213
412-622-3283

American Museum of Natural History
Central Park West at 79th Street
New York, NY 10024
212-769-5000

Peabody Museum of Natural History
Yale University
170 Whitney Avenue
P.O. Box 6666
New Haven, CT 06511
203-432-5050

Dinosaur State Park
West Street
Rocky Hill, CT 06067
203-529-8423

Canadian Museum of Nature
P.O. Box 3443, Station D
Ottowa, Ontario, Canada KIP 6P4
613-990-2200

Royal Ontario Museum
100 Queen's Park
Toronto, Ontario, Canada M5S 2C6
416-586-5551

Field Museum of Natural History
Lake Shore Drive at Roosevelt Road
Chicago, IL 60605
312-922-9410

Science Museum of Minnesota
30 East 10th Street
St. Paul, MN 55101
612-221-9488

Badlands National Park
P.O. Box 6
Interior, SD 57750
605-433-5361

Morden and District Museum
P.O. Box 728
Morden, Manitoba, Canada R0G 1J0
204-822-3406

Houston Museum of Natural Science
One Hermann Circle Drive
Houston, TX 77030
713-639-4600

New Mexico Museum of Natural History
1801 Mountain Road, NW
Albuquerque, NM 87104
505-841-8837

Cleveland-Lloyd Dinosaur Quarry
U.S. Department of the Interior
Bureau of Land Management
P.O. Drawer A.B.
900 North 700 East
Price, UT 84501
801-637-4584

Warner Valley Tracksite
Bureau of Land Management
Dixie Resource Area
225 North Bluff Street
St. George, UT 84770
801-673-4654

Brigham Young University Earth Science Museum
1683 North Canyon Road
Provo, UT 84602
801-378-3680

Utah Museum of Natural History
University of Utah
President's Circle
Salt Lake City, UT 84112
801-581-4303

Dinosaur National Monument
P.O. Box 210
Dinosaur, CO 81610
303-374-2216

Denver Museum of Natural History
2001 Colorado Boulevard
Denver, CO 80205
303-370-6387

Dinosaur Provincial Park
Field Station of the Royal Tyrrell Museum of Paleontology
P.O. Box 60
Patricia, Alberta, Canada T0J 2K0
403-378-4342

Royal Tyrrell Museum of Paleontology
Box 7500
Drumheller, Alberta, Canada T0J 0Y0
403-823-7707

Natural History Museum of Los Angeles County
900 Exposition Boulevard
Los Angeles, CA 90007
213-744-3466

Dinosaurus

This appendix describes the kinds of dinosaurs and provides a Paleo-speak pronunciation key.

Aetosaurus [ae-EE-toh-SAHR-us] (eagle lizard)   Upper Triassic thecodont that, unlike almost all others, appears to have eaten plants rather than meat. It had a relatively short skull and leaf-shaped teeth.

Albertosaurus [al-BURT-oh-SAHR-us] (lizard from Alberta)   Tyrannosaur found in Canada.

Allosaurus [AL-oh-SAHR-us] (different lizard)   The most common of the carnosaurs, found in large numbers in the western United States.

Anatosaurus [an-AT-oh-SAHR-us] (duck lizard)   Among the best known of the crestless duckbills, thanks in part to a mummified skeleton found in 1908.

Anchisaurus [AN-kee-SAHR-us] (near lizard)   Prosauropod that gets its name from being a near descendant of the non-dinosaur reptiles.

Ankylosaurus [an-KYL-oh-SAHR-us] (fused lizard)   One of the last ankies to evolve (surviving to the end of the Cretaceous Period), it is known from fossils found in North America.

Apatosaurus [ah-PAT-oh-SAHR-us] (deceptive lizard)   A big sauropod that gets its name because its bones have been confused with those of other species.

Archaeopteryx [AR-kee-OP-ter-iks] (ancient wing)   The earliest-known bird, combining a number of bird and dinosaur features.

Baptornis [bapt-ORN-iss] (dipping bird)   From the Early Cretaceous Period, this dino had teeth and only the smallest of nubs for wings. It couldn't fly, but was a diver instead, paddling after fish with webbed feet.

Baryonyx [BAR-ee-ON-iks] (strong claw)   This big, crocodile-snouted predator may have lived mostly on fish.

Bavarisaurus [bah-VAHR-ee-SAHR-us] (lizard from Bavaria)   Small, quick lizard found in the belly of a *Compsognathus*.

Brachiosaurus [BRAK-ee-oh-SAHR-us] (arm lizard)   A unique sauropod with front legs that are longer than its back legs, hence its name.

"Brontosaurus" [BRAHN-toh-SAHR-us] (thunder lizard)   Turned out to be the same as *Apatosaurus*, the official name. Most people know the name "Bronto," though, so it still gets used.

Camarasaurus [KAM-ah-rah-SAHR-us] (chambered lizard)   Has chambers in its vertebrae that make them more lightweight, as do many other sauropods.

Carcharodontosaurus [kahr-KAHR-oh-DONT-oh-SAHR-us] (great white shark-toothed lizard)   Candidate for the largest land predator ever.

Carnotaurus [KAHR-noh-TAHR-us] (meat-eating bull)   Carnosaur whose bull-like appearance results from two horny crests growing out of its forehead.

Ceratosaurus [serr-AT-oh-SAHR-us] (horned lizard)   Twenty-foot-long horned ceratosaur.

Chasmosaurus [KAS-moh-SAHR-us] (opening lizard)   Ceratopsian named for the big windows in its frill. It has left fossilized skin impressions that show it was covered with big, round scales.

Coelophysis [SEEL-oh-FY-sis] (hollow form)   A pack-hunting ceratosaur.

Coelurus [seel-OOR-us] (hollow bones)   A coelurosaur resembling *Ornitholestes*.

Compsognathus [komp-sohg-NAE-thuss] (pretty jaw)   A chicken-sized coelurosaur, one of the smallest dinosaurs with a close resemblance to *Archaeopteryx*.

Corythosaurus [koh-RITH-oh-SAHR-us] (helmet lizard)   A duckbill with a crest shaped like a big, high mohawk hairdo.

Daspletosaurus [das-PLEET-oh-SAHR-us] (frightful lizard)   Canadian tyrannosaur, slightly smaller than *Tyrannosaurus*.

Deinocheiris [DY-noh-KYR-us] (terrible hand)   Large bird mimic, known from impressive forelimbs.

Deinonychus [dy-NON-ik-us] (terrible claw)   An obscure and ignored raptor for more than 30 years until a better specimen was discovered in 1969, which reopened the bird-origin controversy.

Deinosuchus [DY-noh-SOOK-us] (scary croc)   The largest crocodile ever was this 50-foot long Cretaceous beast.

Dilophosaurus [dy-LOHF-oh-SAHR-us] (double crest lizard)   Ceratosaur with a V-shaped crest on its head.

Dimetrodon [dy-MEH-troh-don] (two sized tooth)   Meat-eating fin-backed pelycosaur.

Dimorphodon [dy-MORF-oh-don] (two-shaped teeth)   Pterosaur with an unusually deep, rounded skull. It may have eaten insects and small animals. It had a tail but no skull crest.

Diplodocus [dip-LOD-oh-kus] (double beamed)   Sauropod that gets its name from the extra ridge on its vertebrae that lent added support to the neck and back.

Dravidosaurus [drah-VID-oh-SAHR-us] (Dravid lizard)   Stegosaur from India.

Dromaeosaurus [DROHM-ee-oh-SAHR-us] (swift lizard)   A primitive, founding member of the raptor clan with smaller claws and larger jaws than the other sickle-toed raptors.

Dromiceiomimus [drohm-ih-SEE-oh-MYM-us] (emu mimic)   A bird mimic coelurosaur.

Dryptosaurus [DRIPT-oh-SAHR-us] (wounding lizard)   Theropod originally called *Laelaps* but renamed by Marsh.

Edaphosaurus [ee-DAFF-oh-SAHR-us] (Earth lizard)   A plant-eating fin-backed pelycosaur.

Edmontonia [ed-mon-TOHN-ee-ah] (from the Edmonton rock formation)   Late Cretaceous nodosaur with particularly long spikes coming out of its sides and shoulders.

Elasmosaurus [ee-LASS-moh-SAHR-us] (plated lizard)   Long-necked plesiosaur.

Enantiornis [en-AN-tih-ORN-iss] (opposite bird, so called because it has an opposable claw for perching)   Sparrow-sized bird of the Late Cretaceous Period. It was a good flyer and good percher. *Enantiornis* is a single genus that also gives its name to all the sparrow-sized, perching bird species of the Late Cretaceous Period. Fossils of these birds have been found all over the world.

Erythrosuchus [ee-RITH-roh-SOOK-us] (red crocodile; the first fossil specimens had red stains on them)   The largest land animal of the Lower Triassic Period, reaching lengths of more than 16 feet. This beast dominated the Triassic Period, nearly wiping out its competitors—the early mammal-like synapsids known as therapsids. Like modern crocodiles, it may have spent much, but not all, of its time in the water.

Eudimorphodon [yew-dih-MORF-oh-don] (true two-shaped teeth)   An early, primitive gull-sized pterosaur that had peg-like teeth as well as sharper cutting teeth. It had a long tail but no crest on its head.

Euoplocephalus [YEW-oh-plo-SEFF-ah-lus] (true armored head)   One of the largest ankylosaurs, weighing about 2 tons. It had horn-like spikes sticking out the back of its head, and it also had sheets of bone on the skin covering its head to provide extra protection for the skull.

Gallimimus [GAL-ih-MYM-us] (chicken mimic)   Bird mimic coelurosaur.

Garudimimus [gah-ROOD-ih-MYM-us] (Garuda was a mythical bird)   Bird mimic coelurosaur.

Giganotosaurus [jy-gan-OHT-oh-SAHR-us] (gigantic southern lizard)   Contender for largest land predator.

Gorgosaurus [GOR-goh-SAHR-us] (terrible lizard)   Alternative name for *Albertosaurus*.

Hadrosaurus [HAD-roh-SAHR-us] (bulky lizard)   Crestless duckbill discovered in New Jersey, the first dinosaur to be found and identified in North America.

Herrerasaurus [her-RAER-ah-SAHR-us] (Herrera's lizard)   Early four-fingered meat-eating dinosaur.

Hesperornis [hes-per-ORN-iss] (western bird)   Was a flightless diving bird like *Baptornis*. Because it was adapted for diving, its bones were heavier than bones of flying birds. Like *Enantiornis*, *Hesperornis* gives its name to a whole group of similar birds—divers with teeth and webbed feet.

Heterodontosaurus [HET-uh-roh-DONT-oh-SAHR-us] (different toothed-lizard)   A speedy, 3-foot long dinosaur who may have holed up in burrows every summer. It had three different kinds of teeth and chewed by grinding its lower teeth lengthwise across its uppers.

Homalocephale [HOMM-ah-loh-SEFF-ah-lee] (level head)   One of a group of pachychephalosaurs whose domeheads were less thick and pronounced than the others. Homalos grew to be about 10 feet long.

Hylaeosaurus [hy-LEE-oh-SAHR-us] (woodland lizard)   An ankylosaur, among the first dinosaurs to be named.

Hypsilophodon [hip-sih-LOHF-oh-don] (high, ridged tooth)   Ornithopod dinosaur once thought to live in trees, but now believed to be one of the fastest running Ornithischian dinosaurs. In addition to teeth for grinding food, it had a horny beak for cropping vegetation.

Icarosaurus [IK-ah-roh-SAHR-us] (after Icarus, the mythic Grecian boy whose father made him wings out of wax)   Triassic gliding lizard that had rib-extensions for wings.

Ichthyornis [IK-thih-ORN-iss] (fish bird)   A bird that looked and lived like a modern sea gull. It was a strong flyer but may have scavenged the coastline as well as hunted for fish from the surface of the sea.

Ichthyosaurus [IK-thih-oh-SAHR-us] (fish lizard)   Dolphin-like marine reptile that gave live birth.

Iguanodon [ih-GWAHN-oh-don] (iguana toothed)   One of the earliest known dinosaurs, equipped with a famous thumb spike. This ornithopod had teeth only along the sides of its jaws and relied on its beak for taking bites.

Kentrosaurus [KEN-troh-SAHR-us] (spiked lizard)   An 8-foot-long stegosaur.

Kronosaurus [KRO-noh-SAHR-us] (time lizard)   Short-necked plesiosaur.

Lagosuchus [LAHG-oh-SOOK-us] (rabbit crocodile)   A small and quick thecodont from the Middle Triassic Period that may be the closest relative yet found both to the dinosaurs and to the pterosaurs. It ran on two long, slender legs.

Lambeosaurus [LAM-bee-oh-SAHR-us] (Lambe's lizard)   A duckbill with a crest that looks like a huge pompadour haircut.

Lesothosaurus [lee-SOH-toh-SAHR-us] (lizard from Lesotho)   A fabrosaur.

Lewisuchus [LOO-i-SOOK-us] (Lewis's crocodile)   A scuted (shielded) thecodont.

Maiasaura [MY-ah-SAHR-ah] (good mother lizard)   Named because it is known to have cared for its babies, based on the discovery of nests of fossilized young ones.

Mamenchisaurus [mah-MEN-chee-SAHR-us] (Mamenchin lizard)   Sauropod dinosaur with a very long neck.

Megalosaurus [MEG-ah-loh-SAHR-us] (big lizard)   A carnosaur, the first dinosaur to be named as a separate species. It earned its moniker even before *Iguanodon*, whose bones were discovered first.

Melanorosaurus [mel-AN-ohr-oh-SAHR-us] (black mountain lizard)   One of the most sturdily built of the prosauropod dinosaurs.

Microceratops [MY-kroh-SERR-ah-tops] (mini horn-face)   A dwarf ceratopsian.

Microhadrosaurus [MY-kroh-HAD-roh-SAHR-us] (mini duckbill)   A dwarf duckbill dinosaur.

Micropachycephalosaurus [MY-kroh-PAK-ee-SEFF-ah-loh-SAHR-us]   A little dome-headed dinosaur, also the dino with the longest name.

Microvenator [MY-kroh-vee-NAE-tor] (a little killer)   Small coelurosaur.

Mononykus [mah-noh-NY-kus] (single claw)   Probably a flightless ground bird of the Late Cretaceous Period. It had short, thick wings, each of which looks more like a claw sticking straight out from its body. Each claw is actually made of fused wing bones. It was a good runner that may have occupied a desert environment. One of its bird-like characteristics is its large breast bone, which many birds use to brace their flight muscles. In many ways, however, *Mononykus* looked like a dinosaur, with strong legs and a long tail.

Mosasaurus [MOH-sah-SAHR-us] (lizard from the Meuse)   Cretaceous aquatic reptile.

Mussaurus [muss-SAHR-us] (mouse lizard)   The smallest dinosaur ever found, at 8 inches long.

Nanotyrannus [NAN-oh-ty-RAN-us] (dwarf tyrant)   A tiny, full-grown tyrannosaur from Montana.

Nodosaurus [NOH-doh-SAHR-us] (nodular lizard)   Covered in bands of armor of alternating large and small knobs. Like other nodosaurs, its armor may have been fringed with spikes around its sides and shoulders.

Ornitholestes [or-NITH-oh-LESS-tees] (bird robber)   Coelurosaur resembling *Coelurus*.

Ornithomimus [or-NITH-oh-MYM-us] (bird mimic)   Coelurosaur.

Ornithosuchus [or-NITH-oh-SOOK-us] (bird crocodile)   A smaller thecodont of the Upper Triassic Period that may have been capable of rearing up and running on its hind legs, despite its crocodile shape. Its skull and jaws closely resemble those of a small T-rex.

Oviraptor [OH-vih-RAP-tor] (egg thief)   Ungainly looking coelurosaur, misnamed "egg thief" because it was thought to be stealing the eggs it was tending.

Pachycephalosaurus [PAK-ee-SEFF-ah-loh-SAHR-us] (thick-headed lizard)   A big, 26-foot dome-headed animal with a skull three times as long and three times as thick as that of *Stegoceras*.

Pachyrhinosaurus [PAK-ee-RYN-oh-SAHR-us] (thick nose lizard)   A rare ceratopsian with a flat, boney growth instead of a horn.

Panoplosaurus [pan-OPP-loh-SAHR-us] (fully armored lizard)   One of the few nodosaurs to survive to the end of the Cretaceous Period.

Parasaurolophus [PAHR-ah-sahr-AH-lohf-us] (similar lizard crest)   Duckbill with a crest shaped like a giant boomerang.

Pinacosaurus [pin-AK-oh-SAHR-us] (plank lizard)   One of the smaller and skinnier ankylosaurs, at 16 feet long.

Plateosaurus [PLAET-ee-oh-SAHR-us] (flat lizard)   Prosauropod that gets its name from its flat teeth.

Procompsognathus [proh-KOMP-sohg-NAE-thuss] (before pretty jaw)   Small, big-hipped coelurosaur.

Protarcheopteryx [proht-AR-kee-OPP-ter-iks] (first *Archeopteryx*)   Candidate for earliest-known bird.

Proterosuchus [PROH-ter-oh-SOOK-us] (before crocodile)   Among the first thecodonts to appear during the Lower Triassic Period. Unlike later thecos and crocs, which developed a more upright stance, *Proterosuchus* walked with its legs sprawled out to the side.

Protoavis [proh-toh-AE-vis] (first bird)   Controversial candidate for first bird.

Protoceratops [proh-toh-SERR-ah-tops] (first horned face)   Had the famous frill, but not the horns. It was one of the smaller frillheads.

Psittacosaurus [sih-TAK-oh-SAHR-us] (parrot lizard)   A marginocephalosaur 6 or 7 feet long found in Asia.

Pteranodon [terr-AN-oh-don] (winged but toothless)   A member of the largest group of pterosaurs, with a large bony crest counterbalancing its long, toothless beak and only a very short tail.

Pterodactylus [terr-oh-DAK-tih-lus] (wing finger)   One of the first pteros to be discovered. The name also refers to a whole group of short-tailed pterosaurs.

Pterodaustro [terr-oh-DAWS-troh] (southern wing)   Known from fossils found in Argentina. This ptero has a long, weird-looking beak filled with hundreds of long, needle-shaped teeth, evidently designed for combing plankton or little sea creatures from the surface of the water.

Quetzalcoatlus [ket-SAHL-koh-AT-lus] (named for Quetzalcoatl, an Aztec God who took the form of a feathered serpent)   The largest-known pterosaur, a kind of *Pteranodon* with a wingspan of 50 feet.

Rhamphorhynchus [RAM-for-RINK-us] (narrow beak)   Had a long beak with sharp teeth, a long tail, but no crest. It also had a large breast plate where powerful flight muscles were attached. This was evidently a fish-eating ptero—fish remains have been found where its stomach used to be.

Saltasaurus [SALT-ah-SAHR-us] (lizard from Salta, a province in Argentina)   Sauropod with bony armor on its back to protect it from predators. Some of the other sauropods may have had this kind of protection, too.

Sarcolestes [SAR-koh-LESS-tees] (flesh robber)   A vegetarian nodosaur wrongly named as a meat-eater.

Saurolophus [sahr-AH-lohf-us] (lizard crest)   Duckbill with a crest shaped like a single horn sticking out backward from the top of its head.

Scelidosaurus [SKELL-ih-doh-SAHR-us] (limb lizard)   Only tentatively classified as an ankylosaur. This is a primitive armored dinosaur of the Early Jurassic Period with no tail club. It is known from a partial skeleton found in England.

Seismosaurus [SYS-moh-SAHR-us] (seismic lizard)   A contender for the longest-known dinosaur, with an estimated length of 120 feet from head to tail. Discovered in the mid-1980s in Utah as a nearly complete skeleton, this sauropod may have stood 18 feet tall (not counting the neck) and weighed 80 to 100 tons.

Sinornis [syn-ORN-iss] (Chinese bird)   One of the oldest birds (from the Early Cretaceous Period. Unlike *Archaeopteryx*, it has teeth and a short, birdlike tail; it also could fold its wings tightly across its back, and its claws were evidently adapted for perching in branches of trees.

295

Sinosauropteryx [SYN-oh-sahr-OPP-ter-iks] (Chinese lizard wing)   Small coelurosaurian-like dinosaur covered with feather-like structures found in China.

Sordes pilosus [SOHR-des] (hairy devil)   Pterosaur that appeared to have hair or fur.

Spinosaurus [SPYN-oh-SAHR-us] (spine lizard)   Carnosaur with a huge fin-like, fan-shaped crest growing along its spine.

Stegoceras [steg-OSS-err-us] (covered horn)   The name shouldn't be confused with the more famous *Stegosaurus* (covered lizard), which belonged to a different family; this was one of the smaller pachycephalosaurs, growing to be only about 6 feet long.

Stegosaurus [STEG-oh-SAHR-us] (covered lizard)   Thyreophorans with small heads and plates running down their spines.

Struthiomimus [STROOTH-ee-oh-MYM-us] (ostrich mimic)   Very similar to *Ornithomimus*, except in the proportion of its limbs.

Struthiosaurus [STROOTH-ee-oh-SAHR-us] (ostrich lizard)   The smallest nodosaur.

Stygimoloch [STIHJ-ih-MOLL-ok] (devil from the river Styx)   A pachycephalosaur with elaborate knobs and long, horny growths surrounding its high dome, which gave it a devilish appearance. Its horns—combined with the fact that it was found in the Montana formation known as Hell Creek—led its discoverers to name it after the mythical river Styx that bordered Hades, the ancient Greek underworld.

Styracosaurus [STYR-ah-koh-SAHR-us] (spiked lizard)   Ceratopsian with a frill edged with six spikes. It also had a single horn growing out of its nose.

Supersaurus [SOO-per-SAHR-us] (super lizard)   Sauropod known from 8-foot long shoulder blades, a 6-foot wide pelvis, 10-foot ribs, and 4 $\frac{1}{2}$-foot vertebrae. These fossils were discovered in Colorado in 1972. Depending on the unknown length of its tail, it could have been 140 feet long, the longest-known dinosaur.

Syntarsus [sin-TAR-sus] (fused tarsus)   Ceratosaur from Zimbabwe closely related to *Coelophysis*.

Tarbosaurus [TAR-boh-SAHR-us] (terror lizard)   Tyrannosaur found in Late Cretaceous Mongolia that closely resembles T-rex.

Tenontosaurus [teh-NON-toh-SAHR-us] (sinew lizard)   Twenty-foot-tall ornithopod.

Titanosaurus [ty-TAN-oh-SAHR-us] (titanic lizard)   Misnamed sauropod found by Marsh.

Torosaurus [TOR-oh-SAHR-us] (piercing lizard)   Ceratopsian with the biggest frill.

Triceratops [try-SERR-ah-tops] (three-horned face)   The best-known ceratopsian—as well as the biggest, reaching 25 feet in length and 9 feet in height.

Troodon [TROH-oh-don] (wounding tooth)   Raptor with great intelligence and agility.

Tsintaosaurus [SIN-toh-SAHR-us] (Tsintao lizard)   A Chinese duckbill with a crest like a horn sticking forward out of its head, making it look like a unicorn.

Tuojiangosaurus [TWAH-JEAHNG-oh-SAHR-us] (Tuojiang lizard)   A stegosaur from Mongolia.

Tylosaurus [TY-loh-SAHR-us] (swollen lizard)   A mosasaur with a short neck and large head.

Tyrannosaurus [ty-RAN-oh-SAHR-us] (tyrant lizard)   Not all tyrannos were T-rexes, but all were big meat-eaters.

Udanoceratops [oo-DAHN-oh-SERR-ah-tops]   A large proto-ceratopsian from Mongolia.

Ultrasaurus [ULL-trah-SAHR-us] (ultra lizard)   Probably the tallest dinosaur at an estimated 55 feet—as well as the heaviest at 100 tons. Discovered in 1979 in Colorado, it is known chiefly from a 9-foot shoulder blade—the largest dinosaur bone ever discovered—and some 5-foot vertebrae.

Velociraptor [vel-OSS-ih-RAP-tor] (speedy thief)   This overnight success is not only a movie star (*Jurassic Park*, 1993, and *Lost World*, 1997) but a basketball star, too (the NBA's Toronto Raptors were established in 1993).

Yangchuanosaurus [YANG-CHWAN-oh-SAHR-us] (lizard from Yang-ch'uan)   Near cousin of *Allosaurus* found in China.

Paleo-Glossary

This list of paleontological terms comes in handy when studying dinosaurs.

absolute dating   A method of determining the age of a fossil in terms of the number of years old it is. Contrast with *relative dating*.

adaptation   The advantageous conformation of an organism to changes in the environment.

adaptive radiation   Takes place when a number of new, interrelated species develop in a fairly short period of time. This frequently happens after a mass extinction has occurred.

aestivation   The practice some animals have of resting dormant through the hot, dry summer season when food is scarce. Compare with *hibernation*.

altricial   Creatures that are helpless at birth and need to be tended until they become strong enough to care for themselves. Contrast with *precocial*.

arboreal   Tree-dwelling. The arboreal theory of the origin of flight holds that wings evolved for gliding in creatures who climbed trees.

articulated   Bones that are connected to one another in their original configuration. When an articulated fossil skeleton of a dinosaur is discovered, it means the bones have remained undisturbed since the death of the dinosaur millions of years ago.

battery   Any group of similar things that are used together for a single purpose. This term applies well to the many cheek teeth that grew several rows deep in the jaws of duckbilled dinosaurs.

binomial nomenclature (Latin for two-named naming)   The scientific practice of identifying a creature by its genus and species name.

bipedalism   The ability to walk on just two feet, a trait found in people, birds, and many dinos. Bipedalism evolved separately in birds and in people.

bolus   A wad of vegetation that is swallowed without being chewed. Plant-eaters without highly developed teeth, such as the sauropod dinosaurs, swallow boluses, leaving the task of grinding them to their digestive tracts.

carnivores   Creatures that live exclusively on meat, such as most theropod dinosaurs.

catastrophism   The view that extinction takes place when God periodically annihilates living things by means of a flood or other disaster. This view reconciled the idea of extinction with biblical thinking during the mid-19th century.

clades   Groups of living things organized according to evolutionary relationships.

cladistics   A system for organizing life forms that shows their evolutionary relationships.

cladogram   A drawing that represents a clade.

convergent evolution   Occurs when different groups evolve common traits independently of one another. When animals are lumped together on the basis of convergent traits, the result is an unnatural group.

cursorial   A theory that flight evolved in creatures who ran on the ground.

derived trait   A trait that has evolved from a more primitive ancestor that did not possess it.

ecosystem   Interdependent system of living things. Plants feed plant-eaters, plant-eaters feed carnivores, carnivores feed other carnivores and, when things die, they all feed the plants.

ectothermic   "Cold-blooded" animals, which rely on the heat of the sun for warmth and tend to both eat less and move less than endotherms.

endothermic   "Warm-blooded" animals, which are self-heating and keep themselves warm by means of their metabolic processes.

evolution   Change in the genetic composition of a species of organism with time. Every species undergoes evolution.

extinction   The dying off of all members of a group of living things.

fauna   Animal life. Scientists often talk about specific faunas, the kinds of animals that may be found at a particular time and place.

flora   Plant life.

fossil record   The total amount of evidence of the existence of creatures no longer living. The word "fossil" comes from a Latin term meaning "dug up."

gigantothermy   The heating strategy of maintaining a constant temperature by virtue of being large in size. Living gigantotherms of today include giant sea turtles. The larger dinosaurs may also have been gigantotherms.

Gondwana   An ancient supercontinent made up of present-day South America, Africa, India, Australia, and Antarctica.

half-life   The length of time it takes for half of any amount of an isotope to decay. This rate of decay is constant regardless of the amount of the isotope.

herbivores   Plant-eaters, such as cows, horses, and caterpillars.

hibernation   The practice of lying dormant during the winter. Contrast with *aestivation*.

holotype   A fossil skeleton that best represents the species to which it belongs. Other skeletons can be compared to the holotype in trying to determine what kind of dinosaur they are.

isotopes   Atoms of a particular element that have more neutrons than the element usually has. Some isotopes are unstable and give off energy; some decay into more stable atoms.

Laurasia   An ancient supercontinent consisting of present-day North America, Europe, and Asia.

marsupium   A pouch in which a newborn, undeveloped baby can stay and feed until it becomes mature enough to stand on its own two feet. This pouch is found only in marsupial mammals such as kangaroos and koalas. Contrast with *placenta*.

mass extinction   The dying off of many species within a limited span of time.

morphology   The study of the physical shape of living things. Even subtle differences in the shapes of different dinosaur skeletons are important in determining the species to which a dinosaur belongs and how different species are related.

natural group   Made up of creatures from a single line of descent.

natural selection   A theory explaining why evolution occurs. It states that some organisms reproduce in greater quantities than others and thereby transmit more of their genes to the next generation.

niches   The various ecological spaces creatures occupy.

omnivores   Animals that eat both meats and plants. Omnis include bears, many kinds of birds, and human beings.

opportunism   The idea that evolution takes place not just through competition, but as a result of new space opening up for creatures who will adapt to the new conditions.

osteoderms   Bones that are not attached to the skeleton but that lie embedded in the skin. Osteoderms include *Stegosaurus* plates and *Ankylosaurus* armor.

paleontology   The scientific study of prehistoric life, including the study of dinosaurs. It often combines many scientific fields, including geology, biology, chemistry, anatomy, and archeology.

Pangaea   A huge continent made up of all the land masses on earth. It was formed during the Permian Period at the end of the Paleozoic Period.

phylogeny   The study of how species evolve—what characteristics they inherit from previous species and what traits are new—and how species are related to one another.

placenta   A mammalian female organ that connects the mother's bloodstream to her babies', supplying them with all their physical needs. Contrast with *marsupium*.

pleurocoels   Hollow spaces in the vertebrae of many sauropods. These keep the skeletons light without weakening them too much.

precocial   Creatures that can take care of themselves as soon as they hatch. Contrast with *altricial*.

predator trap   A place where large numbers of meat-eating creatures have died after getting stuck.

primitive trait   A trait that has not newly evolved but that is present in an ancestral group.

pubis   A bone arch in front of the pelvis. The two main groups of dinosaurs—saurischians and ornithischians—are distinguished by the direction this bone points. In saurischians, the pubis points forward; in ornithischians, it points backward.

radiometry   A technique for calculating the age of rock by measuring minuscule amounts of radioactive elements within it. This is the most useful method of absolute dating.

relative dating   The process of determining the age of a fossil or rock formation in relationship to other rocks and fossils. Relative dating can be used to compare fossils all over the world.

scutes   Bony shields sticking up out of the surface of the skin of some dinosaurs and other creatures.

selection   What happens when creatures with certain traits survive while other creatures with other traits die out.

sexual dimorphism   The appearance of different shape or size characteristics in males and females of the same species.

specialization   Occurs when a species adapts in unusual ways to occupy a niche that most other creatures cannot fill. An example of specialization in a living animal is the long, sticky tongue of the anteater, which allows the animal to eat even more ants than a human over twice its size.

strata   Layers formed from sedimentary residue left from each of the periods of geologic time.

stratigraphy   The science of interpreting layers of sedimentary rock.

taphonomy   The study of what happens to old remains from the time of death to the time of discovery, including how bones turn into fossils. The word comes from the Greek words *taphos*, for burial, and *nomos*, for law.

tectonic plates   The huge slabs of rock that make up the Earth's crust and that float on top of the slowly convecting rock beneath the Earth's surface.

unnatural group   Includes creatures that did not evolve from a common ancestor. "Flying animals" is an unnatural group made up of insects, birds, and bats, three evolutionarily distinct groups. This grouping should not appear in a cladogram.

variation   The difference between different living things. All creatures tend to vary and to reproduce themselves in ways that are not exact copies of the original.

Relatives Under the Skin

These seven phylogeny tables will help you see the evolutionary relationships among dinosaurs and other creatures. The groupings go from general to particular—big groups to smaller ones.

Table 1   An Outline of Tetrapod Clans

TETRAPODS:	Creatures with four legs and their descendants, including humans, birds, and even snakes.
AMPHIBIANS:	Tetrapods that do not have an amniote embryonic membrane in their eggs. This means they need to lay their eggs in water. Amphibians include modern frogs and salamanders. Ancient amphibians often grew to be much bigger than those of today.
AMNIOTES:	Tetrapods with an amniote membrane, including creatures that lay eggs with hard shells and those who give live birth.
SYNAPSIDS:	This group includes mammals and their ancestors, the pelycosaurs, therapsids, and theriodonts. These creatures have an extra hole in their skulls behind the eye socket, in addition to eye holes and nostril holes.
SAUROPSIDS:	This group includes modern reptiles—turtles, lizards, snakes, and crocodiles—and their ancestors, as well as dinosaurs. The sauropsid group is outlined further in Table 2.

Table 2   An Outline of Sauropsid Clans

SAUROPSIDS:	These creatures have two holes in the roof of their mouth.
ANAPSIDS:	Members of this group—including living turtles—have no extra hole in their skulls other than eye sockets and nostrils.
DIAPSIDS:	These creatures have two extra holes in their skulls behind each eye socket.
LIZARDS AND SNAKES:	This group includes your pet chameleon and your pet boa constrictor.
EURYAPSIDS:	These creatures have a single extra hole in their skulls behind the eye sockets, although different members of this group may have evolved this way independently of one another. In other words, euryapsids may be a polyphyletic group. All euryapsids are extinct.
ARCHOSAURS:	These are the "ruling lizards." They have an extra hole in front of the eye socket and two extra holes behind the eye.
THECODONTS:	The earliest, ancestral archosaurs, now extinct.
CROCODILES:	Gators are part of this group, too.
ORNITHODIRES:	These creatures developed straight ankle hinges enabling increased activity.
PTEROSAURS:	These are the great flying reptiles of the Mesozoic Period. Their front limbs evolved into wings through elongation of their ring fingers; some even had fur.
DINOSAURS:	The "terrible lizards," still alive today as modern birds. Dinos are outlined further in Table 3.

Table 3   An Outline of Dinosaur Clans

SAURISCHIANS:	The lizard butts.
THEROPODS:	The meat-eaters, outlined further in Table 4.
SAUROPODOMORPHS:	The big "bronto"-like vegetarian dinosaurs, outlined in Table 5.
ORNITHISCHIANS:	The bird butts.
FABROSAURS:	Primitive plant-eaters with no cheeks like *Lesothosaurus*.
GENASAURS:	Plant-eaters that have developed cheeks for more efficient eating.
CERAPODS:	This group has specialized teeth for grinding and slicing vegetation. Cerapods are outlined in Table 6.
THYREOPHORANS:	Heavily armored dinosaurs outlined in Table 7.

Table 4 An Outline of Theropod Clans

THEROPODS:	Predacious lizard butts with three-toed feet like birds.
CERATOSAURS:	These dinos have four-fingered hands. The group includes *Coelophysis*, *Dilophosaurus*, and *Ceratosaurus*.
TETANURANS:	Killer dinos with three-fingered hands.
CARNOSAURS:	Big killers, including *Allosaurus*.
COELUROSAURS:	General small killers, although this group includes *Tyrannosaurus*.
ARCTOMETATARSALIANS:	This diverse group includes the big tyrannosaurs and the small, toothless ornithomimosaurs.
OVIRAPTORS:	Odd dinosaurs misnamed "egg-thieves."
MANIRAPTORS:	Vicious, agile group that includes *Velociraptor*. These are the ancestors of modern birds.

Table 5 An Outline of Sauropodomorph Clans

SAUROPODOMORPHS:	The long-necked vegetarian lizard butts.
PROSAUROPODS:	The somewhat big sauropodomorphs, including *Anchisaurus* and *Plateosaurus*.
SAUROPODS:	The very big and huge sauropodomorphs. These include the *Diplodocids*, *Camarasaurs*, *Cetiosaurs*, *Brachiosaurs*, and *Titanosaurs*.

Table 6 An Outline of Cerapod Clans

CERAPODS:	Ornithischian dinos with cheeks and specialized teeth for eating vegetation.
ORNITHOPODS:	Cerapods that generally stood on their hind legs, these include the *Heterodontosaurs*, *Hypsilophodonts*, *Iguanodonts*, and the duckbilled *Hadrosaurs*.
MARGINOCEPHALIANS:	"Edge heads," including frill-headed dinosaurs, beaked dinosaurs, and dome-headed dinos.
CERATOPSIANS:	The parrot-beakeddinosaurs, including the frill-headed *Triceratops*.
PACHYCEPHALOSAURS:	The goat-like, bone-headed dinosaurs.

Table 7   An Outline of Thyreophoran Clans

THYREOPHORANS:	Armored vegetarians.
STEGOSAURS:	Pin-headed dinos with plates running down their spines and spikes on their tails.
ANKYLOSAURS:	Slow-moving, heavily armored dinosaurs. Many have clubs on their tails.

Digging Deeper

Here's a list of books on dinosaurs for further reading.

Bakker, Robert. *The Dinosaur Heresies*. New York: Wm Morrow, 1986.

Colbert, Edwin H. *The Great Dinosaur Hunters and Their Discoveries*. New York: Dover, 1968.

Costa, Vincenzo. *Dinasaur Safari Guide*. Stillwater, MN: Voyageur Press, 1994.

Currie, Philip J. and Kevin Padian, eds. *Encyclopedia of Dinosaurs*. San Diego: Academia Press, 1997.

Desmond, Adrian. *The Hot-Blooded Dinosaurs: A Revolution in Paleontology*. New York: Dial Press, 1976.

Fastovsky, David and David Weishampel. *The Evolution and Extinction of the Dinosaurs*. Cambridge University Press, 1996.

Glut, Donald F. *The Dinosaur Scrapbook*. Seacaucus, NJ: Citadel, 1980.

Gould, Stephen Jay. *Bully for Brontosaurus: Reflections in Natural History*. New York: Norton, 1992.

Lambert, David. *The Ultimate Dinsosaur Book*. New York: DK Publishing, 1993.

Lessem, Don. *Kings of Creation: How a New Breed of Scientists is Revolutionizing Our Understanding of Dinosaurs*. New York: Simon and Schuster, 1992.

———, and Donald Glut. *The Dinosaur Society's Dinosaur Encyclopedia*. New York: Random House, 1993.

Lucas, Spencer G. *Dinosaurs: The Textbook*. Dubuque: William C. Brown, 1997.

McGowan, Christopher. *Dinosaurs, Spitfires, and Sea Dragons*. Cambridge, MA: Harvard University Press, 1983.

Norell, Mark A., Eugene Gaffney, and Loweel Dingus. *Discovering Dinosaurs*. New York: Peter N. Nevraumont, 1995.

Norman, David. *Dinosaur!* New York: Prentice Hall, 1991.

——*The Illustrated Encyclopedia of Dinosaurs*. New York: Crescent Books, 1985.

Parker, Steve. *Identifying Dinosaurs*. Edison, NJ: Chartwell Books, 1997.

Paul, Gregory. *Predatory Dinosaurs of the World*. New York: Simon and Schuster, 1988.

Weishampel, David B., Peter Dodson, and Halszka Osmolska, eds. *The Dinosauria*. Berkeley: University of California Press, 1990.

Index

G-H-I

U-V

W-X-Y-Z